$\mathcal{P}raise\ for$ **ANTI DIVA**

AN OTTAWA CITIZEN BEST BOOK OF THE YEAR

"An entertaining, saucy, naming-names kind of book that no fan of rock 'n' roll in Canada ought to miss." *eye* (Toronto)

"Pope's humour and sexual bravado have translated well onto paper. *Anti Diva* is a subtle but scathing attack on those who have drifted into complacency both on a cultural and personal level. It is both a challenge and an invitation, especially to women and cultural producers, to keep kicking at the pedestals." *National Post*

"Pope...distinguishes herself by her frankness.... [Her] confessions are those of an unreconstructed celebrity." *Elm Street*

"Those hungry for bits and pieces of dirt won't be disappointed. Pope is a world-class namedropper (and I mean that in the best sense of the word)." *Mirror* (Montreal)

"[*Anti Diva* is] a titillating walk on the wild side." *Maclean's*

"Carole Pope manages to dish the celebrity dirt in an attractive manner by not taking herself—or anyone else—too seriously." *The Vancouver Sun*

"A provocative and enjoyably trashy autobiography." *The Edmonton Journal*

"It's the personality behind the words that makes *Anti Diva* an enticing read." *Chart* magazine (Toronto)

ANTI
diva

an autobiography

CAROLE POPE

Vintage Canada
A Division of Random House of Canada Limited

VINTAGE CANADA EDITION, 2001

Published in Canada by Vintage Canada, a division of Random House of Canada Limited, in 2001. First published in hardcover in Canada by Random House Canada, Toronto, in 2000. Distributed by Random House of Canada Limited, Toronto.

Vintage Canada and colophon are registered trademarks of Random House of Canada Limited.

National Library of Canada Cataloguing in Publication Data

Pope, Carole
    Anti Diva : an autobiography

ISBN 0-679-31137-8

1. Pope, Carole. 2. Rock musicians—Canada—Biography. I. Title.

ML420.P66A3 2001 2001   782.42166'092   C2001-900862-7

Lyric excerpt from "Everything Reminds Me of My Dog"
Written and composed by Jane Siberry
© 1988 Wing It Music
International Copyright Secured. All Rights Reserved.
Used by Permission.

Except where noted, all photographs and images appear courtesy of the author.

www.randomhouse.ca

Printed and bound in the United States of America

2 4 6 8 9 7 5 3 1

This book is dedicated to Howard Pope.

ACKNOWLEDGEMENTS

Thanks to
my editor Anne Collins and everyone at Random House;

Ann Dean, AA Bronson, Andrew Alexander, Art Metropole, Kenny Baird, Tim Blanks, Bob Blumer, Tim Curry, Sandra Faire, Fred Nicholitas, Sam Feldman, Bernie Finkelstein, Louise Garfield, Barr Gilmore, BJ Cavnor, Michael Demayo, Marilyn Kiewiet, Ingin Kim, Anya Varda, Rosie Shuster, Kinnie Starr, kd lang, David Marsden, Keith McKie, Paul Oberst, Markus O'Hara, Mimi Paige, Elaine Pope, Hendrick Riik, Bob Smith, Mike Smith, Clive Smith, Christine Degado, Lisa Vogal, AnnMarie Guy, Jenoa Harrison, Kevan Staples, David Ramsden, Sandy Stagg, Gina Stepaniuk, Vicki Wickham, Bernard Zette, Su and Holly.

CONTENTS

Carole, why now? why this book now. . . . why?

I hate having to answer that question. It's worse than having to explain why I wrote a song. After years of silence, a dam broke within me and I had to spew 80,000 or so words out of my brain . . .

Did I do it for the money? Yeah. Did I do it because friends nagged and prodded me? Partly. But once I started writing, it was better than going to a therapist, and infinitely better than an acid flashback. I worked out so much stuff. It explained a great deal of my abnormal childlike behaviour. I was reliving the pieces of the puzzle that is my life, although sometimes it was like ripping open a wound.

I'm going through serious performance withdrawal, because I've been writing this goddamned book forever. I've discovered the experience is nothing like writing song lyrics. I've had to stop myself from using the same adjectives over and over, and I still have no concept of where a comma goes.

When Kevan Staples and I created our band, Rough Trade, we just wanted to play. We didn't expect anything except the thrill of getting our songs out there. We ended up pushing musical and sexual envelopes. We morphed androgyny, humour and various musical genres into one twisted freakish phenomenon. We became a myth, a cult, something for people to cling to: an echo of a blip in time that encompassed the late seventies and the eighties, when we thought we were invincible. Some people are nostalgic for those days. I'm not, but it was a trip going back there and reliving how driven and naïve we were.

I've been watching people forever and apparently I've been taking notes. I've always been a narcissist and a voyeur. As a writer, I've been obsessed with sex simply because it's so funny. It's nature's perverse joke, and a neverending source of material for me. We're all slaves to urges we have no control over and some of us are utterly guilt-ridden when those urges surface. I love that.

This book deals with my denial and discovery of my true sexuality, and how all that has affected my life and art. We have come so far, but still stand at the foot of a mountain of ignorance.

What else?

I'm obsessed with show biz and the cult of personality. The cutthroat food chain of flesh and fantasy that destroys everyone in its path. It's a world in which I feel so at home, a world where a diva, like me, gets to live in a bubble of her own creation. I've had people shake in fear over meeting me. That is an unsettling experience. If only people could see the sad (yet self-empowering) way you have to psyche yourself up in order to get out on that stage or in front of that camera.

I embrace my sick world. I crave all the trappings of success, and yet I'm so disdainful of them. I admit it: I'm a hypocrite. Most of us are fascinated by stardom, even the tasteless no-talent brand that takes up so much of popular culture today. We thrill to the disintegration of the golden boys and girls as they fall off their sun-drenched pedestals into a morass of drugs and alcohol.

I'm quite shameless about namedropping in this book, but I'm only following the example of Truman Capote and Dominick Dunne, two of my favourite writers.

I wanted to write about what it's like to be in a band because, first and foremost, that's what makes me *me*. After the first trembling moments of fear, the sheer adrenaline rush of standing on a stage is the most freeing and addictive experience I've ever had.

THE SIXTIES
(What were we thinking?)

I have to bear the flower-bedecked cross of the baby boomer. For me the sixties consisted of taking every drug possible, hallucinating Shiva and Vishnu cartoons on hardwood floors, and having really bad sex with everybody. I almost forgot—we actually thought you could deal with your emotions with the aid of psychedelics, and yes, we did try to perpetuate the myth of a Utopian, Atlantis-like lotus land where we could live together in peace and harmony. Yeah, right. Put me in a room with those losers now and I would run screaming to the nearest exit.

I moved away from home when I was eighteen. My family was living in Don Mills, a suburb of Toronto. The landscape was flat and monochromatic, relentless in its conformity. I knew I'd lose whatever semblance of sanity I had if I stayed in that house. I was the oldest of four kids. My childhood had been heaven until my father decided we had to move from England to Canada. My parents, my baby sister, Diane, and I had lived in a beautiful house in the country outside Manchester, amongst verdant rolling hills. We had an English bulldog, a green parrot and chickens running in the backyard. I liked to survey my little fiefdom while blowing bubbles in my white clay pipe. The house belonged to my grandmother, who we called Nanny. She lived with us and I absolutely adored her.

One afternoon I was confronted by my godparents, who were standing in the hallway of our house looking devastated.

We watched as a coffin was carried down the stairs by under-takers. Not making the connection as to what a coffin was, I asked them what was going on. They told me "Nanny's gone to heaven." Soon after that we were on a boat to Canada.

Even as a toddler, I knew that my mother was unhappy. I could see her face change when she talked to my father. He was constantly on her back, nagging her about something. My first conscious memory of my father was sinking my teeth into his flesh. This strange man came up to me and I bit him. I didn't know who he was, he was away from home so much. My second conscious memory was music, which was always playing somewhere in the house. My mother started singing to me and taking me to the theatre when I was a babe in arms. From my baby point of view, the theatre seemed like a sparkly shiny place where my mother would fall into a trance. I soon followed her.

My parents, Jack and Celia, were an odd match. Dad was a Canadian who'd moved to England in the forties. He dressed like a gangster, favouring black shirts with white ties. He had wavy hair and a pencil-thin mustache. He was, quite frankly, wacko—a certified manic depressive. He was sexually Victorian and politically left-wing. He was always running some kind of scam. During the war he had done duty as a fireman and he openly admitted to me that he'd ripped off people's belongings while putting out fires in their houses. He'd won my mother over in a three-month courtship. They were both into ballroom dancing and that was how they met.

When Diane and I came home after hanging out with our friends, he'd call us sluts. After we left England, we moved every year of my life, because he had grandiose ideas that the next place would be better, that he'd make more money or whatever delusional shit was going on in his head. For most of those years, he worked as a tire salesman. My sister Elaine was born in Montreal, the first stop on the dysfunctional trip we were on. As a teenager, Elaine used to try to reason with Dad about his moving mania. She was the responsible adult to his irresponsible child. She'd ask him if he'd picked up our report cards and school records before we moved, and he'd lie and say he had. I had long since given up, and the more we moved, the more introverted I became. I spent most of my time in the parallel universe of my fantasy world. I was a poor student except in art, history and literature. I had the extra added pressure of being the "new meat" in my various schools, which to me were more like volatile, intimidating cell blocks than places of learning. When I asked my father to help me with my math homework, he'd get abusive, calling me stupid if I didn't get the right answers.

At one time Jack had been a stilt walker and he said he'd replaced Cary Grant in the Manchester circus he'd worked in. Elaine and I used to pretend we had different dads—William Powell, Fred Astaire or Robert Conrad. We'd fight over William Powell. Jack did have a dark, sarcastic sense of humour that three of his offspring inherited. Only Diane didn't venture over to the dark side with the rest of us.

My mother, Celia, was British, blond and beautiful. She had olive skin and brown eyes, and resembled the actress Gena Rowlands. It seemed to me that she walked around shell-shocked. After we moved to Canada, she told me repeatedly that she was sorry the day after she married my father. That is a steaming load of angst to dump on a child. All us kids would make fun of my mother's accent, and she was not amused.

Mom had been a singer and dancer in British musical theatre. She wanted to continue singing after my parents were married but Dad wouldn't let her. He was insanely jealous and possessive of her. Celia filled our heads with stories about the life she had left behind. She was from an upper middle class family. She showed us a photograph of herself as a teenager, being dragged along by two Russian wolfhounds on leashes. She kept a box of photographs of the people she worked with in the theatre: dancers; a man dressed as Dick Whittington's cat; and headshots of her gal-pals, including Ida Lupino, who had been a member of the same theatre company. The photographs that I was fascinated with were tableaus of nude women covered in body makeup to make them look like classical Greek statues. That's how people got to see a little "artistic" tits and ass. During the Second World War, Celia had worked part-time in a munitions factory, like all patriotic British girls. She'd tell us how frightened she was, hiding under her flimsy kitchen table, listening to the whistle of the German V-2 missiles as they flew over London.

From the moment I set my tiny British sandal-clad foot in Canada, I began to indulge in a rich fantasy life. On that dark day, I moved into an emotional netherworld. The basic theme of my escapist wet dreams was myself turning into an icon worshipped by everyone who laid eyes on me. This helped me evade the grim reality of our first apartment in Montreal, where I contracted every kid disease you could get. I wrote my first song in the bathtub, where I spent a lot of time covered in calamine lotion. To make matters worse, Diane and I were confronted with the fact that Celia was pregnant. We both resented our new baby sister, Elaine, because she got most of the attention. Elaine wants me to stress the fact that she was the beautiful sister.

Two years after we landed in Montreal, we took off for Aldershot, a rustic suburb outside Hamilton, Ontario. We had a white frame house on an acre of land. Dad was on the road a lot with his rubber products. My guilt-filled daydreams at that time involved impressing cute girls. Diane had a whole ménage of invisible friends. Elaine rolled around on the living room floor and had tantrums. We moved on after a year and landed in the west end of Toronto, moving from house to house. By the time Elaine left home, the Popes had moved eighteen times.

At nine, I was given a guitar, which I learned to play badly. I'd pose in front of a mirror, dressed in capri pants and a plaid shirt, with my Matty Mattel fanner-50 cap gun strapped around my waist, and visualize myself singing before an audience and being showered with love and adoration. I became an expert at singing into a hairbrush while gyrating like Elvis. Around this time my mother stopped showing me physical affection. Maybe she thought I didn't need any more touchy-feely stuff. That kind of rejection is something you never get over. I tried to get love from my parents by showing them drawings, usually portraits, which I spent hours labouring over. My sisters and I used to put on shows. We sang show tunes that we learned from the records my mother listened to. Though I liked singing to myself, I was very surly about singing in front of anyone, and Diane and Elaine had to prod me into it. In one of our many houses in the suburban nether regions, we had a next door neighbour, Bill, who was a sculptor. He created statues of religious figures for churches. He let me come over while he worked and taught me how to model clay. Bill was encouraging and inspired me to entertain thoughts of becoming a sculptress. He was my first positive adult role model.

My baby brother, Howard, magically appeared in our lives while we were living somewhere in the depths of Scarborough. Apparently divorce was taboo in the forties when my parents took the plunge. My parents' quick-fix solution for the problems with their marriage was to have more kids. Howard served as a toy for my sisters and me to terrorize. He was cute, with a sweet disposition. We were so awful to him. We liked to hide in his closet until Mom put him to bed, then jump out and scare the hell out of him. We were a satanic version of the Avengers.

When we first heard the Beatles, all three of us were in the frightened "Bambi" phase of adolescence. We were living in Guildwood Village, another stop in Scarborough. We fell in love. We were allowed to see their first show in Toronto at Maple Leaf Gardens. We sat way in the back of the arena in the crappy grey section. We had to endure the screams of thousands of kids. We were outraged by all the hysterical chicks, because we were there to listen. The Fab Four were tiny specks on the stage. The sound system was prehistoric, two spindly PA columns. After seeing the Beatles, we were united in our quest to be cool, swinging and free, like everyone from London. We discovered a new band called the Rolling Stones. They had bad skin and, unlike the Beatles, were dangerous and threatening. In our basement rec room with wall-treatments of simulated burled Carpathian elm, we'd crank up forty-fives of the Stones on our Seabreeze record player and lip-synch to them. I was Mick.

I finally made it to high school. I was studying graphic design at Cedarbrae, a suburban school, where social outcasts like future female impersonator Craig Russell, who was president of the Mae West fan club, and studmuffin Klaus Kassbaum, future bass player for Steppenwolf, sauntered down the hallways. There was the requisite stacked sexy blond girl with attitude oozing out of her pores who everyone said was the school slut. Her blatant sexuality, which turned me on, was the inspiration for Rough Trade's biggest hit. Sex was becoming an obsession with me. I used it as a shock tactic to get attention. I loved the way people would react to my sense of humour, which was riddled with sexual innuendo. For the first time in my life I felt connected with a group of people. I felt an affinity for the kids in my class. We were all dispossessed art students who shared the same warped outlook on life.

But we were soon ripped out of school again by Daddy Dearest. His erratic behaviour was taking its toll. Celia was in tears as we helped her pack. I didn't know how to console her, since we were all trapped in the same hell. My poor little family piled into a Chevy station wagon and drove across the U.S.A. and Canada to Vancouver. Diane and I missed our friends, and I even missed some of my teachers, but the west coast was heaven to us. It was lush and beautiful, with breathtaking mountains. We all loved it there, even though we moved three times in nine months. Celia was actually happy, because she felt a connection to the ocean, and the climate was almost English.

While we were living in West Vancouver, Diane and I went out to clubs like the Blues Palace and saw R&B bands play. Diane would sneak her boyfriend, Gordy, into our basement room so they could make out. One week Diane was on a local teen dance show. The entire family thrilled to her version of the Mashed Potato. I hung out with friends who were as obsessed with music as I was. We'd play R&B records and get lost in the music, which was passionate and raw, unlike the homogenized sound of white artists. Soul music reached into my ravaged heart and moved me like nothing else.

The kids in my new school were tough. Some of them had carved their initials in their flesh. One night a pile of us climbed into two cars and careened all over the mountain roads, ending up at an abandoned shack at a fish cannery. We drank lemon gin until we puked.

Our somewhat idyllic life was shattered by my father's announcement that we were moving back to Toronto. It was always the same broken record—he had some scam going on that was going to make us rich. We wanted to kill him.

———————

Don Mills was the catalyst that pushed Diane and me over the edge. We went back to school, and Jack was on our backs about everything we did. We lived in the middle of a cul-de-sac, where all the neighbours could watch us turn the street into a drag strip when our parents went out. We were supposed to be babysitting Howard, and would threaten to have our boyfriends beat up Elaine if she ratted us out. Boys would tear into our driveway in their Corvettes or on Harleys. They'd make a shitload of testosterone-induced noise. It was all show. We weren't bad girls. It makes me cringe to even use that term. Diane met a boy named Danny on the midway at the Canadian National Exhibition. Both my parents disapproved of him, so she started sneaking out at night to be with him.

I desperately wanted to go to the Ontario College of Art, but Jack wouldn't let me. He didn't consider art a money-making career. He told me to get a job. I dropped out of high school and went to work with Diane at Philco, a factory that manu-factured televisions. Working on an assembly line was an unre-lenting nightmare, standing for eight hours a day putting thirteen resistors in a circuit board every minute. You were allowed to take breaks to go to the nurse's office for Valium so you could deal with the monotony. While you were on line you could hear the stereos being tested in another part of the factory. They used the same two records over and over: "Blue Navy Blue" and "Howdy Doody Christmas." Diane and I were traumatized; we both quit after eight months. Diane left home and moved to a room downtown to be close to Danny. I got a job as a junior artist in a business forms printing plant. That job was the begin-ning and the end of my button-down life. I was living every angst-ridden teenager's nightmare. I was rebellious and self-righteous. I didn't want to spend the rest of my life carpooling to some loser job. The insipid cultural vacuum of suburbia would not claim another victim. Right on!!

I started hanging out in Yorkville, which was Toronto's little slice of sixties bohemia. On weekends, my friend Karen and I took the Don Mills bus downtown. Karen was a miniskirted rebel with white lipstick, mod bob and layers of eyeliner. Her needs were simple: a skin specialist and the love of any long-haired boy. My needs were more complicated. The streets of Yorkville were overflowing with kids searching for nirvana. They sat on the steps outside the Grab Bag, the only variety store on the street. They drank coffee at the Penny Farthing. At night there were so many clubs to hang out at—Charlie Brown's; the El Patio; the Purple Onion; and the Mynah Bird, where a woman swayed back and forth, half naked, in a swing suspended from the ceiling. All the cool kids from Cedarbrae went to Charlie Brown's. My future boy lovers performed in bands on the ground floor. The girls would huddle together in an upstairs room and commune with a Ouija board. We liked having seances with the undead. Yorkville seemed like a different galaxy. I ran towards that bright, beckoning, aura-enhanced light.

The first street I lived on was Huron. It was tree-lined, with Victorian houses that had seen better days. I had a room on the top floor. The colour scheme was puce. I surrounded myself with music and books. My first real artistic influence was the poetry of Sylvia Plath. I related to her dark and bitter sensibilities, but I was not crazy about the oven thing. I remember my parents' first and only visit to my cool pad. I'd drawn a picture of Queen Elizabeth on the wall brandishing a huge cock. Jack and Celia dropped by unannounced with a bag of groceries to see if I was still alive. Both my parents eyed the offending piece of artwork and said nothing about it.

I have fond memories of sitting in tactium, listening to the Beatles and Jimi Hendrix over and over. I mean listening to the same song for eight hours straight. Everyone who lived in the house wandered in and out of each other's rooms. There were no locks on the doors. And God, we used to talk for hours, feeling Christ-like—meaningless cosmic drivel involving DNA and how we were made up of atoms floating in a void. All the stuff killer weed can conjure up. I liked to sit at my window and watch my colourful neighbours. A queen named Murray Cooper used to sashay down the middle of Huron Street singing show tunes at the top of his lungs. Two call girls lived directly across the street from me. Their pimps were always wheeling racks of dresses into their apartment. I thought they were fashion models until they invited me over for tea and showed me X-rated photos of themselves. Across the hall from me on the top floor was a student named Peter O'Brian, who is now a filmmaker. We both thought one of the girls in the house was a witch because she was so intense she scared us. If she was in the kitchen the oven door would fall open; we'd attribute any strange occurrence in the house to her. When we were stoned and ravenous, we'd go to Webster's restaurant on Avenue Road. It was a cool hang; "Take 5" by Dave Brubeck always seemed to be playing on the jukebox. We'd cram our bodies into a booth and load up on rice pudding, french fries, strawberries and cherry coke to ease our drugged-out cravings.

I'd stay up late and pass out at work. I decided to quit before they fired me and try to live on unemployment insurance. I spent hours lying on the floor of my "crib" drawing happening celebs. I was inspired by trendy British pop magazines like *Fab* and *Rave*. I sold some of my portraits of pop stars to my landlord and friends for extra cash.

How hot and exciting it was to dress up in op-art dresses, bell-bottoms or miniskirts and melt into the palpable excitement of the street. We were all one. A lava flow of love. Music was my reason for living. We would pour into Maple Leaf Gardens to see the Stones in all their misogynistic fury. *Under my thumb is a squirming dog who's just had her day.* Defiant Brian Jones playing his teardrop-shaped Vox guitar, the bags under his eyes signifying he was deep, that he had experienced things we could never hope to experience. The prancing Mick Jagger seemed ludicrous next to Brian's blond, village-of-the-damned beauty.

Here's an example of a typical day in my life after I quit my job. Wake up around noon. Two cretinous neighbour boys drop by. We smoke thirteen joints. Get very hungry. Nothing to eat but pablum or canned spaghetti. Eat. Go outside. Become one with God and the universe. Get a little frightened. Go back inside. Play lots of records. Play guitar. Cute boy drops by. Keith McKie, singer in a band. Try not to drool at his beauty. Try to follow his drugged-out ramblings. Crave him in a carnal way. He belongs to another. Rumour has it he is hung like a horse. It's true.

The first time I dropped acid, Keith was my guide. Without someone there to babysit you, your first trip could turn into something akin to having an alien life-form try to chew its way through a host body—yours. Acid came in tabs with pharmaceutical names like Sandoz and Purple Owsley. Sandoz was the name of the lab in Basel, Switzerland, where LSD was manufactured. It was discovered by a German chemist named Albert Hofmann in 1938, which in itself is highly suspect. He palled around with writers Aldous Huxley and Ernst Janger. These were men who wanted mankind to evolve spiritually through the aid of psychedelics, which is a true Western cop-out—and I was ready to buy into it. A hit was an eighth of a tab. Any more than that and your brain could implode.

As soon as I started getting off, every inch of my room took on a vibrancy as though the walls were alive and breathing. The colours were lush and intense. Millions of neurons were firing up in my brain. I was overcome with the feeling that I had never really looked at anything before. Keith sat cross-legged on the floor, his hair lit by the sunlight. I contemplated the texture and colour of an orange for God knows how long. The music we listened to felt like it was part of our psyche. I called Celia and told her how much I loved her. I could sense her discomfort at my outpouring of emotion, like I was crossing a line of some sort.

Dropping acid opened a door that forced me to face myself. Each trip I took was like throwing a stone into a lake, creating a ripple effect, each more intense than the last. Under the supportive influence of Keith, I began to write songs, which I was too insecure to play for anyone.

I had crushes on singers, bass players and drummers. We used to frequent a club called Boris's, which my landlord Bernie owned. The walls were Chinese red and the stage was a simple black slab. All the beautiful kids and beautiful bands melted together in a whirling vortex of sensuality. Every weekend, groups like the Ugly Ducklings (a Stone clone band that wrote great songs), Luke and the Apostles, and McKenna Mendelson Mainline let loose on that stage. Go-go dancers shimmied, jerked and gyrated while the bands performed. Sometimes I'd help a friend work his light show, a series of slides projected on the bands. I'd wander around the club and say hi to people. One boy and I had an intense conversation about the little people living on his eyelashes. I sometimes felt immortal.

The bathroom of Boris's was often filled with girls indulging in the strange process of washing their bangs. Each one of them would be plotting out a strategy for who they were going to fuck next. My friend Angie, who I thought was exotic because she was Hungarian, was always telling me what she did in bed with various musicians. I wanted to block my ears and hum while she filled me in on the graphic details of her scatological sex life. It was grisly stuff.

I made it with a few boys, usually once. It was like a formality we had to get out of the way before we could become friends. In my view, the penis has serious design flaws. It's all function over form, like whoever designed it couldn't wait to use it. The helmet thing is great, but then aesthetically the whole structure falls apart. Balls seem like an afterthought. I used to hate when I was with a guy and he'd take what seemed like hours to come. I know that's most people's idea of heaven, but not me, baby. He'd be rutting away and I'd be furtively looking around the room hoping to spot some reading material. Sex with boys wasn't unpleasant. Most of the boys were sweet and still finding themselves, and I'd get close with them every way but sexually.

My biggest crush was on a girl named Zack, who fronted a band called the Knack. (They eventually changed their name to the Dickens; to this day, I question the wisdom of that decision.) Zaharia Malmolli was an Italian Jew from New York, with an Egyptian thing going on. The Liz Taylor mega-dud had been a big influence on fashion. Zack had huge brown kohl-rimmed eyes and a full sensuous mouth. Her hair, like mine, was cut in the classic sixties Vidal Sassoon bob. She had a singing voice like a black angel. I'd watch her with my breath caught in my throat as she stood there like a Babylonian love goddess belting out songs in some club. I wanted her and I wanted to be her.

Zack's pseudo-Moroccan room had all the essential sixties accoutrements: beaded curtains, hookah pipe, throw pillows, delusions of Marrakesh. I would sit hot and feverish while Zack burned incense and told me about her man problems. She'd say, "Carole, I have a big crush on so and so. What should I do?" She'd been involved with the drummer of the Barbarians. He lost a hand and had an attractive hook in its place. Their claim to fame was "Are You a Boy or Are You a Girl?" Zack also had an affair with John Sebastian, the singer of the Lovin' Spoonful. We actually drove to Buffalo and caught their act in a high-school gymnasium. John was very charming, and I tried not to be jealous. I felt like comic-strip heroine Brenda Starr's sexually ambiguous sidekick. To paraphrase fifties lesbo pulp novels, I felt the shameless burn of the love that dare not speak its name.

In retrospect the sixties were not that liberal. Sex had serious side effects. Birth control pills had been tested on women in Haiti and Puerto Rico for two whole years, which is nothing, then foisted on us. You always felt nauseous and bloated, like you were in a constant state of pregnancy. What a sexual turn-on. Condoms, forget about it, the boys didn't want to know. Free love was a contradiction, a concept dreamed up by some straight guy so he could get pussy. Chick love was okay if the boys were in on it, but pretty much *verboten* if they weren't.

I was on a secret mission to find out where the dykes were. I'd walk along Toronto's garish Yonge Street strip, muttering under my breath, "Oh God, Oh God, where are they?" I'd skulk past the foul-smelling bar called the St. Charles. I knew that's where the boys went. I felt like a frustrated sexual freak. My only information on lesbians was a well-worn Wonder Woman comic and a book called *The Well of Loneliness*, a depressing little tome about a woman called Stephen. Perhaps a name change might help? My mother had given me the book to read, then abruptly taken it back. What was *she* doing with it?

The Knack did a gig in New York. I hopped on a plane to be with them. New York in the sixties was a psychedelic mind explosion, a city filled with vibrant colours. Zack, me, John Lyons, the band's drummer, and his girlfriend Lucy Lerner, whose father had written a little show called *My Fair Lady*, picnicked in Central Park. It was safe then.

I walked through Washington Square and fell in love with the city. It was so vital and alive. I went to some trendy boutiques, Betsey Johnson's Paraphernalia, Trash and Vaudeville. I saw the pop art Brillo boxes and the Campbell's Soup cans of Andy Warhol, whose paintings and films, like *Blow Job* and *Chelsea Girls*, blew apart our conceptions of art. I felt "not just stoned, but beautiful." It was so liberating. I wandered into the Bitter End in the East Village, and saw Donovan jamming with Odetta.

One night a whole pack of us went to the Electric Circus, the quintessential psychedelic experience on the club scene. The Knack, me and Von Meter, a comic whose entire career was based on impersonating Bobby Kennedy, filed into the club. I felt like Beatrice descending into Dante's Inferno. I'd never seen anything like it. We stepped over the supine undulating bodies of people in the throes of acid trips. Various circus acts were in progress. A man was hanging upside down from the ceiling, fighting his way out of a straightjacket. Another man walked a tightrope. A trippy psychedelic light show throbbed all around us, a miracle of oil and water. On stage the beautiful, fucked-up and, from all accounts, incredibly annoying Jim Morrison of the Doors was singing "Light My Fire."

In 1967, during the "Summer of Love," my mother had taken Elaine and Howard and moved back to England. I heard from Diane that Jack had followed them and threatened Celia with a gun. She managed to calm him down and get him off her back. They were now relatively happy, living in Brighton by the sea.

I moved into a tiny room over the Penny Farthing, a coffee house on Yorkville Avenue. There was a small swimming pool in the back, where the bikini-clad waitresses could take a dip. Sitting outside drinking coffee, I'd catch fleeting images of visiting rock gods and goddesses, whose limos would inevitably drive along Yorkville Avenue. I remember seeing Cass Elliot and Brian Wilson behind the tinted glass. I wanted to be at least a demi-goddess, gliding along in one of those big black cars.

The real action was down the street at the Riverboat. One night I smoked a whole whack of doobies with Zack and a pal from New York, singer Ritchie Havens, and we went to see the tiny, barely-formed Joni Mitchell sing "The Circle Game." She was the mould, the role model for every babe you will ever see performing in a Lilith concert.

My new landlords, John and Marilyn McHugh, were an eccentric English couple. Once John came to my room to show me his water on the knee. Did he expect me to fondle it?

My next door neighbour, Geordie McDonald, played drums in a band called the Heavenly Government. Beneath Geordie's nerdish exterior was a brilliant man. He wore a flashing light-bulb on his head while pounding the shit out of his drums. Geordie introduced me to Marshall McLuhan. All three of us sat outside the Penny Farthing drinking coffee and talking the whole afternoon. I had no idea who he was. After McLuhan threw out phrases he'd coined, like "post-literate generation" and "the medium is the message," it dawned on me. He studied the media's impact on society and its effects on each individual's senses. The media was obsessed with us. The baby boomers' rebellion against straight society was labelled a "Youth Quake." McLuhan drew me into what was a very illuminating mind-expanding discussion. There is nothing as sexy as intellect. McLuhan's take on where we were headed was eons beyond my insular self-obsessed world.

Greedy real estate entrepreneurs were starting to conspire against us. There was a demonstration on Yorkville Avenue. We, the villagers, were sick of gawking tourists traipsing through our special place, destroying the love vibes. In the spirit of the Love Generation, hundreds of us gathered one day and sat in the middle of Yorkville Avenue chanting, "Close our street," over and over. The cops were not amused. They came at us on horseback. They dragged some kids off to jail while the rest of us scattered. I had a couple of friends who were busted. They said the cops beat them by putting a telephone book on their heads and then hitting the book with a crowbar. That way there'd be no external signs of damage. Beneath Ontario's calm WASP exterior beat the heart of a police state.

My year-long ride on unemployment was over, and I needed a job. I worked as a surly coat-check girl at the Mynah Bird, a club where the "straights" came looking for hippie chicks' free love. That career lasted about two hours. If a man checked out my cleavage, I'd ask him, "What are you looking at?" That was that.

I answered an ad in *The Toronto Star* and got work as a cel painter at a film company that was producing an animated TV series called *Rocket Robin Hood*. Robin Hood goes outer space. It was the perfect gig for a stoned-out chick like me.

A chimp could paint cels. There were animators from all over the world working on this disastrous series. The ink and paint department was in a large room where we sat at long desks with light boxes cut into them. The place was so full of trippy kids, I'd sometimes get overcome by the stench of patchouli oil, which smells exactly like blue ointment, a medication used to eradicate crabs. Since we were allowed to smoke cigarettes, we pushed the limits and lit up joints while we worked. Things would get slightly hysterical. Fran, the woman in charge of our department, would get suspicious and ask, "What are you smoking?" We'd all reply in unison, "Gauloises."

There was such a language barrier between the animators it was difficult for the departments to communicate without interpreters. Whenever we viewed the rushes, there were glaring mistakes. The characters' heads would fall off. The colours were wrong, and some of the cel painters had added their own little touches like peace signs. One time Rocket Robin Hood was waving a giant shlong at the Sheriff of Nottingham.

One of the animators was Clive Smith. He was talented and English, with long blond hair and giant mutton-chop sideburns. He was kind of sexy, and yet at the same time insane, a human version of the characters he animated. He'd played piano back home in England with Arthur Brown, a singer who liked to set his head on fire, and the Bonzo Dog Band, who were like a musical version of Monty Python.

We became a close-knit clique and had great parties. It seemed like everyone working at this way station wanted to be in a band or be involved in something trendy and "now." I bought a caftan from a guy at work. Those of us who were flirting with the prospect of enlightenment went to see "Sexy Sadie," the Maharishi Mahesh Yogi, whose teachings had seduced the Beatles. Their love affair with him was over. We stood in the lecture hall with Toronto's trendy ones, clutching flowers to our breasts, listening to his spiel. The general consensus was that he was a giggling old fool. I went elsewhere to study Tibetan Buddhism, and I started meditating.

Our abrasive bosses, a husband-and-wife act were also trying hard to be "now." The wife was thirty-something, which seemed ancient to us. She was sorely lacking in people skills, calling clients and co-workers "fucking stupid pricks" when she didn't like their ideas, which was always. She wore garishly coloured mod dresses from trendy Toronto boutiques like the Unicorn. She had huge papier-mâché earrings that lacerated her neck when she moved. She and her husband were constantly giving people tours of our ink and paint ghetto. Once they dragged the Velvet Fog, Mel Tormé, through our gulag. As soon as they left we broke into spasms of laughter. The company ultimately went bankrupt. During the last few weeks of business, the husband walked around the office with a gun stuffed in his pants.

I met a girl named Jane when I first moved to Yorkville. She was part Lebanese, an exotic hothouse flower, and her skin was luminous bronze. She always wore thigh-high leather boots, which were threatening and seductive, and she came on like a cross between Natalie Wood and Diana Ross. She used to appear out of nowhere. I got the distinct impression that she wanted something. One day I found out what that was—me.

I'd just dropped acid and I have to say that Yorkville was enhanced by cosmic oneness. People walked by in slow motion, leaving Technicolor afterimages. Jane materialized before me as she was prone to do. I'm not sure how we ended up in my room but the next thing I knew we were writhing around naked. Neither of us had been with a woman before. I still remember the incredible softness of her skin as we slid into and over one another. I didn't want it to stop, it felt so unbearably good. The most seductive thing about being with another woman is that she knows what you're thinking, what you want, how to touch you. That is the double-edged sword of lesbianism. Making love with a woman is like heroin, like jumping off a precipice and falling into a sweet narcotic-like sensuality. That, I would ultimately learn, is the lure and the trap of being with a woman. I walked around in a daze afterwards, and there was no one I could tell about it. All my friends were straight. I retreated back into the closet.

I had a sweet friend named Allen Collins who was a filmmaker. He was shooting a documentary on Jimi Hendrix and called me at work to ask if I would interview Jimi for the film. I got feverish just thinking about it. The Jimi Hendrix Experience was the first multicultural power trio. It had balls on top of balls, and Jimi's lyrical imagery was a lethal combo of sex and science fiction that blew everyone else out of the water.

Allen, his girlfriend, Mary Lou Green, who was a stylist at Sassoons, a cameraman and myself converged on the Coliseum, a large arena on the exhibition grounds in Toronto. We were beside ourselves with excitement. The minute we entered the dressing room I felt I was in the presence of a rock god. The setting was drugged-out and Felliniesque. The drug of choice: LSD. The Soft Machine, who were the opening band, Jimi, Mitch Mitchell, the drummer, and Noel Redding, the bass player, were surrounded by the usual suspects. Mitch and Noel seemed about three feet tall, but had really big hair to compensate. They were buzzing around Jimi like satellites around the moon.

Jimi was wearing a Moroccan black velvet embroidered jacket and had a trace of an English accent. He was chill, digging the scene with a bemused smile, and didn't have any attitude. I was shaking and getting a contact high from the energy in that room. Even though I was a blown-away groupie, it was clear that Jimi was an oasis of sanity in all that mayhem. I tried to pull it together and ask my list of prepared questions. He was magnetic and charming and said, "Baby, let your mind go." I kept thinking, "How can he make so much sense when he's so stoned?" I just wanted to listen to him talk forever. We dragged ourselves out of there when it was time for the band to go on. A horde of hysterical groupies was waiting outside the dressing room, the Canadian version of the Plaster Casters, those girls who fucked musicians and then made plaster impressions of their cocks. They started yelling at me, "How big is it?" Jimi was a legend in the penis world.

During his passionate performance that night, Jimi did all the Jimi things. He played his guitar behind his back. He ran his tongue along the neck of his Strat like it was the body of a woman. He set fire to it, watched it burn and then doused the flames. He was so hot and sexual on stage. He sang, "Let me stand, let me stand, next to your fire." Yeah, baby. The envelope of peace, love and understanding was being bent out of shape.

Keith McKie had other assets besides his voice and equipage. By this time his band, Kensington Market, had incorporated an innovative new instrument called a synthesizer into their act. The huge black monolith took up the whole stage and could make maybe two sounds, but it was the fucking bomb. Ethereal noises floated through the tripadelic atmosphere of the Masonic Temple, where everyone played. You paid a three-dollar cover to see bands like the Who, Jeff Beck,

Emerson Lake and Palmer, the Brian Auger Trinity and Led Zeppelin. Rumour had it that the Beatles heard Kensington Market's music and ripped them off. Every time I saw Keith, he'd ask about my writing, in his endearing little-boy sexbomb style.

I began to feel more confident about my songwriting and kept networking with musicians. I used to hang out with Peter Hodgson, the bass player for a band called Jon, Lee and the Checkmates. Peter always had a slightly bemused look on his face, like he was watching everything around him and filing it away, which was exactly what I was doing. White boys obsessed with soul music, the Checkmates had their own little cult thing going on at a place called the Avenue Road Club. They dressed in iridescent mohair suits and had Fender guitars slung low over their hips. They would emulate James Brown and work that funky shit. They did the whole soul-review bit, including the cape thing where the singer keeps coming back to the stage until one of the band members throws a cape over his shoulders and walks him off. It was flamboyant and melodramatic, and I still don't get it.

In those days I could sit there watching the band and drink twenty gin-and-tonics and not feel a thing. My sister Diane was dating Jon. She had evolved into a killer babe with a rack of death and was finding herself through hunky boys. She had a succession of cool boyfriends who my sister Elaine and I also loved. They were usually drug dealers or had some other sexy criminal edge. She ended up marrying a real straight boy, after leaving Jon and countless others in the dust.

When I got up my nerve, I'd play my songs for Peter when he visited me in my little garret. He would sit on the tree trunk that served as a chair and be so supportive. I was fucking paralyzed at the thought of singing in front of anyone. I felt naked and exposed, but I was driven to do it. I had to release all my pent-up anger, and the sexuality that was the core of my music, or I would explode.

In 1968, I finally auditioned as the singer for a band. The name of the band was the Deva Loca Sideshow. When I showed up at the rehearsal space, there were two nerdish musicians waiting for me. That in itself was shocking. They had none of the studly swagger that was a prerequisite for a musician in a rock band. Their names were Igor and Phil. It turned out they were trained classical players! I jammed along with those two non-threatening specimens of manhood, and it felt so right. Then *he* walked in the room, this gorgeous boy-man with blue-black hair and an aura of sweetness. I was drawn to him like the lost little girl I was. His name was Kevan Staples. Kevan was auditioning as a guitar player for the band. He pulled out a beautiful white Gretsch guitar and started playing atonal Aquarian-like things. That was his sign. The polar opposite of Leo, my sign. Tragically, or maybe not, the Deva Loca Sideshow never happened.

After the audition Kevan and I talked. He was very sweet and non-threatening. He worked as a roadie for the Ugly Ducklings. He said, "Let's go to my place," which turned out to be an apartment on Yorkville, full of *objets d'art*. We smoked hash in his hookah and he played sitar for me. I played him my dark, overtly sexual songs. He said, "I've never heard anyone like you." His taste in music was very eclectic or, as I saw it, his musical education was lacking. I proceeded to turn him on to soul and gospel music. What I really loved about being with Kevan was how we connected on a meta-physical childlike level. We were into exploring our inner child way before shrinks decreed it was a freeing experience. We became inseparable. Kevan took me to meet his parents, who

I found fascinating. His background was Irish. His mother, Ray, had a dry wit and was an upwardly mobile interior decorator. His father was a couturier who designed dresses for women. He was also a talented painter and did needlework. I felt like asking him if his parents were gay. They were so cool, I could see where Kevan got his urbane sense of style.

I'd moved to a room on Madison Avenue. Kevan would come over and we'd lie on my bed wrapped in each other's arms for hours. We dressed in identical black turtleneck sweaters. Sex was not a big motivation in our relationship, although when we did make love, his flesh had an indefinable scent—something like suede—that turned me on. He had a gymnast's body and was very gentle. Ultimately our union was more a cosmic soulmate kind of thing, which, on days when I'm not feeling cynical, I believe in. At that point, our relationship was open. We were both involved with other people.

Kevan and I wanted to start a band together. We had a somewhat warped vision of the kind of band we wanted. It was going to be called O. I'd just read *The Story of O*, and it pushed buttons I didn't know I had. This band was going to be an amalgamation of shocking sexuality and Kevan's cerebral *Lord of the Rings* vision.

At the butt end of the summer of love, things went a little insane at the normally staid O'Keefe Centre in Toronto. It was a venue where you were more likely to see a diva caterwauling an aria to the severed head of John the Baptist than hear rock music. Seeing Led Zeppelin play there was just so wrong, a real slap in the face of convention. The sheer unrelenting volume of the band was enough to make your eardrums bleed. I figured whoever booked them in there was stoned out of their mind. To make it more ludicrous, Donovan, the fairie king of sibilance, opened for them, singing about his candy man getting him high. His friend Gypsy Dave, often mentioned in his songs, was at his side, and somehow we were all in an elevator together . . . but I digress.

Compared to other bands, Led Zeppelin was dark and threatening. At the end of the sixties there was a violent mood swing over to the dark side of the drug culture, which signalled the end of Flower Power naiveté in this wormhole in time. Things were getting lethal. Alex, the bass player of Kensington Market, was found dead in his apartment. He'd been heavily into the occult. Friends started dropping dead from shooting up methamphetamine. An ex-boyfriend of mine died in a car crash.

To supplement my non-existent income, I started selling weed. I hooked up with two Mafioso boys who delivered a kilo of grass to me every two weeks. I packaged it up into ounces, dimes and nickel bags and sold it to friends. One afternoon I answered my front door with my friend Doug. (We were having a cerebral affair, mind-fucking each other.) A man I knew slightly, named Junior, was standing there waving a knife at me, demanding I give him my stash. I left Doug standing at the door with Junior holding the knife on him while I ran to my room, grabbed a couple of ounces and gave it to the guy. Doug made light of the situation saying, "thanks for leaving me with him." (My two Mafioso boys took care of Junior. I didn't ask for details.)

The two girls who lived in the flat next to me were friends with Doris Day's son, Terry Melcher. He came to visit them and filled us in on all the grisly details of the murder of Sharon Tate. The Manson family had been looking for him but found Tate, who was renting his house. We watched Bobby Kennedy get gunned down on live TV. We sat there in shock. I know this sounds trite, but you had to be there to feel the impact these events had on us. Most of my friends were feeling lost, as the last vestiges of our innocence and idealism blew up in our faces.

I introduced Kevan to Clive. There was an instant bonding between the boys, like two alien entities discovering each other. Somehow we got our dream band together. Clive found us a rehearsal space and we practised every day. O was the kind of band that rehearsed forever and never did live gigs, which added, we thought, to our mystique. Clive played piano and Kevan and I played guitar. For a minute we had John Lyons, ex of the Knack, on drums. We took promo shots of us leaping about in the trees in the middle of winter in Queen's Park. I was wearing a white afghan coat that I wish I had now. O's first gig was playing a song on top of a brightly painted bus at City Hall. It was filmed for the upcoming world's fair in Osaka, Japan. We did one other live show, and then the band disintegrated into nothingness.

Celia came back from England with Howard and Elaine. Elaine hated the English school system and was sent off to Montreal to stay with relatives so she could finish her education in Canada. I took Celia to see a lawyer friend of mine so she could file for divorce. She needed a firm guiding hand to get her into his office. When the divorce was finalized, she went back to England with Howard.

I had my first bad trip. Whoever cooked up what now passed on the street for acid had cut it with strychnine. Tripping out while being doubled over in pain was not worth it. Thank god one of my friends had some Valium.

I stopped practising meditation because one night I had a vision of a man's head with flies pouring out of it. I was convinced it was Satan in his incarnation as the Lord of the Flies. To top it all off, our rooming house was sold and all the tenants got booted out. I felt like I'd been blinded by the cold light of reality. The winter of my discontent began and lasted till 1976.

After a couple of ill-fated romantic detours, Kevan and I shacked up in 1969 in a rooming house on Gloucester Street near the gay village. We were friends, committed lovers and, most importantly, wanted to write together and ultimately put together another band. We had separate bedrooms. Every inch of Kevan's room was covered with stuff—very tasteful stuff, thanks to the influence of his mother, Ray. The Staples house was a designer showcase filled with extremely tasteful clutter. I had different needs. The decor in my room was my cat, Mylar, a few kittens who doubled as throw pillows, and a guitar.

When we first moved into the house, it was owned by a woman named Roma Williams Wynn. She lived upstairs with her son, Joe, who was a thespian in every sense of the word. He had a booming baritone voice, and sometimes he'd stand at the top of the stairs and let out a funny operatic laugh to amuse us. Roma, who had a very dry wit, used to invite me into her room for a glass of sherry and tell me stories about her friendship with Bea Lillie, who was Joe's godmother. She would also stand at the top of the stairs and yell down to us kids on the first floor when we were misbehaving.

A strange boy who lived in a little room in the back of the house had a body shaped like a mutant pear and liked to walk around the house naked. Roma was appalled, but only because his particular nudity offended her aesthetic sensibilities. Joe invited us to his room to try out prunes stuffed with hash and soaked in wine. We swallowed the things and were subjected to music by Crosby, Stills, Nash and whatever. I hated the high, the numbing effect of the opiate. I crawled back to my room and lay on my bed. I couldn't tell which end was up and swore off hash forever. Joe had a sex-bomb girlfriend from L.A., named Carol, who was one of the 7-Up heirs. He was completely pussy-whipped by her. When they were eating dinner, we could hear her scream at him, "Joe, eat your fucking peas!" I know it was purely out of love and concern for his health. Carol's brother Bobby had control of the family's fortune. He'd fly in from L.A. to visit, dressed in skintight jumpsuits made out of yellow gingham vinyl or some other equally ridiculous fabric. He always brought his baby, a drooling Doberman on a leash.

When I wasn't selling weed or painting cels, I was working freelance for a company called Cinera. I lived an opium den–like existence with Kevan and the cast of characters we let into our lives. Clive lived nearby with his girlfriend, Trish (who would later play keyboards with us) and a Welsh couple who worked at the Royal Ontario Museum. They had a menagerie of exotic animals: sloths and squirrel monkeys who fucked each other up the ass as they ran along people's clotheslines, and a mutant coatimundi who liked to claw the flesh off your legs. One morning Clive woke up screaming to discover a slow loris's razor-sharp teeth clamped onto his balls.

Kevan and I were nocturnal creatures who sprawled around waxing poetic and writing songs. Most of the bands we saw around town were doing a mix of top forty songs and original material that I found flat and unexciting. Nobody out there had any passion. All my lyrics were sexual or political and Kevan's music was either old school rhythm and blues or cosmic and trance-like. He really was such an Aquarian. When we were writing together he'd go off into Kevan-land and I'd have to call his name several times to snap him back to reality. Around the time of the moon landing, which moved Kevan beyond words, we were lying on his bed tripping out on acid. As usual we were trying to discern the meaning of life. After some profound soul-searching, Kevan said, "Gravity is important." To this day, I tease him about that.

We'd sent out some demo tapes of our songs and we got summoned to a meeting at Quality Records. A personable man with bad seventies hair offered us a publishing contract, which we signed on the spot. Then a month went by and we didn't hear from him. We called Quality and the man was no longer working there. Our contract was invalid. Variations of this scenario have happened to most of the musicians I know.

We decided to start working as an acoustic duo. We christened ourselves the Bullwhip Brothers. We actually got a paying gig at a sleazy hotel, but were fired because the management didn't go for our sexually threatening material, even though we'd gone to the trouble of learning a couple of cover tunes.

Mom breezed back into town in 1970. We like to think she missed us. She and Howard found a flat in the Annex on Albany Street. I introduced her to Kevan and she thought he was fabulous. Elaine had finished school, and she moved into a house across the street from our boarding house.

In the seventies, there was a harmonic conversion of comedic proportions in Toronto. Gilda Radner, Dan Aykroyd, Catherine O'Hara, Martin Short, Andrea Martin and Eugene Levy all together on one stage. Gilda, Marty, Andrea and Eugene had worked together in *Godspell*, a musical celebrating clowns and Christ, which to me was one of the most frightening concepts ever.

We met Dan Aykroyd and Valri Bromfield in 1971 when we worked with them at Global Village, a fringe theatre. Andrew Alexander was a producer there who organized a weekly event called Platform, where Kevan and I would perform our bizarre songs. We found an audience at this venue, and started doing more gigs around town.

When Danny and Val launched into their eclectic improv, it was like watching a cast of twenty people on the stage. They slipped in and out of different characters as effortlessly as breathing. We became instant friends with Valri, who would come over to our house in the guise of one of her characters, usually a guy with a heavy five o'clock shadow, a man sometimes known as Owen Cobb.

Global Village was the creative spawn of Elizabeth and Robert Swerdlow. They both intimidated the hell out of me. The productions mounted in that lunatic space cemented the phrase "bad theatre" into the English language. One play I witnessed involved a man super-gluing a woman's labia shut.

Gilda Radner did some acting in two of the Swerdlow productions, *Fuck* and *Cherry Tart*. The titles give away the plot lines. She was having a relationship with Catherine O'Hara's brother, a handsome babe magnet named Markus who sold tickets at the door. Gilda wanted him so badly she took things from his place until she had so much of his stuff she told him that he had to move in with her. Their circle of friends came out of the fringe netherworld, and included way too many transvestites and drag queens. Gilda told Markus she felt threatened by the trannies because she thought they were more feminine than she was.

Bernie Sahlins and Joyce Sloane, two of the founders of Chicago's Second City, started a company in Toronto in 1973 in a space on Adelaide Street. The first cast included Gilda, Danny, Valri, Joe Flaherty, Eugene Levy, Brian Doyle, Bill Murray and Jayne Eastwood. It was heaven, and it lasted six months—Bernie and Joyce had all kinds of trouble trying to get a liquor licence. With the help of Andrew Alexander, they finally moved into the old Firehall Theatre on Lombard Street. My sister Elaine started out there as a waitress and worked her way up to manager. Andrea Martin, John Candy, Catherine O'Hara, Rosemary Radcliffe and Martin Short were added to the ever-changing cast. Kevan and I liked to blow some weed and catch the show almost every night.

The Second City space was minimalist: a stage painted black with several entrances. There were four chairs, some clothing, wigs and glasses. That was all they needed. As soon as the bodies hit the stage, it was magic time. They had total artistic freedom and went to some pretty esoteric places. It was like taking a crash course in avant-garde theatre that culminated in turning into a mockery of itself. There were parodies of Pirandello and Strindberg. Characters were born on that stage, like Gilda's Emily Latella, who we got to see evolve on *SCTV* and *Saturday Night Live*.

There were parties with Danny and Valri hamming it up. Nobody could get enough of their version of bad performance art. Martin Short injected a cheese factor into things with his impersonations of Sinatra and Bobby Darin, and he would walk around belting out show tunes at the top of his lungs. All the parties seem to melt into one big scene where a group of us are standing around a piano singing, "With a Little Help from My Friends" along with John Belushi, who, sweating and twitching spasmodically, does an all-too-realistic parody of Joe Cocker.

Danny opened a speakeasy called the 505 on Queen Street East. It had a storefront window that faced the street. For some reason Danny was obsessed with cops, and they'd show up and hang out with him. I guess that's why he didn't get busted. He did amazing impressions of them; he'd break into a French-Canadian accent and pretend he was with the Hull police. Maybe it was a little-boy fantasy he never grew out of. Everyone would stay up until dawn hovered over the turbulent Turneresque Toronto skyline. The cast was smitten with each other. Valri, Catherine and Andrea would stage musicals like *Oklahoma!* They'd literally bounce off the walls and bales of hay on the sawdust covered floor, singing "I'm just a girl who cain't say nooo."

Catherine O'Hara and her sister Mary Margaret were originally waitresses at Second City. Catherine had a sweet disposition and a maniacal look in her eyes. While she was waitressing, the real show was in the kitchen, where she kept the staff in stitches. Catherine and Danny started dating and moved in with each other. Catherine is from a large Irish family, and members of the O'Hara clan were always in the audience. (Later it seemed everywhere Rough Trade toured in Canada we'd run into one of Catherine's or Kevan's relatives.)

The notorious Jane would drop by once in a while to keep tabs on Kevan and me. She'd shoot me hot meaningful looks from across the room, which I pretended to ignore. She was also a fan and liked to watch us jam. One night she brought Michael J. Pollard to the den of iniquity we called home. Pollard was a big deal then because of his performance in *Bonnie and Clyde*. He was the first human being I'd seen who had little ++'s for eyes, like a comic strip character. Kevan and I, always the perfect hosts, offered him some weed. Michael was already so out of it he couldn't tell the difference between Kevan and me. That should have triggered a warning signal somewhere in our little pea-brains. We took him to Second City, which was a big mistake. He would not shut up and kept sliding out of his seat like an unruly child. He was digging the show, but kept disrupting it. My mother was in the audience too, and she complained to my sister about the noise. Elaine said, "that's Michael J. Pollard" as if that should excuse his behaviour. My mother in her fabulous upper-middle-class British accent that sometimes could hit a sonic register only perceptible to dogs replied, "I don't care who he is. He should shut up."

Mom and Howard moved to St. James Town, a sprawling, low-rent apartment complex down the street from us. My dad would show up at Christmas. I didn't really have any contact with him. One night Elaine invited Mom and me over to her place. Elaine offered Celia some pot, and they blew a jay together. Mom got a little buzz going, and said she was going to walk home. Almost as soon as Mom walked out the door, Elaine got worried and called her apartment to see if she'd arrived home safely. There was no answer. She got panicky and kept on calling. Finally Mom picked up and Elaine said, "Where were you? I was so worried." Celia replied, "I was looking at flowers dear; they're so beautiful." The thought of her tripping out on nature thrilled us. Howard liked to lie on the middle of the living room floor, a speaker on either side of his head as he listened to Mott the Hoople. He took Mom to a Lou Reed concert, which she loved.

We began rehearsing with a drummer named Donny, aka Knobby. He had a big 'fro and, conveniently, lived in our house. I'd cook meals for everyone and Knobby supplied our beverage of choice, Baby Duck, a sickly sweet mock champagne that we couldn't get enough of. Knobby and Elaine dated for a minute; their relationship seemed to involve playing poker.

Then we hooked up with a bass player, Bob, who had a Charles Manson vibe but was actually sweet and docile. Another Bob—Bob Ablack, who worked as an animation cameraman—played drums. I was obsessed with homosexuals and their lifestyles. I read novels by John Rechy. All his books had the same theme; the idea of gay men being validated as sexual beings by how many times they got fucked intrigued me. I loved the whole leather bondage image of big, butch, Tom of Finland–like gay boys. The first time I heard the term Rough Trade I knew it was the perfect name for our band. After I'd shown him a photo of a stud wearing a leather motorcycle jacket and nothing else, Kevan agreed with me. He'd been around gay men all his life and didn't find them threatening. We were on the same stupid wavelength. In 1975, we did our first gig as Rough Trade at the Roxy, a movie theatre in Toronto's east end. Gary Topp, who managed the theatre, asked us to do a show. He'd seen us rehearse and liked us enough to give us a break. The Roxy was packed—everyone went to its midnight screenings of cult classics like *Faster, Pussycat! Kill! Kill!* We played for about half an hour. It was over so fast and there was no room on stage. We were tightly wedged in front of the movie screen and the experience was scary but exhilarating. It was a complete catharsis for me. I didn't have time to be frightened, or think about what was happening. I was beginning to feel that fronting a band was something I was born to do. If only it was as easy and natural as my fantasies.

Kevan and I moved into one room on Earl Street. The house was owned by the delightfully eccentric June Faulkner, who managed Toronto Workshop Productions, an avant-garde theatre on Alexander Street. I still have nightmares about that room, because I lived there so long. I was feeling trapped, sharing that confined space with Kevan, fighting with my real sexual feelings. I couldn't stop thinking about women.

I'm not sure how it happened. I ran into Jane at a party. It was a sultry summer night, the kind of night that makes you feel overdressed in anything. Jane was sexy as hell, and she'd been patiently waiting for me to get with the program for years. We went back to her place and fucked each other senseless. I felt like I'd fallen into a whole other sexual and spiritual dimension. From then on we were together almost every night. I'd sneak into bed with Kevan at four in the morning. I felt incredibly guilty, although no way in hell was I gonna stop. He was starting to get suspicious, although I knew he hadn't been completely faithful to me during our time together. When I finally came out to Kevan, he was shocked at my tortured admission, and broke down and cried. I tried to explain it to him. I confessed that I'd been in the closet since I was a kid, that I remembered, vividly, repressing my first sexual thoughts as an eight-year-old girl. As painful as the experience was, I felt like I'd been released from a kind of prison.

Kevan moved out. The first couple of gigs we played after the breakup were difficult and tense. Kevan was angry, hurt and betrayed. After a while the tension eased, and inevitably we started checking out the same women in the audience.

I was developing a singing style in which I tried to cram as many lyrics as possible into a line. I'd over-enunciate certain words and let out an "uh" at the end of others. Kind of a Cher, Grace Jones, Bowie kind of thing, only not really. Some people need musical references or they can't deal. The foregoing bullshit is for them. For the rest of you, you know I didn't sound like anybody else. Marty and Valri began to do impersonations of me whenever they saw me. My favourite thing that Marty used to do was an inane impersonation of Trudeau. He'd slap on a bad wig and do a little freaky pirouette-y dance and talk in a bad French-Canadian accent.

Though things were fine, I kept praying Kevan would meet someone, and he did. He had a brief but memorable three-week affair with Betty Thomas, who was in Toronto with Bill Murray and the rest of the Chicago cast of Second City. She was a tall Amazon warrior–like woman, which turned Kevan's crank. I murmured a silent prayer to whoever. They were great together.

Around this time, Kevan and I discovered our inner comedians. During his affair with Betty, he'd started doing scenes with her at Second City. Sometimes he sat in for Del Close and played piano while the cast improvised scenes from suggestions yelled at them from the audience. I signed up for a Second City workshop that was directed by Joe Flaherty. I got to work my warped sense of humour, and I loved doing improv. The people in my class were pretty straight, and I'd get cut down with looks of total incomprehension when I suggested parodying Andy Warhol films like *Heat*, which no one had seen. I stopped trying to be esoteric and resigned myself to exploring the world of parodying dung beetles with my friend

Jasmine. Joyce and Bernie asked me to try out for Second City, but I declined; my first allegiance was to Rough Trade. The relationship between Kevan and me reverted back to its essence. Writing music and performing was, for us, as intense and intimate as any love affair.

I remember barrelling down Queen Street in a van with Kevan and Betty, following a car with a sunroof. Bill Murray was sitting in the back seat with a girl. He crawled out of the sunroof onto the top of the moving car, pulling the poor girl with him. He climbed on top of her and dry-humped her. It was stupid, dangerous and very funny.

In 1975, there were two dyke bars in Toronto. The Cameo was way out in the east end, on the Danforth, frequented by butch women with names like Bobbi, dressed in pastel-coloured leisure suits, drinking beer. Their girlfriends were all femmes. The women seemed to be trapped as characters in a fifties dyke pulp novel. When Jane and I went to check it out, we sat in a corner and vacillated between being amused, disappointed and slightly horrified. We didn't get it. We'd been expecting Paris in the thirties, an Anaïs Nin kind of vibe, sanguine women lounging in tuxedos, drinking absinthe, cigarettes in holders, perhaps the glint of a monocle. Our romantic notions came crashing down around us.

The other club was the Carriage House, a bar in the basement of a hotel on Jarvis Street. The subdued lighting enhanced what we saw as an erotic cornucopia of flesh. The first thing Jane and I did on our first visit was have a threesome, which didn't go down that well. Invariably one of the participants feels left out. The new girl gets all the action, and God knows I couldn't wait to get my hands on her. Jane broke out in tears of frustration at one point. A foursome is a whole other story.

I was like a little kid dyke in a candy store, and I got wired to the seduction and conquest of women. I'd think I was in love, but it was that electro-magnetic connection women have with each other, like entering a blast furnace of touch, taste and heightened senses. I came out with many cool women artists and filmmakers. At first we behaved badly, seducing each other's girlfriends and playing games, but ultimately we began to honour ourselves and respect one another.

Rough Trade started to play at a place called Grossman's Tavern in the heart of the city's garment district. In the beer-soaked atmosphere, barely discernible in the haze of Export A cigarette smoke, we would put on our freaky little show. I was slim with long straight hair. Every night I'd go into a state of near-apoplexy at the thought of singing in front of an audience. I was always terrified until I'd sung a couple of songs. I'd lock myself in the disgusting puce-coloured bathroom and swill Southern Comfort to get my courage up. It tasted vile, but if it was good enough for Janis Joplin. . . .

I wasn't your typical non-threatening girl singer. My voice and sexual androgyny were powerful. I was all about in-your-face sex. Some of the eminently forgettable songs we performed included "I'm Getting Dry Humped in the Hall" and "Lipstick on Your Dipstick." People would line up down the street to see us. Gilda, Danny and Marty came to our shows. Alice Cooper, General Idea and various arty types mingled with the Spadina Avenue crowd. The woman who was to be Mrs. Kevan first saw us at Grossman's. Her name was Marilyn Kiewiet.

Margaret Trudeau showed up one night. She was going through her own personal rebellion, playing around with the Rolling Stones, who were also in town. A chain-reaction of hissing, whispering voices worked its way up to the stage while we were in the middle of a set. *Margaret Trudeau is here*. We remained calm. If she was slumming with us, living the goldfish-like existence of the wife of the prime minister had really pushed Mrs. T over the edge.

In his heyday, Pierre Trudeau was as popular in Canada as the Beatles. Women screamed at him as if he was a pop star. Before he married Margaret, Trudeau had dated Barbra Streisand for a while. It was one of the most glamorous Hollywood-like things to ever happen in Canada. Imagine Barbra as the glittering trophy wife of our hippest PM. Think of Babs belting out "O Canada" at a hockey game. Back to the sad sad reality: Margaret was eagerly being corrupted by Keith Richards, or was it Ron Wood? After the initial shock of seeing her in Grossman's wore off, we all pretended to ignore her.

I started getting hit on by men and women. I became the test lesbian straight women wanted to experiment with. The results varied. Sometimes they ran screaming for the hills and other times things would develop into a short-lived relationship. I was very easily distracted.

I had a fling with the then bi-curious Andrea Martin. She propositioned me at a party at Jayne Eastwood's house one night. I thought she was sexy and talented, a lethal combination. How could I refuse? We were two sexually volatile chicks in our twenties. The sap was running and I had no control over it. I was obsessed with sex. We went to her place and explored the infinite sexual universe together. We couldn't get enough of each other, we made love and made each other laugh hysterically. Andrea was an Armenian-American from Connecticut. That turned me on, but then what didn't?

Andrea had been seeing Bob Dolman during the time we were indulging in our love fest. He still had a key to her house.

One night he walked in on us while I was down on my knees starting to work my way between Andrea's thighs as she sat at the piano in her living room. She had been playing Chopin and something very George Sand–like had come over me. We pulled ourselves together in a nanosecond and tried not to look too guilty. Bob was not the first straight man who had shot daggers at me from across a room.

Bob's sister Nancy eventually married Marty. Bob married Andrea. Then Bob dumped Andrea for Mary Steenburgen, and Mary dumped Bob for Ted Danson. Kind of a sexual food-chain. It was all so incestuous.

One weekend Andrea and I were shacked up at the trendy Windsor Arms Hotel, then Toronto's fuck pad for the rich and famous. There's something about sex in hotel rooms— maybe it's that you don't have to change the sheets afterwards. There was just one problem. Marty kept phoning every ten minutes pretending to be the Silver Fox, who was Xaviera Hollander's pimp.

Although he existed in a parallel show biz dimension, I loved Marty. I was crazy about his Bobby Darin impersonation. You literally had to drag his ass off stage or he would go on all night.

A couple of years later, Kevan and I asked Marty to open for us at a club called the Edge, the CBGBs of Toronto. So many great bands worked there, thanks to the Garys, the two Toronto promoters who ran the club. (Gary Cormier was at that time one of our interchangeable managers.) At the Edge you could experience the warped sensibilities of groups like the all-girl band the Slits, the singer of which screamed in the middle of a performance, "I HAVE MY BLOOD." Hey, thanks for sharing that with us. You could thrill to the lamentations of the dulcimer-plucking Nico, the hip junkie chick singer, ex of the

Velvet Underground. You could lust after the untouchable cool (male equivalent of ice maiden) boys in Ultravox and marvel at the size of Sting's ego.

The night of the Rough Trade show, the place was packed with the array of freaks we liked to call an audience. Marty had written a set that incorporated witty references to Camus. He said he wanted the audience to turn to each other and say, "exactly." Marty was visibly nervous—he'd never done standup before. The audience hated him on sight and started booing him. Someone was bleating like a sheep. Marty opened with a show tune, such a bad choice for that audience. Then he launched into his monologue. He was halfway through his show when somebody sprayed beer all over him. Marty tried to make a joke out of it and quickly fled the stage. Afterwards, Kevan and I apologized for the audience's behaviour and tried to soothe Marty, telling him the show had to go better the next night, but he didn't want to have to face an audience that was hungry for his blood. He was so traumatized by the experience that he still tells the story on talk shows. I'm thrilled to have my name bandied about on late night TV in whatever context. Marty claims it was the worst gig of his life, and it was the first and last time he attempted standup.

My true kindred spirit in the group was Gilda Radner: we'd both spent our childhoods in imaginary worlds putting on shows in our bedrooms.

When Gilda first started working on *Saturday Night Live*, I'd pal around with her. She was skinny and filled with kinetic energy. She had a funny staggering kind of walk, like she was about to trip over her feet. She was like a kid, always excited about the big toy called life. John Belushi seduced her away from Second City to work on *The National Lampoon Radio*

Show and tour. I saw them perform together at the El Mocambo. They were perfect foils for each other. In one sketch, Gilda played Rhoda Tyler Moore, a blind girl, waving a cane around and tripping over things. She was so completely in character, with a beatific blind girl face, a kid trying to make it in the big bad city. Belushi played her boyfriend. Changing his voice, he'd pretend to be a gang of thugs beating her up, and then he'd revert back into her boyfriend's voice and pretend to save her. During the sketch she slammed herself into a wall, which looked really painful. Like Lucille Ball, she was a great physical comedian.

I remember when Gilda was approached by Lorne Michaels, a Canadian producer she'd worked with before, to do a live comedy sketch show called *Saturday Night Live* on NBC. Gilda vacillated. She was slated to do the *David Steinberg Show*, which she thought was a sure thing, but she finally let herself be persuaded to take the risk and go to New York to join the Michaels cast. She rented an apartment on Charles Street in the Village. In her living room was a raised platform that she used as a stage to perfect her tap-dancing routines. The first time I went to her apartment, she put on a little-girl show for me. When Gilda threw parties, she'd tap dance for her guests. At one of her parties, Tom Schiller (who did a feature called "Schiller's Reel" for *SNL*) showed us a preview of "La Dolce Gilda," a black-and-white homage to Fellini in which Gilda played a decadent Roman sex-bomb.

Gilda was one of the sweetest souls I've ever known. She was very nurturing and tried to make sure that everyone around her was taken care of. When she lived in Toronto, she would bake cookies for Christmas at her house on Pears Avenue and hand deliver them to us. But she had problems. There was a food thing, not on the scale of Karen Carpenter, but there was some bingeing and purging going on. She'd been plagued with weight problems for most of her life. She was obsessive about food and her favourite restaurants. In New York, we'd go out for a big meal, then go back to her place where she'd retreat to the bathroom, telling me she was going to make herself throw up. I'd kind of stand around, whistling tonelessly under my breath, trying to act casual while I waited for her to come out.

During her stint at *SNL*, Gilda was involved with some men who didn't realize what they had. She had a boyfriend named Gary Wiess who conceived and shot edgy short films for the show. He took her completely for granted. I was always lecturing her on men. It was easy for me, since I had nothing invested in them. I'd tell her, "Ignore the men that come on to you, play hard to get and they will be your love slaves." That was hard for her. Gilda once floored me by asking, "Carole, if I was a lesbian would you sleep with me?" Such a typical straight girl question. I lied and told her I would.

Whenever I went to visit Gilda at *SNL*, I'd meet her in the cast and writers' offices on the seventeenth floor in Rockefeller Plaza. The place was charged with electricity. Gilda and I would cruise down the hallway together, and she'd stick her head in office doorways and check in with everybody to see what was going on. When she was working on a character called Candy Slice, a punk rock chick based on Patti Smith, she asked me for some insight on what it was like to be a chick singer. I told her to work her attitude. Gilda's way of creating her characters and making decisions about her life was to get input from all her friends and then make a choice.

One week Candice Bergen was hosting the show. She was flawlessly beautiful, the quintessential twenty-something WASP girl, fresh off some film project. Gilda introduced us, and Candice took my hand and told me she loved my blue nail polish. I was breathless. We talked a little about her work as a photo-journalist. She wanted to hang out with us later, but Gilda passed. I bit my lip in frustration. Besides being drop-dead gorgeous, anybody who had to compete for attention with a brother named Charley who was a wooden ventriloquist's dummy would have an interesting story to tell.

There was a different drama going down in every room. Some people were naturally high from the rush of adrenaline induced by the pressure of having to be on every week. Others got stoned on all manner of stimulants. I sometimes joined in. Performing sketch comedy on live TV was cutting edge. Nobody had done it since the fifties, not since the days of Ernie Kovacks and Sid Caesar. It had to be incredibly nerve-wracking. The other women in the cast, Jane Curtin and Laraine Newman, never got to shine like Gilda, who'd been accepted into the boys' club and knew how to play them. She worked her way into that bastion of male egos, competition and rampant testosterone. Gilda was their non-threatening mascot, and they all loved her.

On Saturday night, during the taping of the show, there was always a play within a play unfolding backstage with Gilda and the boys, a celebration of the dysfunctional, where the cast reworked their scenes and kidded around with each other. Chevy Chase was the handsome preppy jock. Danny was, well, Danny. He was very young, twenty-three or so, but always acted much older. There was only one word to describe Bill Murray—insane. He was always grabbing Gilda. John Belushi told Gilda to "eat a bowl of fuck." It was a routine they'd go through. He thought it was funny. She looked at him like his kid sister would. She wouldn't say anything, and he'd say it again like a bratty little boy. Belushi was staggeringly talented but his destructive streak stuck out a mile. One time Danny and John were running through a scene about the infamous short order cooks, Pete and George. They repeated the word "cheeseburger" over and over.

Sometimes I'd run into Danny and John at the Mudd Club. Belushi could not get drunk or stoned enough. Michael O'Donoghue was a presence who hovered around the periphery of all the madness, low-key compared to the rest of the cast. As a writer and actor, he injected his dark comic sensibilities into the show. He played a warped character called Mr. Mike, who was the kind of man who wondered what it would be like to plunge fifteen-foot-long needles through Elvis Presley's eyes. He eventually married Cheryl Hardwick, who played piano in the *SNL* band. Gilda and I used to visit with Cheryl and her roommate, an androgynous girl named Pinky, before she defected to the other side.

Those early shows left an imprint on my friends and me. Catchphrases used by *SNL*'s sick and disturbed characters were quickly assimilated into our childlike vocabularies. The "Ooh noo" we heard weekly on the *Mr. Bill Show* was a prime example. It was a warped parody of a children's show. Sadly it was all too evocative of my childhood—I liked to torture my dolls, too. I mean, who else could you vent your hostilities on at six? Mr. Bill and his dog Spot were claymation models mutilated weekly by Bill's traitorous best friend Sluggo and a human hand called Mr. Hand.

Whenever I could, I shamelessly hustled to get Rough Trade on the show. I had the support of the cast, but Lorne was another matter. The prospect was held over me like a dangling carrot, and he wouldn't commit either way.

Backstage at *SNL* there was always a crowd of celebrities, watching each other and getting swept up in the rush of what was then a trendy new phenomenon. Some became regulars, like seventies supermodels Cheryl Tiegs and Lauren Hutton, who had a contagious energy. One minute I'd be getting stoned with a poncho-wearing Elliott Gould, the next I'd be dragged away by Gilda for some little crisis, and then I'd be watching the show backstage from an ever-changing vantage point, as . . .

One week Marianne Faithfull was the musical guest. She was obviously stoned on some very bad shit. I couldn't imagine performing in that state, and it was excruciating to watch her sing in a junkie-like trance. Mick Jagger stood backstage, fidgeting nervously, willing her to make it through.

There was always a party after the show in some trendy restaurant, laden with piles of food and alcohol that the cast was usually too exhausted or hyped up to appreciate. Coming down off a high like that is similar to postpartum blues. You've created this great thing and now it's over.

I was still beating the Rough Trade thing to death. By then we'd released our first album, a direct-to-disc effort that was eclectic, expensive, and difficult to find. We never had good management, so most of the time we had to fend for ourselves in the sad reality of a music business controlled by fucked-up white guys. Lorne was resistant, even though *SNL* did support bands who didn't have deals. But I had no clout with Lorne and, at that time, I didn't have the finesse to get my way with him. Damn, it was annoying, because men are usually easy to manipulate.

I lost contact with Gilda in 1979 after she became enmeshed in a one-woman Broadway show that Lorne was producing called *Live from New York*. She left *SNL* for good in 1980, and made a series of strange career choices. For instance, she turned down the role of the cancer patient ultimately played by Debra Winger in *Terms of Endearment*. Markus told me he had been visiting Gilda in her dressing room during her run on Broadway, and Robin Williams had come back to see her. He'd been trying to talk her into playing the role of Olive Oyl next to his Popeye in the Robert Altman film. Gilda was angry at Markus for letting Williams into her dressing room; she'd been trying to avoid him because she had no interest in playing the part.

In the early eighties, I'd still show up at a taping every once in a while. Kevan and I were friends with Howard Shore, the show's music director. I saw Gilda at a party right after she married G.E. Smith, the guitar player in the *SNL* band. I'd had no idea they were an item. Their ill-fated marriage did not last. The more famous Gilda became, the more paranoid she became. She couldn't walk down the street without being besieged by fans. She hired a bodyguard and shut herself off. When she married Gene Wilder, her close friends claimed he was too possessive of her, but maybe he was just protecting her. The film projects they worked on together were disappointing. The last time I saw Gilda was in London in the summer of 1986. She was walking down Sloan Street with Gene. We stood on the street reminiscing about the old days. She exuded serenity and seemed very happy.

In 1989, two months before she died, Gilda was in Toronto and went to see Markus at his Queen Street bar, the Squeeze Club. She travelled with a black female bodyguard, an ex-marine who was skilled in all the martial arts. Gilda's hair was short, just starting to grow back after extensive chemotherapy treatments. She ran around the room in her funny Gilda way, and apologized to Markus for cutting off her Toronto friends, including his sister Catherine. At Gilda's memorial service, which was attended by nine hundred people, Markus said that Bill Murray got up and in a cryptic statement condemned Gene Wilder. Some people at the service cheered. The incident was never reported in the press.

By 1976 Kevan and I had morphed into queens of androgyny. We were a combination of punk, bondage and glam. We were into marketing. Our band slogan was "repulsive yet fascinating." Clive designed a flyer that depicted a cut-out doll with a bondage outfit and accessories. He also designed a chrome baby that we used as a logo for our first T-shirt. Two of my friends started a company called Imagician. I was their test subject. They conceived a new look for me and gave me a frightening makeover that consisted of highly flammable ciré jumpsuits and the first of many bad perms.

One afternoon Patti Smith and Lenny Kaye were in town doing a show and they turned up at Imagician's studio, a minimalist loft space. Patti had an artist's pallor and seemed very introverted. We talked about music and literature. I asked her to sign my copy of *Seventh Heaven*, a book of her poetry, which had become my bible. She wrote, "Rough Trade, Smooth Blade," and drew a picture of a razor blade dripping blood that turned into a diamond. We went to see her show that night. She was savage and wild, a rock 'n' roll poetess, a whirling dervish spinning in total abandon. She had a weak bladder and in the middle of her show pissed her pants and didn't seem to give a fuck about the audience's reaction.

We opened for Roxy Music, a band fronted by the suave Bryan Ferry. He was smooth and clever, crooning his songs like Noel Coward. The members of Roxy were some of the most innovative musicians around, their sound dense and sophisticated, and you just knew they all went to art school. Brian Eno played keyboards and was a pioneer of the ambient movement. I had a little thing with a girl who had lived with Eno and wanted me to pound the living shit out of her. I like to blame him for my subsequent forays into the world of S&M. Bryan Ferry was very grand and married well, to a woman named Lucy who had a title. An avid reader of *Tattler* and a lifelong anglophile, I was jealous. I would kill for a title (if only I could have married Princess Diana).

Everything about Roxy Music seemed seamless and calculated. Some of their album covers reminded me of Über Nazi art, a homage to a non-existent master race, athletic images of blond women with torpedo breasts throwing javelins. On stage, two such women accessorized Roxy Music as undulating eye candy.

This was the first time we'd played Massey Hall. I was shaking with stage fright. I unzipped my jumpsuit as far as I could and went into shock for most of our set. It must have gone all right because Elton John was in the audience that night and later, in a radio interview, was very complimentary about us.

We began playing the Colonial, a cavernous club downtown on Yonge Street. It was the last bastion of jazz, a showcase for greats like Thelonious Monk, Charles Mingus and Rahsaan Roland Kirk. We started working downstairs in a room called the Meat Market. We opened for Momma Cooper, the drag queen I'd seen strolling down my street in the sixties. He shared the secrets of crossdressing with me. I found out where he hid the lump of flesh between his legs, and how two bags of rice and an excess of body fat could simulate a pretty good set of tits. We soon became regulars, and the management of the Colonial bumped us upstairs into the big league.

While singing on the Colonial's stage, I was mesmerized by the large spinning mirror-ball hanging above me that always gave me vertigo. By now I could actually perform without the aid of mood-altering substances. The Colonial was a hotbed of repressed sexuality and cheap cologne. On a typical night, a film of a sex-change operation was projected on the wall beside the stage before our show. Garishly dressed pimps and their ladies lined the bar. I was inspired by them and wrote an anti-prostitution number called "Song to My Pimp." It went right over their heads; they loved it. Our fans sat up close, yelling out requests. Xaviera Hollander pushed her girlfriend on a table and climbed on top of her. Micky Spillane's wife, a sexy blond bombshell named Jerri, introduced herself to me and said she was a fan. Elton John worked the dance floor with a boy-toy.

We had to play Saturday matinees, which filled me with hatred. Inevitably somebody in the band was late. It's inhuman to ask a musician to get up in the afternoon; after all, we are the Lestats of show biz. Sometimes unruly cocks would pop up in the audience. I'd point them out and humiliate their owners. Kevan and I thought of Rough Trade's music as sexual parody. We were always surprised when fans took our satirical songs seriously enough to unleash their man things.

Kevan and I went to see *Women Behind Bars*, a Tom Eyen play in New York. It starred Divine, the anti-Christ of drag, three hundred pounds of pseudo-woman with a mohawk. She was the epitome of trailer trash glam. Billed as "The Most Beautiful Woman in the World" by John Waters, who directed all her films, Divine, whose real name was Glenn Milstead, hailed from Baltimore, where she started out as a hairdresser. She leapt into cult stardom via her role as a disgruntled housewife in *Pink Flamingos*, a film in which she ate dog shit. My favourite was her role in *Multiple Maniacs*. One of the highlights of that epic was a scene in which Divine and actress Mink Stole are making love in a church. Mink inserts rosary beads into Divine's ass, and they hallucinate the seven stations of the cross. In *Women Behind Bars*, Divine plays a sadistic prison matron who terrorizes the inmates and, of course, fucks them. There was something sweet about Divine. Kevan and I both fell hopelessly in love with her.

I had this idea for a stage show incorporating Rough Trade songs with theatre, really bad theatre involving my favourite themes, sex and bondage, with sapphic undertones. I loved S&M because it was a visual image that flouted sexual taboos. We called Ron Link, who had directed *Women Behind Bars*, and Divine's manager, Bernard Jay, and met for lunch at a restaurant on Columbus Avenue. Divine's hair was close-cropped and blond. She had a mischievous bad-little-boy quality, both shocking and cute. I'm not sure how that worked, but it did. Kevan and I did all the talking and Divine did all the eating. She showed some interest in the project between bites. That afternoon Divi taught us one of life's great lessons: how to walk out on a cheque in a restaurant. I think she was testing us and we passed.

At that time we were managed by Fran Pillersdorf, who also worked for lighting designer Jules Fisher, a Tony Award–winning genius who lit all the big Broadway shows. Somehow she persuaded him to design the lighting for our extravaganza. Fran knew how to hustle. She was connected with Tony DeFries, who managed David Bowie. She called DeFries and got him interested enough to meet with us. Fran and I marched into the Central Park West offices of his Main Man Records, a label that specialized in signing sexually ambiguous acts. Some of the artists on Main Man had been Bowie's love toys, like Dana Gillespie, whose song "Weren't Born a Man" was a big hit in my circle. Tony was extremely charismatic, with wavy grey hair, and there was an air of decadence about him. Still, he appeared imposing and managerial behind his big desk. We pitched our idea to him. He seriously contemplated our ridiculous concept. He dug it, and why not? It was a great tax break for him. We were on. Daddy wrote us a cheque.

Elaine was writing comedy and had a radio show on the CBC called *The New Bob Harper Show*, which, in her words, was funny because there had never been an old Bob Harper show. Elaine, along with regulars Rick Moranis and Catherine O'Hara, did a weekly tongue-in-cheek satire of radio talk shows, which, again in her words, was witty, brilliant and controversial. Some of the audience thought it was brilliant and some people took it literally and called in asking where they could get the products they were advertising in the fake commercials.

I got Elaine to help me write the script for *Restless Underwear*. We became a parody of writers in forties movies. We paced, we typed, we smoked cigars, and it was done. Kevan hired CBC veteran Peter Mann as music director. Peter was never seen without a cigarette fluttering nervously in his hand, and always wore a wool cap that sat over a bad wig. Even now, he still works on every CBC variety show, the ice-skating specials and the Juno awards. I have a bunch of Junos and I use them as nasty giant sex toys.

Somebody conned the CBC into giving us some rehearsal space, and Divine and Ron Link flew up to Toronto. We'd have meetings and work on songs. Ron was suave and handsome, with a shock of black hair and a Machiavellian edge, and he couldn't keep his hands off Kevan. Kevan humoured Ron and his unwanted attentions in his Canadian passive-aggressive way. I kept asking Divine about his infamous shit-eating experience. I'd say things like "Divi, did you get worms?" She'd say, "Yes, I got worms" and make an evil little face. Then I'd feel slightly sick. Divine had a voracious appetite and was easily pacified by being placed in front of a refrigerator. We began teaching her how to sing. She didn't have much experience. She'd paraded around on stage during an Elton John concert, and that was the extent of it. She couldn't differentiate between a verse and chorus in a song. I'm not sure she ever figured out that concept.

Divine and I did a photo shoot and pre-show interview with Lawrence O'Toole, a writer for *The Globe and Mail*. Divine arranged herself on a couch, as sweet and seductive as honey. O'Toole asked Divine what her voice was like. Divine answered, "It's a great voice. You've heard of Leontyne Price? Well, she's a little darker, that's all."

The focal point of the show was a giant whorish round red bed. Elaine had come up with some brilliant kitschy vignettes. One was called "Truck Stop Gal," in which Divine was to portray a tacky waitress in a diner looking for love. What a stretch. Her other "acting" role was as an evil gossip columnist. Divine and I took a little trip through the CBC costume department. It was gigantic, packed with gowns and tons of accessories. A girl could get lost in there. Divi utilized her formidable shoplifting skills by picking up a few new outfits, and calmly walking out of wardrobe with them hidden under her sweater.

It's hard work being a parody of a woman. Divine worked with a tag team of attendants to create her look, which had been fossilized in *Pink Flamingos*. There was a hair boy, a dress boy and a bum boy. There was no shortage of boys who wanted some Divi love. Frankie Piazza was responsible for Divine's makeup, and Larry LeGaspi always did her gowns. Divine was one of the most professional and undemanding performers I've ever worked with.

On the night of the show—December 19, 1977—Massey Hall was packed. The audience piled into the faded elegance of that beautiful old concert hall, which was tarted up like an old queen. Netting was wrapped over the plaster scroll work to keep pieces of it from falling on the audience. Punks dressed in leather and kids from the burbs sauntered to their seats. People were more than ready for the twisted shit we had to offer.

Divine was sweating under her wig and layers of pancake makeup, but she was so damned sweet and easy to be with. Her first costume was a two-piece tiger-skin number that revealed the vast expanse of her stomach. The members of the band were dressed like sailors and shunted off to a corner of the stage. We had two superfly bad sisters, the Dykettes, for me to fondle for the "special ladies in the audience." One was Jo-Ann Brooks and the other was Luci Martin, who went on to sing with Chic. Kevan's roommate, hunky David Whito, writhed around on the bed in leopard-skin briefs. He had on a collar and a leash so we could drag him around when he was ba-ad. I had to discipline him repeatedly during the show. Underwear was hurled into the audience.

Divine sat on the red satin-covered bed and sang "Sob

Sister," and I strangled her with my nine-foot bullwhip. In the dramatically challenging "Truck Stop Gal" sketch, I was the other waitress in the diner, talking *Mildred Pierce* trash. Divine desperately needed a man. Joanne and Luci, dressed like five-foot-tall boys, attempted to gang-rape her. Trying to hide her obvious delight, she flicked them away like flies off horseshit.

Divi and I also did a homage to Carol Burnett and Julie Andrews in the form of a trashy duet—me in a bondage rig with long black gloves and fetish heels, and Divine in a gold lamé muumuu that reflected the light off her like laser beams, partially blinding the audience. We sang "Auto Erotic Love," my ode to masturbation, and played with ourselves.

During a quiet moment in the show, I stood under a street lamp wearing a trench coat and sang "Grade B Movie," a song inspired by Kurt Weill, which we'd written while painting somebody's living room for some extra cash. It's all about loving a no-good man named Johnny. I fell on the floor of the stage in a swoon at the end of the song. The audience loved it.

Throughout the show, I had a hard time holding back my laughter as I tried to project the image of an evil dominatrix. The show made no sense. It was titillating and stupid. In short, it was everything we aspired to. The critics unanimously panned it. They were straight and, although they claimed otherwise, had no concept of camp. Our work was done.

In 1980 we did a production of *Restless Underwear* in New York at the Beacon Theater, and it was a complete and utter disaster. We were somewhat hesitant about attempting it in such a large venue, but Vicki Wickham was managing us at the time and she thought it would be a good career move. Elaine wrote some new (dramatic) pieces for the show. One was the "Crass Elliot Story." Divi was Crass, the overweight lead singer of a group that very much resembled the Mamas and the Papas. The rest of us played band members. Divine got to do a dramatic death scene in which she choked on a ham sandwich. She had lines like "I'm a jumbo and I need fuel." In a sketch called "The Lesbian Tenement," Divine played a teenage girl named Sue Stopadopolus who discovers she's a raging bull dyke and seduces an innocent girl named Ginger. For that scene, Elaine wrote one of my favourite lines ever: "A broom handle lay broken on the floor from their mannish lovemaking." Sue is ultimately gunned down by the cops for her perverse ways.

The cast was comprised of Divine, the band, and Brenda Bergman, a blond bombshell/junkie/actress. Brenda had worked with Divine in another Tom Eyen play, *Neon Women*, and she had an intense junkie mystique. She was damaged goods wandering around in a trance, a lost little girl not unlike Marilyn Monroe. We were in awe of her. Somehow being a junkie in New York had more cachet than lying in a gutter in Toronto.

For the New York show we used a new band. Terry Wilkins, an Australian with dark good looks, a total babe magnet, was on bass. Buckey Berger played drums; he was short with a receding hairline and, no matter what was going down, always had a grin frozen on his face, which was sometimes disconcerting. Dave McMorrow, tall, laid-back and sensitive, played keyboards. For musicians, they were low-maintenance. There was only one diva in this band, as opposed to five. We'd turfed the last load of musicians in 1978 when they insisted on having band group-therapy sessions.

On the day of the show, we ran our scenes in the cavernous theatre. I could not get enough of watching Divine work. I wished Elaine could have been there, but she was busy working on another project.

The problem with the production was that half the audience was there to see Divine in what they thought was going to be a play. The other half was there to see us. When I say there was hostility in the crowd, it's an understatement. The audience was split into two warring factions. Those for us and those against us. What a stimulating climate to perform in. We got through the show somehow. Thankfully it was only a one-night deal and I seem to have blocked out most of it. Perhaps with years of therapy more of the ugly images will come back to me.

I never saw Divine again. Six years later, I was visiting L.A. and heard that she was slated to do a guest spot on *Married with Children*. That night I called her at her hotel and made arrangements to meet her the following day. The next morning Elaine called me and told me to turn on the TV. Divine had gone to sleep and had never woken up. A master of the theatre of the absurd, Divine is now part of pop-cult history.

I Like It, but Is It ART?
(My heart belongs to Dada.)

I first met the trio of artists known as General Idea—AA
Bronson, Felix Partz and Jorge Zontal—at Grossman's Tavern
when they came to check out Rough Trade. They walked into
the bar and scanned the room like artists do, looking for
useful material to archive in the back of their minds. AA
appeared deceptively innocent and boyish with blondish-red
hair that had two blue streaks on the sides. From the moment
I met him, I believed that he had a fascinating hidden agenda
I would never become privy to. Felix, who I always called by
his real name—Ron—was the most open and gregarious of
the three. He was droll, with a sensuous face framed by dark
longish hair. Men and women were drawn to him, and I mean
that in a purely sexual way. Jorge was an intense Latin from
Venezuela with a receding hairline and a heavy beard. He was
brooding and had a sardonic sense of humour that made me
like him right away. Jorge and AA had studied architecture
and Ron was a painter. Even though I knew them for years,
they remained a fascinating enigma to me and to others who
were part of their circle.

GI operated as a collective, recruiting other artists into the
fold, but the core and real creative brilliance came from the
boys. As artists, they played with cultural phenomena and
iconography. They employed shock tactics and humour in
their work. They were so in sync with each other that the

body of work they produced seemed to flow from one mind.

The collective spanned Canada and included a group of artists called the Western Front. Eventually I was introduced to more artists, whose names were as surreal as their physical appearance: Granada Gazelle, Chick Rice and Vincent Trasov, who, in the guise of Mr. Peanut, his alter ego, walked around dressed in a Planter's Peanut suit (he ran for mayor of Vancouver and placed third). A woman named Donna Dogmatic got her creative kicks from wearing a dog head. Dr. and Lady Brute dressed in leopard-skin fabrics, and the Lady made some kind of artistic statement by climbing trees and posing like a jungle cat.

Ron, AA, Jorge and Mimi Paige, who became the first Miss General Idea, had lived on Gerrard Street in 1969. That area was a little annex of Yorkville, with a row of trendy boutiques, including The Unicorn and a zebra-painted store called Bizarre. Granada Gazelle lived across the street from GI, and they became good friends and moved in together. Granada was a voluptuous woman with a quirky sense of style and humour, which made her a natural candidate for the collective. She was running a group called the Film-Makers Distribution Co-op, and would bring movies home to play in the living room. She was into retro dressing and was always on the lookout for vintage clothing.

Granada connected them up with a woman named Sandy Stagg, who sold antique clothing at a flea market in Trinity Square, where the Eaton Centre is now. Sandy was originally from London and had come to Canada with her husband, a travelling salesman. He set her up in an apartment in the 'burbs, then took off on a sales trip. She decided she didn't want a split-level kind of life and left him. She had a real eye for antique clothing and art deco. Her ex-lover, Paul Oberst, describes her as "a creature of fierce loyalties who has an amazing ability to catch people's eyes." Sandy started visiting the GI boys and soon became part of their scene. With her luminous pale skin, she was destined to become a GI model.

GI moved into 241 Yonge Street, a loft space that became their headquarters. Think of it as a surreal version of MTV's *The Real World*. The front room of the loft was painted shocking pink, and Jorge created a green jungle room next to that. Two long corridors went all the way to the back of the apartment, where everyone had bedrooms. At one point, the collection of roommates included Mimi, Felix, Jorge, AA, Danny Freedman, an actor who won a Genie for his part as a bum boy in the film *Fortune and Men's Eyes*, and Pascal, a beautiful, high-maintenance drag queen. Paul Oberst, a carpenter, architect and artist, completed the group. He was also connected to Granada, who captured his heart, he says, "when I first saw her beautiful collarbones and body swathed in monkey fur."

The group started making mail art, which involved creating and mailing postcards out to other artists and getting their work in return. They applied for an arts grant from the Canadian government, but were turned down. Oberst says, "AA fired up his afterburners and went after the money and the government. He had a way of making people look stupid, which forced them into giving him what he wanted."

In 1975, GI began to publish an art magazine called *File*. The original logo looked exactly like the logo for *Life* magazine, which resulted in the Time Life conglomerate coming down on GI hard, even though *Life* magazine had ceased publishing at that point. They charged GI with stealing their copyrighted logo, stealing their audience and taking unfair advantage of their audience. The claims were ridiculous, as GI's lawyer pointed out. You only had to look inside *File* to see that the content was the polar opposite of *Life*. There was a series of letters exchanged between Time Life and GI, which GI expropriated and made into art. GI's whole *oeuvre* was about zoning in on whatever was *au courant*, chewing it up and regurgitating it with a different spin.

They got great publicity out of the charges. Two features appeared in *The Village Voice*, and even the art reviewer of *Time* denounced the whole thing. Still, in the end, GI had to change its logo, but not without sending a letter admonishing the giant publishing corporation that it, in turn, could not use the *File* logo in any of their publications. It was amusing for all of us to watch the corporate and art worlds clash.

Kevan and I were drawn into the General Idea circle, the precursor to the Queen Street scene. Sandy Stagg turned herself into a kind of self-proclaimed patroness of the arts. Her leg, encased in a high-heeled fetish shoe, graced the cover of the *File* issue on glamour. She organized get-togethers in her loft space, a seventies update of the salons of the demimonde, a very civilized environment where we were treated to Sandy's fabulous spreads. We became part of a growing clique that showed up at each other's exhibitions, gigs and mock executions. At that time Toronto was alive with creativity and no one seemed to feel threatened by anyone else. In those days the arts community operated on a much smaller scale, and the scenes were so closely connected and interlocked that they energized each other.

Sandy, who has been described as *Ab Fab* heroines Patsy and Edina morphed into one trend-setting entity, placed ads in *File* for her antique clothing store, Amelia Earhart. She got plenty of business because of the cachet of her association with GI. Customers like Steven Strange and David Byrne were lured to her store. GI club membership gave her entrée into hip scenes in London and New York where she could run wild with trendy vacuous Euro-trash.

One night an artist named Flaky Rosehips walked into Grossman's dressed as Adolf Hitler. Mr. and Mrs. Grossman were at the bar, and Mrs. Grossman freaked out. We tried to placate her by telling her that Flaky was an artist who used shock tactics to make a statement. She was not amused, and who could really blame her? She'd flipped out when she'd heard our song "What's the Furor 'bout the Führer?" but we'd begged her to listen closely to the lyrics and she had figured out that it was an anti-fascist rant. In a fit of insanity, Sandy Stagg, Murray Ball and Mary Lou Green decided to make Flaky up to look like the Führer for an opening at the Art Gallery of Ontario. They couldn't have thought of a more offensive idea.

Rough Trade took part in Going Through the Motions, a larger-than-life art extravaganza. With AA acting as emcee, GI put the audience of eight hundred through a rehearsal of reactions: laughing, applauding and cheering for a mythical beauty pageant—Miss General Idea 1984. These reactions were videotaped and archived. We supplied the music.

The pageant "contestants" glided along a runway dressed in venetian blind–like structures—three triangles of metal piled on top of one another like fifties lampshades. The models' bare arms poked out of the slats. We wrote two songs for the occasion. "I Like It, but Is It Art?" was a tongue-in-cheek critique of the art world with a latin beat that went something like this: "Sylvia Plath getting gassed, Warhol getting shot by Solanis, I like it, I like it, I like it, but is it art?"

The other song, "Beauty Queen," was an ode to every kind of queen I could think of. "You're not a drag queen or a dinge queen or a rice queen or a dairy queen, a rim queen; you're a beauty queen." It soon deteriorated into sheer stupidity, but it had a catchy Vegas groove, and I delivered it in a laid-back Sinatra style. It was such a high to camp it up at the AGO. Under the guise of art, people will tolerate almost anything.

While all this Dadaist stuff was going down on stage, actress Suzette Couture, in her role as the spirit of Miss General Idea, delivered an inspiring monologue while she searched for a seat in the audience. Actors stood in the lobby playing celebrities being interviewed by other actors portraying the media.

Through Robert Handforth, who was the curator of A Space, I got involved in an event called "Torch Song Showcase" with Dianne Lawrence, Suzette Couture and the fragile, otherworldly Brenda Donahue, who was called back to the great beyond soon after this event. We were just four women doing our interpretations of Cole Porter, Bessie Smith and sixties pop songs. Three of us wanted to strangle Dianne. I'd known Dianne forever. Once we went to a Warhol book signing and made him autograph our bare shoulders and, believe me, he didn't want to touch our flesh. Then we had Jorge photograph us as though we were art. Dianne was over-the-top and talented, but she had an unfortunate habit of rubbing people the wrong way. When it came to "Torch Song Showcase," she thought she was running the show. It was my first taste of chick show-biz drama, and I was secretly hoping there'd be a catfight. To promote the event, we were photographed at night wearing long dresses, standing ankle-deep in Lake Ontario holding flaming torches aloft. The image of that photo shoot has stayed with me.

There were other female hijinks. Granada, Dawn Eagles and photographer Isobel Harry conceived of a fashion show called Glamazon, which featured clothes from 1940 to 1979. They used a cutout of Jane's head and arched neck coming out of a shoe for the poster and dubbed her the Glamazon Amazon. (Yes, that Jane—who was by then a percussionist with Rough Trade, as well as being a drop-dead gorgeous homewrecker.) Granada and Dawn recreated a Dior dress from nothing and constructed a metal Paco Rabanne ensemble. The show used fashion as a schema of the past and took an anthropological approach to how women saw themselves and were seen in the years represented. The models were depicted in everyday situations on campus, on the beach, and getting married, pregnant, divorced and under the influence. Everything about the show was so painstakingly accurate you almost felt like you'd stepped back in time, although true to the GI credo, every dress and accessory was fetishized. I coordinated the music for the event, researching and finding a popular song for each year represented in the show. Suzette Couture, who had the style and panache of a sophisticate, did the colour commentary. Isobel was one of the models in the show. In one segment she was watching *Concentration* in black Carhart jeans and a muted green sweater. And then she had to run some errands, so she slipped on her green vinyl mules and beige leather clutch coat, made to look like leatherette.

Isobel's work as a photographer included a series of self-portraits in the style of Cindy Sherman. I had such a crush on her. She had a beautiful face with fine lines around her eyes and the corners of her mouth, and there was something ethereal about her. Her hair was cut into an inverted wedge. She was on an artistic quest for something vague and unattainable. She photographed me lit by shafts of light through window blinds. We had a flirtation, but it led nowhere. Her real love was a man named Burt, and they are still together today. I think that was the last time I felt truly innocent and romantic. There was a photograph of us in an issue of *File*, walking down the street arm in arm with Ron and AA. Isobel is quoted as saying, "This is the year to look like everyone else."

When we did our first album cover, we chose GI to shoot and design it, and the boys were instrumental in helping us create an image for Rough Trade. Glamour was always part of their credo; their art was devoted to redefining it and making it their own. (They delivered a treatise on glamour in *File*, in the issue with Sandy's foot on the cover: "We knew that in order to be Glamorous we had to become plagiarists, intellectual parasites. We moved in on a history and occupied images, emptying them, reducing them to shells. We filled these shells with glamour, the cream-puff innocence of idiots, the naughty silence of shark fins slicing the waters.") Jorge spent hours photographing us and he used to say that no other photographer could make me look as great as he could. Jorge painstakingly retouched the skin around my eyes to get the intense expression that my myopic orbs radiated. The first album cover GI designed and shot for us was *Avoid Freud*. It was the beginning of a theme in which I was always on the front and Kevan on the back. Wearing Thierry Mugler suits with massive moulded shoulder pads, with our flesh bronzed and then literally air-brushed with makeup, we were made over into beautiful iconic beings. On that first cover, I held a martini glass and Kevan a tuning fork. The resulting image remains powerful and unique.

The art world was just one of the scenes that was exploding in Toronto in the seventies. Living at Earl Street gave me first-hand access to the theatre world. My landlady, June Faulkner, was an innovative producer who was not afraid to experiment—as proven by the shows she chose to mount at Toronto Workshop Productions. I sometimes felt I was existing in a rarefied atmosphere that cultivated artists like the exotic creatures we think we are. The actor Cedric Smith lived in a tiny room next to mine and he didn't always close the door completely; it seemed he was always being straddled by some actress, the strangled cries of orgasm reverberating out into the hallway. June often threw parties, and her living room was always full of actors and actresses, some of whom I may have inadvertently slept with.

I remember when June lured the Lindsay Kemp Mime Troupe from England to do their productions of Genet's *Our Lady of the Flowers* and *Salomé*. The company consisted of boy angels with stunning pre-Raphaelite faces and one exotic woman. Kemp created a surreal persona for himself that he lived every day. He'd more or less assumed the identity of his elder sister, who died while he was a child. I never saw him without white pancake makeup on his face, which gave him the appearance of a male geisha. He was involved with one of the members of the troupe, and there was some intense drama going on between them. I'm no fan of mimes, but I was engrossed by their performance. The actors brought the tortured sexuality of Genet's work to life in stark black-and-white. A character would suddenly burst into song or occasionally utter a word, then retreat back into silence. I was sucked into the twilight netherworld of a Paris populated by pimps and sailors. And I'd never seen anyone milk a curtain call the way that company did. They took their bows in agonizing slow motion, and they were so achingly beautiful you didn't want them to stop.

June also staged a production of *The Club*, a play I'd seen three times in New York. An all-female cast portrayed Victorian gentlemen at a men's club. They sang turn-of-the-century songs objectifying women. That was the first time I'd seen drag kings, and women dressed in men's clothing was a painfully erotic turn-on for me, and for most of the boys in the audience. (June had asked me if I wanted to be in the production, but Rough Trade's schedule conflicted with that of the show.)

Around 1977, Sandy Stagg decided she wanted to open a restaurant on Queen Street, which she thought was an up-and-coming neighbourhood. She found a roach-infested diner called the Peter Pan, renovated it and turned it into a trendy hangout. GI had just moved their studio into the neighbourhood and A Space soon followed. The Peter Pan became hot, and was one of the first successful eateries on the two blocks of desirable Queen Street West.

I took my mother to dinner at the Peter Pan so she could meet AA, Jorge and Sandy. The thing I haven't been telling you is that Celia had been very ill with colon cancer and had undergone surgery. For years, she'd suffered from stomach trouble, which her doctor, dismissing the complaints of a middle-aged woman, misdiagnosed as indigestion. I had gone to visit her in the hospital with my lover at the time. Kevan and I had just won a Genie Award (the sad Canadian version of the Oscar) for scoring a film called *One Night Stand*, and I wanted her to see the gold statuette. We'd been tentatively trying to connect with each other. She had come to some of Rough Trade's gigs, which thrilled me, as I was still trying to get her approval. That hospital visit was my way of coming out to my mother. I knew that she would pick up on the relationship between Paula and myself, even though we didn't say a word about it. Paula left us alone for a while and Celia quizzed me about her life and career, and that's when I knew she knew.

In the late seventies the Toronto music scene was incendiary. A punk club called Crash and Burn on Pearl Street imploded into business. The bar was a door sitting on two garbage cans, at which only Molson's Black Label beer was served, a punk aesthetic, perhaps. Making an anti-establishment statement, the club sometimes forgot to charge admission. Bands like the Dead Boys, the Dishes, the Curse, the Diodes, the B Girls, Martha and the Muffins and the Viletones all vented their caustic, warped sensibilities there.

One of the girls who ran the club was Anya Varda, this ripe sexy thing that every boy within a ten-mile radius homed in on. The boys of GI were no exception. They loved her, and she became their muse. Anya has an indefinable accent reminiscent of Audrey Hepburn; she was the punk Holly Golightly. She switched her hair colour from blond to black, and became a *File* magazine cover girl. Jorge photographed her, and Ron and his boyfriend Tim Guest lusted after her and tried to talk her into having a threesome with them. Anya eventually moved into a back room in the Earl Street house. She was a kind of sexual catnip, constantly being pursued by well-known musicians who fell madly in love with her.

So anyone who wanted a taste of the underground went to Crash and Burn to watch the bands and soak up the punk ambiance. One night the club held an anti-beauty pageant, and the most talked about contestant was Miss Curse, who wore a dress covered in tampons and sanitary napkins smeared in fake blood. The Horseshoe Tavern on Queen Street was a big venue for punk bands with events like The Last Pogo, and Celia, God love her, showed up to support her kid, like any show-biz mom. I have a photograph of us backstage and I'm hugging her close to my punk self.

Kevan met Marilyn Kiewiet through Sandy Stagg, who brought her to the Forge on St. Joseph Street to hear us play. Marilyn was tall, hovering around six feet. She was a stunning brunette with fashion-model good looks. She was not without baggage, which came in the form of a six-foot boyfriend named Tom. She took off for Holland the day after the gig, but when she returned, Kevan arranged to meet her. He was smitten. He took her to the Planetarium so they could gaze at the stars, and it was very romantic and Aquarian. The beginning of their relationship was tumultuous, though, because Marilyn had to disentangle herself from Tom, and he did not leave willingly. Marilyn moved in with Kevan in April of 1977.

Kevan and I were big fans of the Clichettes: Louise Garfield, Johanna Householder and Janet Burke. These three performance artists did a series of pieces that involved lip-synching and cross-dressing. They struck a chord of insanity in me and I got addicted to their spacey shows. The first show I saw was called

Half Human, Half Heartache, which was about three alien space girls who land on earth. Nonetheless, there was something very Berlin-in-the-thirties about it. In a later show, called *Up Against the Wallpaper*, the three played pieces of furniture and walls in an empty house. They also worked with us on several occasions. We persisted in having people like the Clichettes open for us, although they often did so at their own peril, since audiences who have been sitting in a bar drinking for a couple of hours are not always blessed with camp sensibilities.

In 1978, we performed for GI's tenth anniversary on the top of the brand new CN Tower, which lords over the cityscape like a phallic obelisk from a Jetsons cartoon. The first time I stepped out of the elevator, I felt like I'd walked into a science fiction film. The problem was, there was only one elevator, which didn't make it easy to cart up our equipment, let alone the hundreds of guests. The top of the tower revolved so you could gaze out onto the city below, or not, if you suffered from vertigo. The soirée was packed with the hippest of the hip from the art scene and Queen Street. There was a fashion show put together by David Buchan, an artist who coined the term "geek chic." Most of his work featured his alter ego, the swinging La Monte Del Monte. Working with GI was always an incentive for us to try something different, even if it was just a new hair colour. Some of the guests suffered from motion sickness; there was some projectile vomiting and that wasn't pretty. The evening wound down and eventually all the guests were escorted out by the nervous CN Tower officials.

Sandy, always the restless entrepreneur, decided to unload the Peter Pan and move on. She and Murray Ball, the lead singer of the Dishes, formed a partnership and opened a place on Yonge Street called the Fiesta. GI's art adorned the walls, which were painted in pastel colours. My baby brother Howard worked there as a waiter. Sandy and Murray came up with a menu that included dishes like chicken in bondage, which was chicken bound up in licorice ropes. The food was never really that good. The Queen Street crowd spent hours in this new hot spot almost every night; it became an extension of the Stagg salon. Howard remarked to Steven that I spent so much time at the Fiesta I should have my mail delivered there. Steven Lynch (who is now a successful makeup artist) and the rest of the Fiesta staff couldn't resist making fun of Sandy. Steven and Howard used to put on English accents and parrot, "I can't run the Fiesta, be patroness of the arts, seduce young boys and be Sandy Stagg all at the same time," which made Sandy nuts. Sandy loved men but didn't always make the smartest choices. She took up with Steve "Nazi Dog" Leckie, the lead singer of the punk band the Viletones and, no surprise, it was a disaster. One night he broke into the Fiesta and stole all the liquor. (He is now a born-again Christian.)

One night Anya and I went to see Japan play. Unlike so many eighties bands, they were actually talented musicians, but they were full of themselves. After the show, someone suggested they come to the Fiesta. As soon as they walked in the door, the singer, David Sylvian, said, "This is the worst possible place you could have brought us." Frightened of another outburst from the male diva, everyone steered clear of him, huddling together at tables to escape his wrath.

On New Year's Eve it became a tradition for me to rent a limo with Sandy Stagg and AA Bronson and go from party to party, crashing the ones we weren't invited to and generally being obnoxious and loud. We were sometimes accompanied by a gang of art chicks, dressed in men's tuxedos with pencil-thin mustaches drawn on their upper lips. We were wild on other nights of the year, too. One Halloween, AA's costume was a conservative tweed suit and a paper bag held close to his body. I peeked inside the bag and there, protruding through a hole in the bag, was his cock. Elizabeth Chitty, a friend of AA's, put her hand into the bag and screamed. She thought AA had hidden a mouse in there.

By its tenth anniversary, GI was in the art world big league. The boys were represented in Europe by one of the most powerful artist's agents, Lucio Amelio. If he saw potential in an artist, he could take them very far. The GI boys went to Amsterdam to shoot a video called *The Colour Bar Lounge*, featuring Billy Pano, a beautiful blond boy GI liked to use as a model. Kenny Baird, the art director on the project, and Billy went to Amsterdam on their own to meet up with GI. Tarted up in colourful Gerald Franklin leathers, they ended up travelling on the same flight as the Stones, who were dealing with Canadian drug busts. Customs officials assumed Billy and Kenny were part of the entourage. They were pulled off the plane and busted. After a night in jail, they were released and went on to Holland.

There were GI posters plastered all over the streets of Amsterdam, with Billy as the "Nazi Milk" boy. Bill already looked like a role model for Aryan youth, and he had been photographed by Jorge with a Hitler-like milk mustache. Memories of the Nazis were burned into the Dutch psyche. There was negative feedback and open hostility against GI. In spite of the Dutch reaction, GI was hugely successful in Europe.

Back in Toronto, GI seemed to have a monopoly on the grant system and by the early eighties there was a backlash against them among struggling artists, who were bitter. Jorge and AA decided to relocate to New York, leaving Ron behind in Toronto.

During the first years of their work as a collective, GI tried to obscure their individual identities, but that changed with a number of self-portraits called the *Three Men Series*. One of the portraits was part of a larger series called *Mondo Cane Kama Sutra*—the artists in full poodle drag posed against a pink background, their eyes gazing towards the heavens. GI's 1985 exhibit at the Art Gallery of Ontario was a series of paintings of a ménage-à-trois of poodles humping each other in a parody of neo-classical art. The pieces are rendered in a precise mechanical style that is both titillating and humorous. I attended the opening with Kevan and Marilyn. We overheard a woman remark, as she stood stunned by the vulgar intensity of the paintings, "Well, the colours are nice." This series included embroidered poodle crests and fragments of wall sections from a poodle tomb covered in poodle hieroglyphics.

In 1985 Jorge tested positive for HIV and Ron fell ill two years later. The fact that they were positive was not common knowledge. I had no idea they were sick until someone still close to them told me in the nineties. The years 1983 to 1988 were ground zero for GRID (Gay Related Immune Deficiency), later called HIV. The first virulent strain of AIDS was so strong it sometimes took people out in two to three weeks. After Jorge got sick, he and AA decided to move back to Toronto, and they scored an incredible penthouse apartment on top of the Colonnade in Toronto. The apartment was huge and aesthetically pleasing to the eye, and there was a small swimming pool on the roof.

GI's first AIDS logo appeared in 1987, appropriating the design and colour scheme of artist Robert Indiana's *Love* emblem. Not only did GI hang paintings of the logo in art galleries around the world, posters and billboards of the work appeared on the streets of New York, Berlin and San Francisco. They followed this with other AIDS-related works, one of which was large constructions of AZT tablets entitled *Placebo*. The artists had shown us the reality of AIDS. There is no cure. We are all affected by that fact no matter how AIDS impacts our lives.

The last time I saw Jorge alive was in Los Angeles. He was teaching a course at Santa Monica College, and he took me out to dinner. It was the first time we talked about his illness. Then I spoke to him on the phone on the night of his fiftieth birthday; he was lying in his bedroom at GI's apartment, surrounded by all his friends. His voice was hoarse, and I had no idea that he'd gone blind. Kevan was there and sat at his bedside holding his hand. Within two days, he was dead. The year was 1994. Ron died a few months later.

As I was researching this chapter I came across a piece that was not fully realized by GI, called *From Fin de Siècle*— another extension of the *Three Men Series*. It's a vast expanse of a glacier with three baby seals lying on one of the outcroppings. I couldn't help but think of the artists as victims.

Last year AA, the only survivor, did a one-man show. It was a huge blow-up colour photograph of Ron lying in bed, surrounded by his favourite possessions, his body wrapped in Missoni sheets. His eyes were open and blank, and the flesh was falling away from his face. He looked like a skeleton. The photograph was taken three hours after he died. I went to see the show with friends and we were shocked. We stood there speechless, unable to figure out AA's rationale for this invasion of Ron's privacy. And then someone said, "Maybe AA was depersonalizing death. Blowing the image up to the size of a billboard was the ultimate public act." Which, I guess, was in keeping with what General Idea was all about.

I do believe that AIDS has had a major impact on the death of art. So many people who were on the verge of changing the world, in every conceivable way, are no longer on this earth, and I feel bored and jaded by the numbing sameness of the regurgitated pop culture that passes for art. I don't want to think that all these people died in vain without leaving a legacy. Every once in a while I see something that jolts me, something true and subversive, and I'm somewhat reassured that not all art has been reduced to empty hype or a pretty face staring indolently from the pages of *Interview* or *Vanity Fair*.

When I first met Bob Ezrin in 1971, he was a rich, long-haired kid from Forest Hill with a pseudo-hippie thing going on. He bore a resemblance to the actor Al Pacino, and seemed serious and self-important for an eighteen-year-old. He was already married to his childhood sweetheart, Arlene. In our incarnation as the Bullwhip Brothers, Kevan and I played a couple of our songs for Bob in an office he shared with a friend in Yorkville. He was experiencing his first taste of success, on the heels of his innovative work as the producer of an album for the godfather of Goth, Alice Cooper. I was nervous and cannot clearly remember his reaction to our songs. I think he was tactful and encouraging.

The Bullwhip Brothers, identically attired in terry-cloth jumpsuits like our heroes John and Yoko, went to see Alice's show at Varsity Arena, a soccer field in Toronto, which on that particular day was transformed into a battlefield strewn with the bodies of wasted acid casualties draped in flowers. The humid air was permeated with the smell of incense and hash. Alice Cooper was out to shock, which in those days didn't take much. His band wore women's dresses, ugly print numbers that a Russian housewife might own. Alice seemed to be making some kind of a chicken statement, since he kept throwing the poor birds around during the show. I didn't witness any bloodletting, or any introduction of foreign objects into their little chicken bums, but they didn't seem to be too happy about being tossed into the crowd.

We didn't see Bob again until the mid-seventies, when he came to see Rough Trade work at a club called the Forge, accompanied by Bernie Taupin, Elton John's songwriting partner and lyricist. After our set, Bob told us he liked what he'd heard and said he wanted to meet with us. Kevan and I made arrangements to get together with him at his house the next day. After the gig I went to Bernie Taupin's hotel room with Prakash John, an extraordinary bass player, along with his blond girl. Almost as soon as we got there, Bernie started to hit on me. His seduction technique was as subtle as a swarm of locusts flying against a windshield. In a whiny, bratty, little-boy voice, he loudly asked me to sleep with him. I said no. He asked me again. I said, "No, I'm a dyke." That only made him more determined. It was an uncomfortable and embarrassing situation for everyone, and Prakash and I decided to take off. We left Bernie sitting and fuming on the floor of his suite. Strangely enough, the blond girl stayed behind.

The next day Kevan and I went to Bob's house. He was ingratiating and flattering and obviously used to getting what he wanted, but when it came down to it, he made us an offer we could refuse.

He wanted to produce an album for us in exchange for fifty percent of everything. When it came to that kind of heavy-duty life-changing proposition, we had no negotiating skills whatsoever, but we knew we didn't want to sign over half our lives.

Around that time, Motown approached me about signing with the label. They weren't interested in Rough Trade or Kevan, and wanted me to record different material. They were saying, "We like you, but we don't like anything you're doing." I'd heard such horror stories about Motown from singer Rick James that I never seriously considered their proposal.

Ezrin and I started to connect. He called me into the studio to sing backup for a guitar player whose album he was producing. There I was singing vocals with a shy English guy named Peter Gabriel. I had no idea who he was, since I wouldn't have been caught dead listening to Genesis. Bob was very intriguing to me. He was rich, powerful and intelligent, and there was a dark side to him. He was a control freak who exercised his power in two ways: he was either sensitive and caring or blatantly rude and abusive to the artists he worked with. The first time I saw him go a little over the top, he was producing a band called the Babys, four pretty young dudes with shag haircuts. The singer of the band was John Waite. Bob was verbally intimidating them. I had the feeling that if one of the band members had called him on his behaviour, he would have backed off, but no one did. It was all some kind of male power thing that I don't pretend to understand.

As I got to know Bob, he told me he was a manic depressive, just like my father. He confided in me that his IQ was off the scale—was he trying to impress me? It was obvious from the moment I met him that he had some heavy frontal-lobe action going on. I was very attracted to Mr. Ezrin, so much so that we actually did it. He was a sensitive lover, and not surprisingly, women were all over him. Power was the lure and aphrodisiac that drove me into his bed; also, the fact that he'd had an affair with Julie Christie factored in there somewhere, in a six degrees of sexuation way. While I was wrapped up in this strange infatuation, I kept asking myself what the fuck I was doing. Maybe I was just checking to make sure I was still gay, and yes, I was. It was the last time I would ever have sex with a man. I'd always had a problem with male authority, and sex with men, no matter how sweet they might be, felt like an invasion of my body. It's a trip, looking back on your life and trying to analyze your erratic behaviour years after the fact. Maybe I had some deep psychological Daddy issues that I needed to work out with him. Our relationship, whatever it was, turned into a friendship, though every once in a while Bob would hit on me. After all, he is a man.

Lily Tomlin was in town doing her one-woman show *Appearing Nightly*, and Elaine and Lily had worked together on a project. We went to see her, and she was nothing short of brilliant. Carol Channing came backstage after Lily's show and invited us to see *Hello, Dolly!* which she was on the road touring. That show was like a karmic albatross hanging off her. So Elaine, Lily and I went to see Channing the following night. I couldn't imagine how she could still get it up for that part, but she did. I had to wonder if she had any other facial expressions besides the semi-maniacal smile that was always plastered on her face. After the show, there was a party on the roof of 21 McGill, an exclusive women's club in Toronto that, sadly, no longer exists. The party was just Carol, cocktails and God knows how many male dancers and queens running around in a drunken frenzy.

Elaine and I took Lily to another party, where we were put in the position of acting as her bodyguards. It was in an artist's loft in a warehouse and everyone in the room converged on Lily at once. Elaine and I stood guard on either side, like two of Charlie's Angels. We were Lily's only protection, and it was a job the Pope sisters took seriously.

Bob was producing an album for Tim Curry called *Read My Lips*. He asked Kevan and me if Tim could cover one of our songs, "Birds of a Feather." We said yes, of course, and ended up signing over a percentage of the publishing to Bob. I met Tim at Nimbus Nine in Toronto, where they were recording. In the control room, Bob was goofing around with Michael Kamen, the arranger on Tim's album. Bob was running around the control room letting loose a stream of comic nonsense. All of a sudden Bob and Tim launched themselves at Michael and gaffer-taped him to his chair. Then they pushed him out the door of the studio into the middle of the street and left him there to die! Fortunately for Michael, it was not a heavy traffic area.

Ezrin and Curry had hooked up through Jerry Moss, the co-owner of A&M. Bob was impressed with the way Tim carried himself, the way he walked into a room like he owned it. He took an instantaneous liking to him and decided to produce him.

Tim was very charismatic and had a seductive vulnerability about him. It wasn't easy to get to know him—you'd have to work for it, peeling away layer upon layer of information, to reveal his essence like a glittering prize. And you'd enjoy every minute of it. Tim had an eclectic sense of humour and did a caustically funny shtick featuring Edith Sitwell and members of the Bloomsbury Group. I thought he was far too brilliant and sensitive for his own good. Tim's acting career was diverse and had included a stint with the Royal Shakespeare Company in London. But the part that firmly entrenched him in the cult of personality was that of the cross-dressing Dr. Frank N. Furter in *The Rocky Horror Picture Show*.

Bob was having a thing with the actress Madeline Kahn, who was shooting a film in Toronto. He had to work late one night, and asked me to amuse/babysit her. I took her over to Peter Mann's apartment, because he worshipped her and I knew he would fawn all over her, and that would make her happy. We smoked a joint, and I persisted in telling her what a brilliant comedian she was, but she kept correcting me, telling me she was an actress, not a comedian. She did, however, tell us about working with Mel Brooks on *Blazing Saddles* and how she had come up with the idiosyncrasies of her character, Lili Von Shtupp. It was an honour to spend a few hours with her, but I was discovering that actresses and actors were the most difficult and temperamental of creatures and had to be handled like rare, exotic and sometimes deadly flowers.

We started socializing with Tim, and one claustrophobic summer day, several of us took a ferry out to Hanlan's Point, on the Toronto islands, for a picnic. The setting was as civilized as possible. We sat under a tree looking out onto the almost stagnant water. Tim's manager, Clauda, actually waded into scary Lake Ontario and started swimming straight for the other side. It looked like she might make it to Buffalo, but some power-tripping water cop in a boat made her turn back.

The Curry project moved to New York, where Bob kept an exclusive apartment on the Upper East Side, just down the street from the digs of the elusive Garbo. Bob was raking in the dough from working with bands like Kiss. Not only did he produce their albums, he took a very active part in writing the material. Bob was a classically trained musician, and there was a grand piano in the apartment's sunken living room. Sometimes he'd let me use the place when I was in town. I loved staying there. I felt very Jackie O–like, or maybe I was more like Eloise at the Plaza, hanging out in Bob's love shack.

I started seeing Luci Martin, one of the backup singers I'd worked with in *Restless Underwear*. She'd relocated to New York. There was nothing heavy between us, just cheap meaningless sex. Luci was one of the two girl singers in Chic, the creation of producers Nile Rodgers and Bernard Edwards, who were hot and in demand because of the uniqueness of Chic's sound. The actual members of the band were almost eclipsed. I went to visit her while they were recording, and I wasn't allowed inside the control room. We had to sit and talk in the lobby of the studio.

If Luci and I were partying at Bob's place, we'd roll around on his wall-to-wall bed and watch videos like *Behind the Green Door* or *Deep Throat* on his big bulky 3/4" tape deck, now as antiquated as an eight-track. Those porn epics were considered a big turn-on and milestones of sorts. People couldn't get enough of Linda Lovelace. In her dual role as a housewife and porn star, she could, and did, wrap her mouth around two cocks at a time. It wasn't pretty to look at. In the late seventies the sexual climate of America, especially in New York, was open and promiscuous for gays and straights alike. Wife swapping was a party game, and clubs like Plato's Retreat, where straights participated in sex orgies, were what was happening. Lovelace was interviewed on prestigious talk shows like Dick Cavett's.

The recording of Tim's album was intense and exhausting. Tim's voice was powerful, his range diverse, and the material on the album all over the map. One cut was a metal version of an old Scottish folk tune and featured a Highland regiment pipe and drum band. Tim also did a cover of "Anyone Who Had a Heart," and I got to sit in the old Columbia recording studio in New York while a string section laid down a track. Tim's working situation with Bob was turning into a nightmare for him. Kevan and I spent a long sleepless night in New York talking with Tim. He was a mess, and he poured his heart out to us about the complexities of Bob. He felt he wasn't getting any respect as an artist or a human being, that Bob was doing too much coke and was suffering from all the side effects. Bob seemed paranoid and threatened by Tim. We were in the unusual and difficult position of trying to comfort someone we considered to be an icon. I know I did talk to Bob about the situation, but I didn't want to push things. In the end, the album turned out incredibly well and was a real showcase for Tim's talent.

Bob's life was complicated. He and Arlene had divorced, but he was very involved in being a father to his son. Like all of us, he was doing too many drugs, and I worried that he had somehow got to the place where he relied on drugs as a dangerous emotional bandage. It seemed to me that he was in serious pain. (He is light years away from that person now.)

I was no prize myself in 1978. I had become obsessed with an obnoxious straight girl who had substance-abuse problems. My self-esteem must have been at a low ebb or I wouldn't have been remotely interested in her or so enamoured of everything Ezrin. Bob was this bright shiny object that sometimes distracted me from what was going on in my life. It wasn't until years later that I realized that kind of behaviour was a pattern with me. I would let people distract me from the grim reality of events in my life.

I'd been living with the shocking news that Celia's cancer had come back with a vengeance. She was intent on fighting it and took an aggressive stance. She was working on changing her diet and lifestyle. When I was with her, we'd talk about food. The English diet we'd been raised on was a colon-clogging nightmare of overcooked vegetables and meat. My eating habits had changed, and Mom was game for anything, so we both tried a supposedly DNA-regenerating diet that was popular then. Celia was also on a quest for some kind of spirituality. We discussed Buddhism and the beat version of Unitarianism, which she'd embraced in the sixties. But we never got into the dynamics of our relationship. There was something indefinable between us. Some kind of barrier. I felt like I could never really reach her, and that feeling never completely went away.

Mom had to undergo another operation, and the outcome was not good. Every time we went to the hospital to see her, we were given more bad news. The cancer had spread into her lymph system. We were stunned, and all her children went into denial. On the last day of her life, I went to the hospital to see her. She was emaciated, with a bloated stomach. The doctors had removed more of her intestine, and the latest prognosis was that she didn't have long to live. Elaine and I decided we wouldn't tell her that she was going to die, although I'm sure she must have known. I stood next to her in that green silent room and time stopped. I don't know how long I stood there holding her hand. I wanted to say so much, but I didn't. I told her I loved her. I wanted to say, "Don't leave me," but I didn't. I don't know how I left that room, and I hated myself for leaving. She died later that day. Elaine was there when it happened. She was the only one of us who was really completely there for my mother during her illness. Elaine was angry with Diane, my father and me because she felt we were useless in the situation. She was right.

But each of us had a different relationship with my mother. I was the test child; my parents were winging it, usually at my expense. The most traumatic thing Celia did to me was to stop showing me any physical affection. I never got over that rejection. Things got progressively easier for my sisters and brother as my parents relaxed their paranoia and control.

All through my life, Celia told me stories of her mother's death. My grandmother died at fifty-nine from cancer of the small intestine, and her body lay in state in our house for three days. Celia could never get the image of her dead mother out of her mind. She was haunted by it and would share that with me in lurid detail. Celia was obsessed with her looks and aging, and she instilled fear and terror about it in all her children. Now she had died at fifty-nine, of cancer of the small intestine. The night of her death she came to me in a dream, dressed in a hospital gown and looking as she had that day. In subsequent dreams she became younger and more beautiful. When I dream of her now, she is in her thirties, at the peak of her beauty, standing on the beach at Cape Cod, where we sometimes used to vacation.

Howard was especially traumatized by Celia's death. He was only seventeen years old and cast adrift; he would have to leave the apartment they'd shared and fend for himself. He came to my room the day after Mom died. He looked so young and so lost I could hardly bear it. I felt like his sister and his mother. Bob dropped by and was sweet and comforting to Howard (a simple thing but beyond the scope of my dad). Bob talked to him like he was his own son. Elaine and I arranged a memorial service for Celia with a very spiritually evolved female Unitarian minister. At the service, we played music by Billie Holiday and Ruth Etting. All these great women, who were friends of hers, showed up. We found out at the funeral that before she'd become ill she'd been seeing a man who was thirty-five. Celia had this whole other life we knew nothing about.

Shortly after that, Elaine bought a car, packed up her belongings and took off for Los Angeles. She wanted to pursue a career as a writer, and there was nothing holding her in Toronto. Howard found an apartment with two friends. I was an inconsolable mess and submerged myself completely in my music. Music has an indefinable healing power and has saved me from myself on more than one occasion.

We did a show with Tim Curry. Tim knows how to work a stage, and when he's out there, he owns that piece of real estate. He seduced the audience like a lover and then blew them away. He took our song "Birds of a Feather" to a whole other place, making it more dramatic than my campy version. He knew how to integrate rock and theatre. The show got reviewed by Jonathan Gross in *The Toronto Sun*. He loved Tim and somewhat grudgingly liked us, but panned the shoes I was wearing. What the hell did my footwear (transparent jellies) have to do with Rough Trade's performance? Gross had definitely pushed some buttons in me. The media continually used the phrase "raunch queen" to describe me, and I thought I had a little more going on than that. I ran into Gross at a party and went postal on him. All six-foot-whatever of him cowered behind his girlfriend, who had balls to spare. I asked him what my shoes had to do with the way I sang. He didn't really have an answer; he was such a wimp. His girl was all over me like a she-wolf protecting her young. Critics are a bunch of bottom-feeders, as far as I'm concerned.

Kevan and I wanted to get to the next level in our career and find good representation. By the end of the seventies, we'd been through three managers. Our first, Jake Boxstrum, was a business man and part-time race-car driver. He was a great guy but not really connected to the music business. The second was Fran, who wanted to jump my bones, so that didn't last long. Then one of the Garys—Gary Cormier—took a stab at representing us and that didn't work out either.

John Scharer was a Canadian producer who had put together Nona Hendryx's first solo album. He knew we were looking for management and suggested to Nona's manager, Vicki Wickham, that she fly up to Toronto with him to see us play live. We liked Vicki from the moment we met her. Vicki is uniquely British and somewhat eccentric, which goes with the English territory. She is up and enthusiastic about everything. At the time, her hair was cut into a blond shag and she had an outdoorsy thing going on. She was liked and respected in the industry. In the swinging sixties, Vicki had produced a hit weekly TV show in England called *Ready, Steady, Go!* and she knew everybody in the British music industry. I loved her because I could mention an obscure English singer to her and she'd not only know who they were but have dish on them as well. She thought we had potential, understood where we were coming from and was willing to take us on. Vicki immediately started to shop our demos in the U.S.

———————

Through Vicki we met Nona Hendryx. Kevan and I were sitting in Vicki's apartment in New York one night when Nona walked into the room. We both let out audible gasps, she was so beautiful, her African-American and Cherokee bloodlines clear in her striking face. A member of the glam trio Labelle with Patti LaBelle and Sarah Dash, she had spent her life on the road. Labelle had disbanded after some inner diva-like turmoil. Now Nona was having a bitch of a time getting accepted as a black woman singing rock because she didn't fit into any preconceived niche. Kevan and I knew the feeling. We asked Nona to perform at a couple of our Toronto shows, our "theme concerts" like "Twilight Women" and "Gidget Goes Mondo." The Garys booked Nona at the Edge. We ended up writing with each other and performing on each other's albums.

In my misery after my mom died, I decided it was time to move out of Earl Street. It seemed unbelievable that I'd lived there for eight years. I found a new apartment—directly across the road from my old one.

Somewhere in the mid-seventies, every social outcast and struggling artist I knew who was looking for a way to vent, an outlet, found his or her way to New York. Musicians were on the same cerebral wavelength; it seemed like bands were reproducing like a virus trying to infect us with a new way of being. Glam was over; we were sick of lamé, cross-dressing decadence. It was all about pushing the envelope. Iggy Pop introduced bloodletting into rock and roll. The New York Dolls fucked with gender and got the best pussy. Sulky Debbie Harry was the untouchable ice maiden who fronted Blondie. Tom Verlaine and Television were punk aesthetes. Richard Hell was unwashed and angry. The Talking Heads celebrated the nerd. The raw, intensely erotic poetry of Patti Smith had a stunning impact on me, or perhaps it was just her presence. The disenfranchised, their blue-white skin casting an unearthly glow, went on a nightly migration, moving from Max's Kansas City to CBGBs to the Mudd Club. The punk sensibility rose out of a milieu in which every individual was a walking disaster.

I was on fire, hooked on performing. I wanted to be loved; I wanted to expose myself and my sexual politics. Singing is a seduction that you have to pull off every night, and it made me feel totally and utterly alive. We did a three-week gig at Trude

Hellers's in the Village. It was a cabaret club that had taken a right turn into the twilight zone. The club was decorated in black-and-white faux deco. Two indolent go-go dancers stood against a wall, dispassionately shaking their booty. Somehow it worked. The audience we attracted was eclectic. I was lucky enough to meet theatre producers such as Hal Prince and Joseph Papp, who was an advocate of free public theatre. In the crowd there were actors, musicians and people stoned on meds meant for outpatients of mental institutions. One Latino girl kept yelling "Elton John" at us while we played. It seemed he was her only frame of musical reference. Our drummer at the time, Rick Gratton, was short, his upper body pumped up with muscle—he looked like the Michelin man. He was hyper and neurotic, which I viewed as an asset. Peter Hodgson was on bass. He had his own language, a land of "Peterspeak." (When someone wanted to get laid, he'd remark that "they had that special look of insertion.") Mike Fonfara, our keyboard player, believed in better living through chemistry. During one of our gigs, he slumped over his keyboards, fast asleep, and I had to go over and prod him into consciousness. Jo-Ann Brooks, the daughter of Dianne Brooks, one of Canada's great unknown rhythm-and-blues singers, sang back-up vocals. Unlike her mother, she sometimes sang flat. She really got on my nerves. She'd say things to me like, "I've decided not to sleep with you, Carole." Like I'd ever ask her.

A man in the audience jerked off into his shoe during one of our sets. We could see him shooting his load from the stage. The band couldn't get enough of that. The burning question was—did the guy put the shoe back on his foot?

Lou Reed came to several of our shows because Peter and Mike had worked with him. He'd bring along his lover, Rachel, the stunning, high-maintenance transvestite he was living with. Joanne and I liked to gossip with her between sets.

She was a total babe, which turned us both on. Rachel was jonesing for a penthouse on Park Avenue. She told us she wanted Lou to shower her with jewels like she was one of the Gabor sisters. Anytime Lou and I attempted to have a conversation, he was totally incoherent. Each time he came to the club, he was high on some kind of volatile drug cocktail.

Andrea Martin had an apartment in the city, and she showed up at Trude Hellers several times to lend her support and her general fabulousness to the whole thing. After the show, we'd go out and carouse in the big urban amusement park that was New York.

Rough Trade's review in the *Daily News* stated that we "worked out of the basement of the psyche" and that we "celebrated and satirized those regions of carnal knowledge that society prefers to keep underground."

Walking the streets of New York was euphoric, better than any drug. I liked to wander for hours, getting lost in the city, just feeling the vibe. On one of my walks, I ran into some members of Blondie in the Village. The scene was so vibrant then, we all felt connected, like we were part of something bigger than us. They turned me on to a store where you could buy punk gear. I bought bondage pants that had a strap that attached to both legs so your movements were restricted. It seems strange that we were so wired to physically restrictive clothing as a fashion statement when we were all about rebellion.

I had a meeting with Eddie Kramer at his Electric Lady studio in the East Village (he had produced Jimi Hendrix's *Electric Lady Land*). He was standing there with guitarist Jimmy Page, who was dressed entirely in black. I must say that everything paled next to Page in that room. I'd heard that he was into the cult of Aleister Crowley, an English Satanist from the thirties. I found him intimidating. Kramer was very open and supportive. He said he didn't have time to do anything with us right now, but wanted to keep the door open.

When I was in New York, I'd occasionally crash with Mark Shaiman, who I'd met through my friend Marg Gross. One of his many gigs was acting as Bette Midler's music director. Mark had an apartment on West End Avenue, in a building full of people who were somehow involved with Midler. A bevy of ex-Harletts paraded in and out of Mark's apartment. Staying with him was like living in a 1940s musical. Kids would drop by, clutching their sheet music, nervous and hyped up about their impending auditions, to rehearse their numbers with him. I loved to listen to the diverse, sometimes certifiable, array of talent that came through his door, some of whom went on to be very successful.

With Mark, I got to work my inner queen. (I am the faggiest dyke ever.) Elaine, out in L.A., had somehow gotten a copy of super-agent Sue Menger's address book and had given me the home numbers of stars like Streisand and Woody Allen. (It turned out she rifled through the drawers of every Hollywood celebrity whose parties she went to.) One night Mark and I called everybody, giggling like little kids. We both talked to Jon Peters, Streisand's hairdresser/movie mogul lover. We went to Broadway shows together. Standing outside the theatre, we'd quickly inhale a couple of joints. Warily eyeing the street performers, especially the mimes, we'd plot ways to kill them. We were fans of the dark sensibilities of Stephen Sondheim. We saw his *Sweeney Todd* three times. I loved it whenever Sweeney, the demon barber, slit someone's throat—there was something tantalizing about the way the fake blood gushed out from under the razor he was clutching. Victor Garber played a lovelorn sailor in the production we saw; at one time he'd been the lead singer of a precious Toronto group called Sugar Shoppe. Back in Toronto, I'd fantasized about dragging Sugar Shoppe into a back alley and slapping them around because they were so insipid. But Garber had an amazing voice.

Mark and I were both unnaturally obsessed with Joan Crawford. (Yes, I know it's a cliché.) Strolling around his living room, Mark would direct the light from his table lamps into his eyes in a parody of the way the key lights were used to make Joan look younger when she made her comeback in *Mildred Pierce*. I really pushed the Joan thing when I drew thick eyebrows and painted red lips on Mark's white Husky. Mark loved it so much he took the dog outside for a walk. PETA is gonna shoot me with fake-blood pellets.

One night Mark and I went to CBGBs, which was full of inmates from the asylum I'd escaped from, to see a band called the Shirts. One of Mark's kids, Annie Golden, was their lead singer. I thought the Shirts were hot and would have a successful career, but as usual I was wrong. (Annie did get a gig in the movie version of *Hair*.) That night they were opening for the Talking Heads. I was ready to dis the Heads, since my first impression of David Byrne was that he was a total nerd, with his quirky body language and stilted singing style. But he got to me. His lyrics were all about urban angst, the song "Psycho Killer" being a prime example. The Heads were true artists, and as they evolved, they embraced other art forms, including dance. Byrne worked with choreographer Twyla Tharp on a dance project called *The Catherine Wheel*, and he collaborated with Brian Eno composing ambient music. Together, on an album called *Music in the Bush of Ghosts*, he and Eno sampled random dialogue, sermons by Baptist preachers and

other bits and pieces, and made that part of the music way
before rappers appropriated the idea.

Studio 54 was the Sodom and Gomorrah of the late seventies,
the place where celebrities would go to let it all hang out.
Their names were out of the pages of *Women's Wear Daily*:
Halston, Liza, Bianca, Calvin Klein and David Geffen were
the inhabitants of that decadent nocturnal world. Getting into
54 was a big production. The monolithic doormen were keep-
ers of the gates of this demi-paradise (or hell, depending on
what kind of mood swing you were in). To enter this tacky
temple of trendiness, you had to register on some kind of
trend-o-meter in the bouncer's drug-addled brain. Some nights
Steve Rubell, the club's owner, would stand outside, hand-
picking the action. You had to be somebody or be with somebody who was somebody. Once admitted, you were faced
with a Dionysian display of shirtless bartenders. The air was
thick with sensuality and throbbing disco music. One of my
brother Howard's fondest memories was getting a blow job
from some chiselled hunk up on the catwalk.

One night I sat on a couch gossiping with Nona Hendryx
and super-diva Patti LaBelle. They had the best dish on other
black artists. We sat there immersed in our own little world,
calmly watching Peter Allen, a flaming singer who'd been
married to Liza with a Z, make an idiot out of himself. He
was prancing around the dance floor dragging unwilling partners along with him, practically foaming at the mouth. What
was Liza thinking, with her string of faux marriages?

My favourite club was the Palladium, more tasteful than
the pink glitz of 54. You could schmooze in the minimalist
Mike Todd room. The bathrooms were equipped with all the
accoutrements for a night of drugs and sex. People would pile

into the stalls and snort coke while a world-weary attendant handed out towels to staunch those pesky nose bleeds.

Spilling into the Me Decade, it seemed the gods were finally smiling on Rough Trade. It had been an intense struggle for us. I felt that I was looked on as a threatening entity in the boys' club that ran the music industry. An aggressive, sexually androgynous woman with warped sensibilities did not sit well with them. Our first album, *Avoid Freud*, was licensed to Stiff Records in the U.S., but they went bankrupt. Bernie Finkelstein, the head of the label we'd signed with in Canada, got us licensing deals in Europe with various labels. He also signed a new distribution deal for us in the States with Boardwalk Records, a subsidiary of Casablanca, which was the love child of the late Neil Bogart. That label scored mega-hits with their artists Donna Summer, the Village People and Kiss. In this boogie wonderland, people laid out lines at the board meetings. You just knew Casablanca was flirting with destruction and would ultimately crash and burn.

Boardwalk, on the other hand, was a small operation and all business. Irv Biegel, the head of A&R, was responsible for signing us. He was intent on breaking Rough Trade into the U.S. We sat in hotel rooms for hours taping radio interviews and promo spots that went out to hundreds of stations. At that time, payola was a major influence on airplay, and record companies hired independent promoters to work their product. They were ready to bribe radio jocks with whatever it took—drugs, cash or pussy.

Rough Trade performed on the opening night of the infamous Danceteria in 1982. R.E.M. opened for us. Divine was in the audience, along with our pal Tim Blanks and the hot Youth Quakers of the moment. We were overwhelmed by the experience. Danceteria was three floors of trendiness conceived and managed by Jim Fouratt, a cutting-edge entrepreneur who was instrumental in launching a myriad of New York clubs (including Hurrah, Blitz, Pravda, the Underground and the Peppermint Lounge, where we also played). Jim gave New Yorkers what they wanted before they knew they wanted it. The process of getting nightclubs up and running was politically tense and dangerous. Jim's partner in this venture was Rudolph Pieper, who was married to Diane Brill, a stacked blond socialite/model who acted as the club's hostess. Jim could relate to Rough Trade, because he thought we were talking to him and his life. Danceteria was the kind of venue that made you want to check out all the floors for fear of missing out on anything. For a New York nanosecond it was the only game in town. Some nights, a young dark-haired Madonna could be seen dancing on the third floor.

Through Mary Lou Green, who was now the artistic director of Vidal Sassoon in New York, I connected with the New York art crowd. She'd been cutting my hair since the GI days, and she'd been servicing the heads of the famous forever. Mary Lou was a trip, beautiful with brown eyes and great cheekbones. She was on some kind of permanent wild ride, and once you got on board with her, you were sucked into the vortex.

Hair was an integral part of the music scene, the Flock of Seagulls look being the nadir that so many aspired to. One of Mary Lou's most frightening hair-styling concepts involved cutting someone's hair with a laser, a titillating combination of hairdressing and performance art. The event took place in Las Vegas. Sassoon's had to get NASA to transport the laser by truck across the country for this, the most expensive haircut ever. The price tag was nine thousand dollars. Fortunately, the model Mary Lou used for this experiment in terror had very, very long hair.

Imagine the model strapped down on a cold metal table, her hair trailing out behind her like a photograph by Man Ray. Mary Lou stands over her, a butt jammed in the side of her mouth. She's wearing infrared goggles by Gucci and latex gloves by Rubbermaid. Her cigarette is from the fine people at Export 'A'. Maybe she slaps the model across the face a couple of times before firing up the instrument of death. Then she aims the laser and severs the hair in a beautiful, straight line. There is a barely perceptible odour of burning hair floating in the air.

Mary Lou was always on call for the caprices of Andy Warhol. She styled his wigs for various photo shoots. He alternated between grey and white hair pieces. He had started going bald in the sixties and had devised a way to turn even that into art.

Mary Lou had a thing for musicians. She dated Robert Fripp, guitar god and English eccentric. A founding member of King Crimson, he conceived his own brilliant genre of music, called Frippatronics, a series of hypnotic repetitive guitar loops. Fripp liked to play with his back to the audience. (Apparently he has now stopped talking to anyone, even his manager, to whom he hasn't spoken in three years.) When we went club hopping, Mary Lou clung to Fripp like he was a lifeboat in a sea of insanity. He was constantly besieged by fans. He refused to sign autographs. He told people, "Oh, you don't want that." (Fripp is a very astute man. We once discussed my mother's death, identical to her mother's, and Fripp said, "Perhaps she was following a script." That idea stuck with me. Are we programmed to make the same mistakes over and over because certain modes of behaviour are imprinted in our DNA?)

Kevan and I once crashed at Mary Lou's apartment. There were three other boys already staying with her. Five of us shared her bed. Two of the boys were in a band called the Screamers from San Francisco. (I saw their show in Toronto at the Horseshoe. They ended the night with a song called "Eva Braun." This show-stopper involved the band cranking up their synthesizers to a fevered, repetitive pitch and leaving the stage. That was high art back then.) Two of the members of this cutting-edge unit were Tommy Tomato and Tomata du Plenty. One of the Tomatoes (I can't remember which, and does it really matter?) would pose provocatively on Mary Lou's bed with his package arranged like a homo boy-toy.

One night ML and I were having a tête à tête in her bathroom. While we were talking, the sexy Tomato and another boy came into the room with towels wrapped around their waists and said they were going to take a shower. We both said sure, whatever, and went back to our conversation. They ripped off their towels and stepped into the shower. The male ego being what it is, they were determined to get our attention. They frolicked in the shower, pressing their naked bodies against the glass. They put on an erotic water show, while we kept obsessing about Mary Lou's man problems. Fripp was out of the picture, and she had a big crush on our new bass player, Terry Wilkins.

"Carole, how can I get Terry?" she asked.

Cut to a cock being lovingly soaped up and inserted into a squeaky clean anus.

"Well, you could invite him over and seduce him."

Cut to a mouth gulping down a payload of sperm.

Mary Lou was a relentless party animal. No segment of New York society was safe from her. We ended up in the most remarkable places. I once contemplated a glittering Mount Everest of pink rock cocaine across a table from Clive Davis, the president of Arista Records. Sometimes I went along with

ML while she copped. Scoring coke was a nightmare. I was always nervous because of that nagging little thing about drugs being illegal. I was hesitant about going with her because I thought there'd be thugs hanging around with guns.

We'd go to some pusher man's apartment, usually a penthouse, and she'd whisper reverently, "this is where Keith scores." (The blow was always phenomenal. In Toronto I was used to the stepped-on baby laxative shit. I always thought I'd die after doing a line, but hell, I'd do it anyway.) It has been my experience that dealers are the most boring people you could ever meet. They offer you a bump and you're trapped and obligated to listen to them drone on about something mind-numbingly boring. You hang on their every word like they're the most fascinating people you've ever met so they'll lay out more lines. I often felt like a whore selling myself to a Colombian drug cartel.

One night Mary Lou somehow wrangled an invite to a gala at the Met. Diana Vreeland was curating an exhibit featuring clothing worn by Jackie O during her brief but brilliant reign in a land called Camelot. We all worshipped DV because of her fashion philosophy, her outrageousness and, most important, the fact that she had multiples of the same black outfit. Black was all we little eighties sycophants of fashion ever wore. Our gods were Yohji Yamamoto and Comme des Garçons. Mary Lou took Kevan to the party as her date. He spotted Ms. Vreeland and made a beeline toward her, dragging Mary Lou. He introduced ML to DV like they were old friends. Kevan did have this wild streak in him. I remember once we were on one of our many road trips, driving across the border to play a gig in New York. Right before we went through customs, Kevan rammed a gram of hash in one cheek. I stood there sweating profusely while he calmly made somewhat garbled small talk with the U.S. customs man.

Mary Lou became involved with Robert Mapplethorpe. I was at her place one night and she showed me prints of some disturbingly erotic photographs taken by him, S&M images of naked black males. His work included a series of exotic sensual flowers reminiscent of Georgia O'Keeffe paintings; he insisted that "photographing flowers is no different than photographing a cock." The flower photographs were more sexually explicit, in my view, than the nudes. When Senator Jesse Helms ostracized Mapplethorpe and his work, he failed to pick up on the blatant eroticism of the sexual organs the flower photographs so graphically portrayed.

Mapplethorpe had been Patti Smith's lover and soulmate for years, although their affair was cerebral, not physical. He had a decadent handsome face with penetrating green eyes and dark hair. We'd run into him on our exhausting club crawls at the Continental or Hurrah. Mary Lou had to compete for Mapplethorpe's attention with Lisa Lyon, the body builder, who became his favourite model. He was beautiful and unattainable, and all the girls wanted him.

Career-wise, Mary Lou got me on Glenn O'Brien's cable show. A columnist who wrote for *The Village Voice*, he had a weekly show that was so bad it was good. Taste and content were not an issue: it was spontaneous, free-wheeling performance art.

Anyone who could pay the broadcast fees could have their own show on cable. My all-time favourite was the *Robin Bird Show*, a cultish smut-fest in which Bird lay around on a bed half-naked fondling brainless morons. Now that was entertainment.

We let Mary Lou organize our social lives. That "we" included Terry, who she'd finally managed to seduce. Her whole reason for being was hooking people up with each other. She herded us like trendy cattle and made sure we partied and abused ourselves all night long. One night we spilled out into the street after a trek to the Cotton Club in Harlem, and we were stranded—we couldn't get a cab out of there. It was surreal to be stuck on the streets of Harlem with Klaus Nomi, a Goth operatic performance artist, never seen without his trademark white pancake makeup. He dressed like he was wearing a stage set. David Bowie, always the chameleon, appropriated Klaus's look for his "Scary Monsters" video.

My brother Howard moved to New York in 1982. He, like every other cute gay boy in New York, supported himself by catering and bartending. In a complicated series of manoeuvres and subterfuge (nothing came easy for Howard) he sublet an apartment in Hell's Kitchen, with a roommate, Elsa. She was a talented chef and loved to cook big hunks of animal flesh for us. Howard soon hooked up with the exotically androgynous and genteel Bernard Zette—Howard and Bernard clicked immediately. Zette was originally from New Orleans. He'd moved to New York and founded a dance troupe called Andronyx, which worked at a club called Stillwende. Bernard remembers my brother "as the epitome of a new-wave boy: black pants, white shirt, thin black tie and spiky blond hair. He was just the cutest thing."

I first met Bernard at a party on a boat in New York harbour, where Howard and I were drinking tequila sunrises and schmoozing with Anya Varda, who'd moved to New York from Toronto. Bernard was flawlessly beautiful; I thought he was decadence incarnate. But I'm a sucker for anyone who comes from the South.

Howard worked his way up to running lights for Zette's troupe. Andronyx used to work at Danceteria, which had expanded to five floors, the top being a roof garden that was only open in the summer. One piece they performed to King Crimson's "Sartori in Tangiers"—such an eighties song title. The performance involved the whole troupe in various stages of undress, fighting over an immense slab of bloody flank steak. The piece started on the top floor and the dancers worked their way down to the basement.

Howard and his roommate, Elsa, decided to get married so that he could stay in the U.S. Their new-wave wedding and reception took place in their small, cramped apartment, which was packed with people. The bride and groom were dressed in white tuxedo jackets, their blond hair stiff with gel. They looked cute as a couple. Before the ceremony, Howard and Elsa had had a heated discussion about the wardrobe for their nuptials—there were some issues to be settled about who would wear the leather pants in the family. They both did. They had the nagging part of marriage down.

Howard turned on the radio to a classical station for some ambience. The couple stood framed by the only window in the apartment that didn't face a brick wall and exchanged their vows in front of a Unitarian minister. A row of their friends, most of them illegal aliens, stood behind like a bunch of paparazzi, snapping wedding photos. There was a continuous whirl of Polaroid prints being spit out of cameras. The wedding music started out with strings but, as the ceremony progressed, it rose to a deafening cacophony of horns and tympani, so the minister had to raise his voice louder and louder to be heard. Howard was not amused, but Elsa was trying hard not to laugh.

After the ceremony, I had a couple of drinks and started hitting on a girl named Frances, who turned out to be Elsa's girlfriend. She'd had quite a few drinks and was talking loudly about what a farce the ceremony was, while sitting next to the minister. We both got wasted and took off to my hotel and had cheap meaningless sex. I felt guilty afterward. Not everyone was living my polygamous lifestyle. (Later I apologized profusely to Elsa.) After the reception Howard went out with the boys and Elsa went to bed.

But the marriage was no joke to the Popes. Elsa was a fabulous sister-in-law; we considered her part of the family. Howard brought her up to Toronto one Christmas where she met Diane and her two kids, and my dad, though by then he was living full-time in his imaginary world. Howard and Elaine spent almost every Christmas holiday at my place in the eighties.

Howard was a music junkie; that was his real love. Before he left Toronto, he'd played guitar and bass, and recorded an album with a band called the Biffs, and then went on to do the same with Drastic Measures, a fine band fronted by the talented Tony Malone. In New York, Howard and Bernard formed a band called Zette, and went through numerous creative incarnations I could barely keep up with.

Howard, my slim little brother, also started to work out, intent on getting a buff toned body, which is sexual currency in the boy world. In New York it was no surprise that he became obsessive about it and that somehow, at the same time, his hair started getting blonder. Jim Fouratt remembers that for one summer, Howard was the most beautiful boy in New York. Bernard was crazy about him, and all the love songs he wrote were for Howard. But the feeling was not reciprocated, and things got tense between them. Bernard got a record deal with MCA and Zette released a single, produced by Man Parrish, a version of "La Freak," a song that was originally recorded by Chic. Bernard was on Howard's back about his guitar playing, which even I have to admit just didn't cut it. Howard would procrastinate about practising, a form of self-sabotage; part of him thought he didn't deserve to be in a successful band.

Rough Trade played a litany of New York clubs. The dressing rooms were cramped, graffiti-covered blow-holes in the belly of the beast. And it wasn't like you got paid or anything; it was about putting yourself out there. Howard and Mary Lou were always at our gigs, hyped and full of enthusiasm. Howard was our biggest fan, constantly plotting potential career moves. He knew more about us than we did. I'd scan the audience until I saw his expectant face. It was reassuring to have him there. I'd grown closer to him than anyone else in my family.

One of the strangest clubs we worked at was called Heat, run by trendy gangsta wannabes swathed in black. The stage was high on a platform and underneath it, behind a metal fence, the management kept several pacing, snarling, angry German shepherds. The dogs started barking during our show, but the audience was with us—no really, they were. I remember staring down into the semi-simpatico face of the Eurotrash pretty boy, Prince Egon Von Furstenburg. What insanity prompted the owners of the club to think treating dogs like that was cool? I was so tense after that show that Mary Lou grabbed Kevan, Terry and me and took us out nightclubbing.

Rough Trade appeared on the fledgling MTV, where we were interviewed by video jock Nina Blackwood. She was pretty in an eighties over-the-top kind of way, but no rocket scientist. There was another veejay named Martha Quinn, who had more than a modicum of intelligence, but had the look of a small frightened animal. (Paul Shaffer, who dated her, told me the pressure of working at MTV got to her.) At the beginning, it seemed like

MTV only had about ten videos to air, and because of that, our single "All Touch/No Contact" got into heavy rotation.

The talent from Boardwalk Records all attended the launch of VH1, a new video network that was more middle-of-the-road than MTV. We only had two other label mates. One was bad girl Joan Jett, a sexy little butch number who had a big hit with a song called "I Love Rock 'n' Roll." The other band, Night Ranger, were all about their hair, and for a moment or two they burned their way up the Billboard charts.

Everything was one big camp joke to Howard and me. Howard turned me on to Charles Ludlam, who founded a theatre company in the Village called the Theatre of the Ridiculous. Ludlam always played the female lead in his productions, the most notorious of which was *The Vampire Lesbians of Sodom.* Ludlam was an amazing actor, and his fans included Warren Beatty and Diane Keaton. Howard took me to his production of *Camille.* Ludlam simpered onto the stage like a Charlotte Brontë heroine, dressed in a low-cut gown exposing a hairy chest. An ugly period wig sat on his head. He staggered around calling out the name of his lover, Armand, à la Garbo, in a plaintive keening voice. But he sucked you in until you forgot what he looked like. He played Garbo better than she played herself. His portrayal was both funny and poignant.

Most of my outings with my brother seemed to involve looking for Mr. Goodbar. We'd start at the more upscale boy bars—the Saint, the World, the Hellfire Club and the Pyramid—but the longer the night wore on, the funkier the clubs became. Howard knew every doorman and bartender in town, which is essential for club-hopping. In the early mornings we'd venture into the meat-packing district, to the Anvil and the Mine Shaft. Though I wanted to watch the boys go at it, because I was a woman, I was barred from the room where all the kinky, heavy man-love was going on.

Gay New York was filled with talk about an illness called the gay plague. The first time we heard about it, Howard, Elsa and I had gone to a club called Area to dance and look at boys. Area was a cavernous temple of dance. The entrance was a long hallway with four glassed-in windows where real live human beings were displayed in various stages of eighties-style debauchery. It culminated in a huge space with black steel girders dissecting the room; there was a butch industrial vibe going on. Rumour had it the disease was transmitted by bodily fluids, sweat being one of them. All night long we had a running joke about avoiding the sweating dancers.

The first friend whose illness I witnessed first-hand was Robert Handforth, who I'd met through General Idea. He was the curator of the multi-media gallery A Space, and he seemed to belong to another era—when men were complete gentlemen. He was tall, blond and debonair, his upper lip adorned with a pencil-thin mustache. In Toronto we used to go out dancing all night. He and Sandy Stagg had shared a house together, a homage to another era decorated with Robert's collections of art deco black panther statuettes and mercury glass. When Robert was offered a post as the cultural attaché for the Canadian Embassy in New York, his whole world was magically transported to a brownstone on the Upper West Side. His job was to support and promote Canadian artists who were performing or showing their work in galleries in New York, and he became a driving force in a gallery called the 49th Parallel, designed to expose Canadian artists to the New York scene. It was a gig made in heaven for him.

It was indescribable to watch Robert turn into a frightened ravaged human being. I went to see him at St. Vincent's Hospital in New York. AIDS patients were quarantined like highly contagious aberrations of nature at the time. So little was known about AIDS that the masked doctors and nurses didn't encourage you to touch patients, but to treat them like lepers.

I'd sit with Robert and feel useless. I'd hold his emaciated body in my arms and be speechless. His eyes were frightened, his face covered in lesions, and at the end he was suffering from dementia. Robert's family came to New York from his home town of Ottawa, and I can only imagine what a shock it must have been for them to see their son dying from a disease misrepresented in the media as the gay plague (thus ignoring the millions of straight people in Africa who were suffering and dying from it). So many of our friends were terrified that they would be next. Some men started to practise safe sex, but others believed they were immune, that it could never happen to them. They were in such denial that they became even more promiscuous.

It's true that we were all hedonists and narcissists, self-involved and pleasure-seeking, but art flourished and evolved during the cultural renaissance that took place in those years. Stagnant and pop-ish since the sixties, in the eighties art was in your face and transgressive, like the graffiti cockroaches of Keith Haring. It seemed like there were all these people with the same mindset who were on the verge of changing the world. When I remember the brilliant and beautiful minds I knew back then, I'm filled with unbearable sadness. None of them are here, including my brother. I can't write about Howard's death yet. Sometimes I feel like I'm surrounded by an army of ghosts.

I never got enough love from my beautiful, blond, unattainable mother. Just when I was starting to make a tenuous connection with her, I lost her to cancer. In the fall of 1981, I met Dusty Springfield. She was a blond, beautiful Englishwoman. If you are a lesbian, you know where this is going.

Dusty Springfield was an icon. I loved R&B and thought she was the only white woman who could sing it with the necessary soulful, heart-wrenching intensity. I used to sit around my room on Earl Street, with my lesbo gal-pals, and we'd play Dusty's albums and fantasize about her. She was part of the collective lesbo consciousness. We all knew she was gay. The boys had Rock Hudson. We had Dusty.

My manager at the time, Vicki Wickham, thought the two of us should meet. She had a feeling we'd get along with each other. In another life, Vicki had co-written the English translation of Dusty's hit "You Don't Have to Say You Love Me" with her friend Simon Napier Bell in twenty minutes in the back of a taxi. It was originally a melodramatic Italian pop tune that Dusty first heard at the San Remo music festival in Italy. Italian pop ballads at that time always had a massive Puccini-like string movement in the middle where the audience stood up and cheered. She apparently liked that. I'd heard the stories Vicki would tell about Dusty, and she sounded like a handful, but Vicki believed that you could have any woman you wanted if you put your mind to it. Her mantra—"Every bird is pullable"—had become part of my philosophy.

So I flew to New York to meet Dusty, Queen of the Mods, and see her perform at a supper club called the Grand Finale. Vicki came with me. The place was packed with Dusty fanatics and celebs. The audience included Rock Hudson and Helen Reddy. We sat at a long table with Jane Seymour, who was looking very waif-like. Sitting next to me, fuming with impatience, was the delightfully cranky Fran Leibowitz, who kept smoking cigarette after cigarette and muttering under her breath, "Is she coming on? When is she coming on?" Dusty was two hours late, but it was worth the wait—her voice made me slide off my seat. She gave us everything we wanted and more. She went someplace in herself and pulled out pure unadulterated soul—nobody had a voice like hers. It was amazing to see someone who hated to perform and made such a huge production out of it, move an audience the way she could. She laid every naked emotion out on the line: love, pain and longing.

After the show, Vicki and I left the club. She thought there would be a mob scene backstage and didn't want to deal with it. We were halfway down Broadway when I asked Vicki if I should go back and try to meet Dusty. Vicki told me to go for it. I went back to the club and wandered backstage to stand nervously in the unflattering fluorescent light of her dressing room. Mary Isabel Catherine Bernadette O'Brien (Dusty Springfield to the rest of us) was heavily made up, her eyes rimmed with her trademark heavy black eyeliner. Her hair was white-blond, and she was wearing some kind of sequined beaded number. Her look was over the top in a bad way. The elitist snob in me rebelled, but she was an icon and so was I, albeit in a Canadian, self-effacing kind of way.

My first words were, "Vicki suggested that we meet." Dusty looked at me shyly and smiled. We started to talk and joke around, and within moments began to flirt madly with each other. I inched closer. Dusty's hand reached out to stroke the leather pants I was wearing. She was charming and had a warped sense of humour. She told me that when she was tarted up she felt like a Puerto Rican drag queen. We broke into slang like a couple of cockney yobs. I loved the sound of her speaking voice.

In the middle of our dance of seduction, Helen Reddy came backstage, accompanied by her husband and the singer Jane Olivor, to do the prerequisite fawning diva thing. Jane Olivor— oh, how can I put this without seeming cruel?—was not the most attractive of women. An insipid version of Streisand, she had had a big hit in the seventies with a song called "Some Enchanted Evening." Jane took off, and we all started dissing her—nasty, yes. Then Helen Reddy and her husband left, and Dusty and I turned to each other and said, "Why is she married? She seems like a big dyke." Later that night, Dusty and I went out for a drink and zoned in on the intriguing connection between us. Among other things, we shared a mutual fear of celery.

After I flew home to Toronto, I couldn't get Dusty out of my mind. I called her a couple of times. She was obviously involved with someone, but being the egotistical and callous dyke that I was, I kept piling on the charm. Three months later, we arranged to meet in Montreal, where Dusty was being honoured by B'nai Brith. Since Dusty's views regarding the PLO were slightly to the right of Vanessa Redgrave's, the idea that she should be so honoured was ludicrous. Being the diva she was, I think she simply liked the attention. There's nothing as cold and bitter as February in Montreal. If you're lucky, your limbs retain some sensation as you plow your way through the snow drifts. I tentatively knocked on the door of Dusty's suite at the Ritz Carlton. She answered the door, then stepped back to reveal the rococo decor accented with heavy black and gold striped wallpaper. She seemed shy and unsure of herself, and she was not alone. Her assistant, a girl draped in pearls who epitomized the meaning of the word preppy, was introduced as Westchester. She discreetly left the room. Dusty and I sized each other up—yes, the air was thick with sexual tension.

She offered me a drink, and the next thing I knew, we were all over each other. We tumbled onto the bed half-naked. It was the first time I'd been with an older woman. I found the idea very erotic. I fixated on her sensual mouth and her unfathomable eyes. It was an incredible turn-on to hear her come.

It was a quickie. Dusty informed me we had to drag ourselves to the home of the person who was paying for all this insanity. We'd go on to the award ceremony from his place. The house, not surprisingly, was a temple dedicated to the art of overindulgence. A painting of a little girl by Monet hung over the fireplace. Just to make sure we grasped that fact, a book containing a print of the painting was placed, oh, so carelessly open to the right page on the mantelpiece just below the masterpiece. The rich guy prattled on about nothing, maybe because we were making him nervous. We pretended to listen and, at the same time, tried not to maul one another. I felt like I had tasted the appetizer and was hungry for the rest of the meal. This boy had his own fleet of vehicles, including a helicopter. We piled into one of them and made our way to the banquet room of a downtown hotel.

The award ceremony was predictably boring. We all know the drill: sit at tables in a stupor, pushing inedible food around our plates and zoning out on the long speeches. Dusty was presented with a gold plaque with a map of Israel on it. Afterward, we went out partying with two gay journalists. We didn't know the meaning of discretion. We went to the Velvet Fist, a trendy after-hours bar. Montreal is a city that seethes with repressed Catholic sexuality. The bars are open till four and you can see graphic live sex shows. When it came to partying, I was a lightweight next to Dusty. I could barely keep up with her. We spent the weekend together in a sexual stupor. I vaguely remember flying back to Toronto.

The third time Dusty and I met was on a plane to Amsterdam. She was shooting a television show in Holland and had scammed an extra plane ticket for me. We were to stop in London on the way back. We travelled first class on KLM. This was my introduction to the rarefied world of a pop icon. A smarmy obsequious air steward hovered over Dusty. Champagne flowed as if from a fountain. There was a nine-course meal.

We arrived in the city at night. My first impression of Amsterdam was that it was so clean. Was that a faint odour of disinfectant I detected in the air? Dusty said that when the Dutch spoke they sounded like they were talking with hot potatoes in their mouths. I was impressed by the sense of history that permeated every building, the water in the canals reflecting the moonlight. Falling into Dusty's vampire-like existence, I can only recall seeing the city at night. She was haunted by legions of demons and had trouble sleeping. One night, we toured the infamous red light district. Arm in arm, we wandered through streets where whores posed in windows displaying the merchandise. We went to a sex store that catered to every sick, angst-ridden fantasy you could imagine. We picked up a few items. The night wound down at a gay bar where Dusty was worshipped and fawned over by sweet little Dutch boys.

The studio where the television show was taping was in Hilversum, on the outskirts of Amsterdam. The taping was an unrelenting nightmare. It took hours for Dusty to pull herself together. She was a walking time-bomb of insecurities and the Dutch were perfectionists. They didn't believe in wasting time either and somehow pushed all of Dusty's buttons. The diva reared her regal head. Divas live in their own little delusional world attended by effeminate men and sycophants. She was just impossible. If there was a way for Dusty to complicate things she found it. I wanted to scream, "Shut up and sing the fuckin' song, bitch." I didn't. I was lusting after what was bad for me. The dynamics of our affair would change daily. There were so many red flags, it was like a ski run. Our relationship hovered somewhere between Christmas and the seven rings of hell.

On the way home we stopped over in London. We were picked up at the airport in a Daimler; it was black, sexy and understated. Dusty rivalled Liz Taylor in the luggage department. She had about twenty suitcases jammed to the bursting point.

We stayed at the Four Seasons, where Dusty just waved in the direction of the concierge and we were whisked to a suite. There was a lot of drinking going on. Room service brought up magnums of Tattinger and Dusty's fave, Grand Marnier. I met her very loyal back-up singer, Simon Bell, and her brother, Tom. Theirs was a strained relationship. You could cut the tension with a chainsaw.

We went sightseeing. We ran through Westminster Abbey like children. When we saw the tomb of Mary, Queen of Scots, we fell into the infamous Monty Python routine. In Scottish accents we yelled, "Are you Mary, Queen of Scots?" "No, I'm not." In the Python routine Mary is pounded with clubs every time she denies her identity. We drank and debauched in tony restaurants. We stayed three days; then I flew back to Toronto and Dusty to her home in L.A.

Rough Trade had a break in touring, and I went to visit Dusty. Yes, I knew it was bad for me. She lived in a small house up in the hills in Nichols Canyon. Her neighbour was the ill-fated newscaster Jessica Savitch, who was busy building herself a pretentious dream house up on Mulholland Drive. A house she'd never live in.

Dusty took me on a tour of L.A.—a sprawling suburb connected by mini-malls. We drove around the perfectly mani-cured streets of Beverly Hills. We cruised by endless monu-ments to bad taste, the sinfully expensive Hollywood glitter palaces that the stars called home. Dusty made a special point of driving by Dionne Warwick's house, which was hideous. She and Dionne were rival divas, since they had both recorded Burt Bacharach's songs, classics like "The Look of Love" and "Anyone Who Had a Heart." If you wanted to live, you'd better like the Dusty versions.

We drove by the Ozzie and Harriet house, a white frame house, just like the one on the TV show. Cute.

We visited Forest Lawn Cemetery, which I found over-whelming. The only sound was the hissing of sprinklers feed-ing endless rolling emerald lawns. There were too many movie star stiffs in graves marked with monuments surrounded by reflecting pools covered in water lilies. They were entombed in wooded shrines and in shady grottoes with babbling brooks. Their ashes were interred in niches in endless white marble mausoleums. I started to o.d. on the sheer volume and told Dusty I had to get out of there.

The thin line of reality was stretched further as we careened by the Tate/Polanski house where the Manson family had committed their ritualistic murders. (Years later, Trent Reznor would record the brilliant *Downward Spiral* at a recording studio in that house.) We continued on past introvert producer Phil Spector's compound, surrounded by guard dogs. Dusty was a huge fan of Phil Spector. His innovative "wall of sound" had changed the face of pop music in the sixties. He was the genius behind girl groups like the Crystals and the Ronettes. Spector had been married to Ronnie, the Ronettes' lead singer, and had kept her a virtual prisoner during that time. Dusty told me that, these days, Spector usually sat in his living room, clutching a rifle and nursing his paranoia. Our tour of Tinseltown mercifully came to an end. The only house that blew me away was an octagonal number where Garbo had hung her cloche hat.

Part of my fascination with Dusty was the life she'd led. I could never get enough of her stories. She, the whitest of white women, had sung at the Apollo with Motown artists Stevie Wonder, Martha Reeves and Marvin Gaye. For some reason, Dusty loved food fights; she had had a knock-down drag-out battle in the hallway of a hotel in Australia with Gene Pitney. She hit him with a bag of flour. He was wearing a new suit and was not happy. Another time she lobbed a sardine down the décolletage of one of the Shangri-Las. She liked the sound of china breaking as she hurled it down a stairwell. She fought with drummer Buddy Rich when they were sharing the same bill and she got top billing over him. He insulted her and she slapped him across the face. She told me about the time she went to play some dates in South Africa. She had the musician's union put a stipulation in her contract that she would not perform before segregated audiences. It turned out that the clause was illegal. She was escorted out of the country. Dusty said she was naïve in every way and that it had not been a political act, *per se*. She just thought that anyone should be able to buy a ticket to see one of her shows.

Dusty started her singing career in the fifties as the lead singer in a girl group called the Lana Sisters. They dressed in lamé and recorded some forgettable songs. She was booted out after some chick histrionics between the members of the group. Dusty changed her name when she and her brother Tom and another friend, Tom Field, formed a trio called the Springfields. They performed in a mishmash of musical styles and were given a television series by the BBC before they even had a record deal. Their big hit was a song called "Silver Threads and Golden Needles." Soon after that, Dusty launched her solo career. She was so hot she had four television series in England in the sixties. Her guests included up-and-coming artists like the Beatles and Jimi Hendrix. She and Jimi jammed the R&B classic "Mockingbird," a Charlie and Inez Fox tune, on the uptight BBC. Dusty did a special featuring most of the Motown artists she'd toured with. Thanks to her, artists like the Supremes and the Temptations had their first exposure in the U.K.

She fought hard to get the sound she wanted on her albums. She wanted a black vibe, her version of Motown. She battled to get bass players to use a Fender bass. She recorded vocals in the bathroom at Phillips Studio in order to get enough reverb on her voice. She said the cleaning staff looked at her like she was crazy when they discovered her belting out vocals in the loo. Dusty told me about how frustrated she was, recording in England with the London Symphony Orchestra, "just one blond bird battling a bunch of blokes." Dusty was still upset about how they couldn't get a groove going.

She once offended HRH Princess Margaret at a royal command performance by remarking that there were many queens in the audience and they weren't all in the royal box. One can only imagine Yvonne (which is the gay English nickname for Margaret) in a gin-induced frenzy having a royal hissy fit. Dusty had a framed letter in her L.A. bathroom from one of Margaret's ladies-in-waiting, expressing HRH's displeasure.

One night, during that first L.A. visit, we went to see a band called U2 at the Country Club. I thought they were entertaining. Their singer with the strange name, Bono, had charisma. We ran into Elliott Roberts, Joni Mitchell's manager at that time. He had a little thing for me, but he was a) a man and b) smarmy, and I wasn't remotely interested. We all ended up at a party in a house in the Hollywood Hills. It belonged to a lovely couple who were into some kind of kinky Nazi love play. The *pièce de résistance* in their living room was a clear Plexiglas grand piano. Whoever came up with that idea wasn't into sound quality.

We all started drinking, quickly depleting the supply of booze and food. Dusty and I made polite conversation with our host, who was obsessing about his wife Barbara. He kept repeating her name in a German accent.

The U2 boys were doing a post-mortem on the gig, which always makes me scream with boredom. *You played that chord wrong. You ended the song too early.* That kind of thing. How did I know they would be mega-stars one day? They were Irish and the English part of me didn't trust them. Elliott was hovering around me and pointedly ignoring Dusty. Maybe that explained why I discovered her later sitting on the couch making out with the bass player. My face dropped as if it had been dragged down by centrifugal force. It was too fucking surreal.

I said, "Dusty, I'm leaving, I'm not gonna watch this, I'm out of here." I stormed out of the house. I had no car and couldn't drive even if I did. Dusty eventually came after me, apologized and tried to calm me down. She offered to leave with me, but was too wasted to drive. We ended up getting a ride home with a guy who thought he was running laps in the Indy 500. We veered all over Mulholland Drive in his jeep. We were dangerously close to the edge of the cliff, nothing between us and the sheer drop miles below. I thought we would crash and burn in a fiery inferno. "Oh, get me to a twelve-step program." When we got to Dusty's place, I was a wreck and yet, somehow, managed to let myself be placated by her.

Two years later, Rough Trade worked with U2 at a pop festival in Denmark. We heard them singing hymns and praying before they went on, in their dressing room, which was next door to ours. We let out a collective, "Oh, please."

The next day Dusty was nursing a hangover and I was feeling more than a little gun-shy. To smooth things over, Dusty took me for a drive up into the arid hills, to the Wildlife Way Station, a shelter for maltreated animals. These animals had been abused or abandoned by their owners. There were wolves, bobcats, a tiger, a dwarf-like lion whose growth had been stunted because he hadn't been fed properly. They were kept in large fenced-in areas with plenty of room to run around, but couldn't be released back to the wild because they didn't have the skills to survive. I loved the wolves, especially their penetrating ice-blue eyes. I held a little lynx who had cancer. Dusty walked up to the tiger's pen and started making tiger-like sounds. He sidled up to her and she stroked him. She was in her element. She cared passionately about animals. One of her pet causes was to stop animal testing.

Around that time, Rough Trade made its first trip to L.A. to do a live gig and a TV show. We taped "High School Confidential" and "Grade B Movie" for *Live at the Improv*, a comedy show. I guess they thought we were funny. Dusty sat in the audience with two enabler friends of hers who owned a bar in boys' town. She did a very bad job of hiding the fact that she was resentful that it was me up there instead of her. I got defensive about it, which was crazy.

Los Angeles is a mecca of bad taste. Where else can you see Heather Locklear and Pamela Anderson in a production of *The Trojan Women*? Dusty and I decided that for our bad-taste adventure we had to see Pat Collins, the Hip Hypnotist. I remembered her appearing on *The Ed Sullivan Show* when I was a kid. My big memory of that Sunday night ritual was my dad, who loved the dancing dogs. He would unfailingly call us into the living room to watch them.

But the pooches had nothing on the splendour that was Pat. With her towering blond beehive, her cat's-eye glasses with white frames and her white fishtail gown, she resembled a drag queen gone wrong. She would pick some rube out of the audience, get him on stage, put him under and make him do embarrassing, fifties things, like bark like a dog or sing. It was hard to watch, like *I Love Lucy* when she'd done something that upset Ricky. Still Ms. Collins was appealing, maybe because she was bossy in a dominatrix kind of way and, at that time, women on TV were either subordinate mom types or really nice girls you wanted to slap some sense into.

Collins was performing at a club on the strip, and she was just like we both remembered her. For the first hour it was great. She put members of the audience under and completely humiliated them. When her show passed the two-hour mark, we decided she was on speed. She would not stop. It was worse than seeing Wayne Newton in Vegas. Sitting across from us was a familiar, strange-looking woman, obviously exasperated with the show. She recognized Dusty before we recognized her. It was Martha Raye. She started putting on a little show of her own. She put her glasses on upside down, made distorted faces and pulled out her false teeth. A note was delivered to our table. Did I say note? I meant a scroll, which when unrolled said "bore bore boring," *ad infinitum*. We blew that hypno popstand and ended up going to Martha's house in Bel Air. I had a momentary thrill driving through the gates of the last bastion of old rich white movie stars.

This was years before Martha married the effeminate fashion designer who drained her dry. That night she was accompanied by a lady army colonel in full drag, a tastefully butch mocha-skinned woman. Also along for the ride was Martha's assistant, a dolly bird from Manchester. When Martha opened the door to her house, six small dog-like things ran out to greet her. In the living room, every inch of wall space was covered with photos chronicling her fabulous career. There were movie stills and Weegee style shots from the U.S.O. shows she did with Bob Hope. An Oscar stood glittering in a glass case, the Jean Hersholt Humanitarian Award for her unstinting efforts to entertain "our boys over there." Martha let me hold her Oscar, and the weight of it felt so good. She bombarded us with jokes, and she thought I was funny, too (around two in the morning I tend to get stupid and maniacal from lack of sleep). Martha pulled out some Locker Room, a synthetic and legal form of cocaine, and began snorting it.

Dusty and I had been doing double takes all night. We had a whispered conversation about the relationship between Martha and the colonel, who was intriguing because she rarely spoke, and when she did, it was to say something dry and witty. Martha pointed to pictures of herself in uniform standing with soldiers on war-torn battlefronts. She said she had started working with Bob Hope in 1942 and hadn't stopped entertaining the armed forces until the sixties in Vietnam. When things got really tough, she'd fill in as a nurse. We stumbled out of there into the first pearl-grey streaks of dawn. She'd exhausted us.

There's a joke: what do lesbians do on their second date? Bring a U-Haul.

Well, it's painfully true. In the spring of 1981, Dusty, her two cats and I moved in together. I found a house for us in Toronto's Cabbagetown, once an Irish slum but now an upscale Yuppie neighbourhood. Even as the faithful Westchester was hauling in the furniture, an inner voice was screaming *Noooooooooo!* Two divas under one roof—bad.

Where do I begin? We had stalkers. Ever since I'd started getting any kind of recognition, there had been a little lunatic fringe of people who followed me. They were harmless for the most part. But now Dusty's stalkers and mine had seemed to band together to monitor our every movement and launch an all-out assault. One time the doorbell rang around eleven at night. Four of them were at the door. "We just happened to be in the neighbourhood." They thought we'd be thrilled to see them. We were not amused and threatened to call the cops if they didn't leave. Though we had a couple of other visits, from then on they tailed us at a distance. If only Dusty's pampered cats could have been trained as guard dogs.

Dusty was so insecure about her looks, it took her hours to get ready to go out, which made me nuts. I'd watch her as she checked herself out for what seemed like the thousandth time in the mirror. I'd tell her, "You look fabulous in that Kenzo; that colour is amazing on you." Dusty would say, "My hair is wrong! I can't get it to work." I'd say, "Honey, we have to go. We're going to be late." It just didn't register.

Dusty could be so brilliant and entertaining. She had a wonderful laugh and smile. I was totally captivated by that side of her. When we made love, Dusty would sometimes ask me, half-jokingly, "to pound her through the mattress." After we had our way with each other, we were always ravenous, but neither of us wanted to get up and cook. Dusty would ask, "Where's our Filipino houseboy?" We'd drag ourselves out to dinner at the Courtyard Café, the Toronto eighties hang. Sometimes Kevan, Marilyn and Roy Krost, whose brother was Dusty's L.A. manager, would join us. Dusty would hold court, telling us endlessly funny stories about her recording sessions and life on the road.

But Dusty wasn't working, and she'd turned down almost every offer that came her way. She'd drink, and sometimes I'd join her, though inevitably I fell into a drunken heap hours before she did. When I didn't want to play that game, she'd go out to the Fiesta and drink with Sandy Stagg. They'd hang out till all hours. I'd lie awake and imagine all kinds of scenarios. When she'd try to sneak into bed at dawn, I'd try to articulate how I felt about her behaviour but she'd lapse into silence. In the afternoon, when she woke up, she'd apologize sweetly and act contrite, attempting to lull me into a false sense of security. Dusty was hell bent on destruction, and we both knew it.

The real horror started the day I had to take her on the first of several trips to the emergency room. She was experimenting with other forms of substance abuse. She had taken some pills, coke and God knows what else. Another time, I walked in on her in the kitchen where she'd methodically started slicing the outside of her arms with a knife. I grabbed at her and wrestled the knife out of her hand. Blood was spattered everywhere in our sterile white kitchen. I tried to ignore the faded scars on her arms from other episodes. What kind of self-loathing drove her to that? I was furious. Did she even give a shit what she was doing? These episodes left me shaking and numb. It was frustrating not to be able to discuss her behaviour with her. She would only let me see so much of her. Dusty alluded to the fact that she was the child of an alcoholic mother, and I knew that she and her brother, Tom, were estranged, but otherwise she was silent about her past and the origin of her demons.

Kevan and Marilyn loved Dusty but they were quickly exposed to the flip side of her personality. Howard and Elaine worshipped her. I was looking a little tortured. There were whispered phone conversations while Dusty slept. They were all sympathetic to our plight.

With Dusty I never knew what drama I'd wake up to. Sometimes it was great. On July 29, 1981, we set the clock for five a.m., along with most of the population of North America, so we could wake up to watch the wedding of Charles and Diana. I made a big disgusting English breakfast. You just fry everything in sight. We sat in bed propped up by pillows and cats. Dusty filled me in on all things royal. She knew the names of all the regiments in the wedding procession and the duties of the Queen's guard, the Royal Hussars, who had the sexiest army drag going. Dusty was positively psychic when it came to the Windsors. "Baby, the Queen Mother will be wearing a yellow dress. Beryl's [that's Queen Elizabeth] frock will be blue. Yvonne's already had two gin and tonics; her dress will be tangerine." Dusty was right. That really blew me away.

While Dusty was living with me, Kevan and I were recording our second album, *For Those Who Think Young*. It was the follow-up to *Avoid Freud*, which had gone platinum (in the U.S. that would automatically make you a millionaire but in Canada, a thousandaire if you were lucky). Still, we felt some pressure to come up with the goods again. We were recording at Manta Sound, with Gary Gray engineering and Eugene Martynec co-producing with us.

We asked Dusty and Howard to sing background vocals on a song we'd written called "The Sacred and the Profane." Just for a change, it was about a woman. Under the influence of my twisted Catholic girl, my brain was inundated with images of Fellini films and Catholic morality. I think the Catholics have the kinkiest religion going. Images of Christ on the cross and the beatific and suffering saints turn me on. Don't get me started on the Archangel Michael or Satan.

I think Dusty was in shock over how quickly and efficiently we recorded. It was Canada and we were on a budget. Dusty and Howard walked into the control room at Manta and met everyone. We were psyched about having Dusty sing on our album. She was a little tense, but sweet Howard put her at ease. He was into being Dusty's brother-in-law. Howard's singing voice was the male version of mine. They went into the studio, worked out harmonies and sang their parts. Dusty was very self-critical, but Eugene and Kevan kept stroking her and telling her she was great.

Rough Trade's sessions were amazing. Kevan and I got to behave like kids, and some of our fantasies were realized on record. After Dusty and Howard were finished, we sat in the control room devouring sushi and listening to the finished product. The song was phat, that's the only way I can describe it.

About six months into our catastrophe, Dusty left for Los Angeles. She took her cats with her. She made sure to erect a tent as a shelter for any stray cats that might show up in our backyard. She couldn't deal with the thought of a cat freezing to death in the winter. I phoned her and told her a cat had moved into the tent. She asked me what he looked like. I told her he was white, ginger and black, and beat-up looking. Dusty said his name had to be Sir Edmund Hillary. I brought him inside out of the cold, and he slept at the foot of our bed.

I started going to Al-Anon meetings so that I could cope with living with an alcoholic. I found it very hard to open up, because of my celebrity status, though I was somewhat relieved to be in a room full of people as obsessed as I was.

Dusty was starting work on a new album called *White Heat*. A diverse group of songwriters were attached to it, including Elvis Costello, who was a big fan of Dusty's. Kevan and I contributed two songs. One of them, "Soft Core," was about loving an alcoholic. It was ironic that Dusty ended up recording it.

I went to visit her in Los Angeles. Things were tense between us, since Dusty wanted to see how far she could go before I'd stop loving her. We went to AA and Al-Anon meetings. People poured out litanies of pain, which was somehow reassuring. Dusty was very mischievous. After the meetings she kept blowing the cover of celebrities who were drinking and using. My mouth would drop open as she rhymed off an A-list of stars who were wired on blow and booze. The whole point of these twelve-step programs was to protect your anonymity.

Dusty was sneaking drinks, usually vodka, because she thought I couldn't smell it on her breath. I'd ask her if she'd been drinking. She'd look at me with a mixture of guilt and anger on her face and reply, "No, I haven't," in a tone that would make me not want to push it. She'd hide liquor around the house, but in such obvious places I'd always find it. I think she wanted me to confront her. I felt like a cop monitoring her every move and I hated it.

I visited the studio where Dusty was recording. It was the first time I'd been to a studio in L.A. Talk about stereotypical. Even before I walked into the control room, I could hear the sound of chopping, a razor blade against metal. One of the producers Dusty was working with was meticulously pulverizing rock cocaine on a metal tape reel. It was such a ludicrous image, I had to laugh.

I watched her go through the painful process of recording. She was such a perfectionist. She worried over every infinitesimal nuance of her performance, sometimes recording a vocal word by word. If anyone in the control room ventured to say a take was good, Dusty would just glare at them. She had her own agenda when it came to what was good enough for her. It was the polar opposite of the way I worked. I was happy if I stayed in key. My singing is all emotion and passion, and as soon as I start to think about what I'm doing I lose it. I was in awe of the painstaking ordeal Dusty put herself through. The results were well worth it. The cuts on the album were a mixture of dance, rock and ballads. Dusty's voice had never sounded better.

Dusty never came back to Toronto. We broke up in L.A. I told Dusty I was being torn apart by her behaviour. She was very sweet and resigned. It was heart-wrenching. I finally accepted the fact that I had no control over her behaviour. I was vain and naïve enough to think that my loving her would make everything all right. She was so lost and I cared deeply about her, but it was fucking up my life. I didn't have the tools to deal with her problems, and I could barely contain my anger and resentment. The twelve-step programs I had to suffer through finally made sense. Let go and let God. When you live with an alcoholic you develop the symptoms of their disease. Their self-loathing is a poison that eats away at you.

We did keep in contact by phone. I sent her flowers. I loved her and wanted her to get better. *White Heat* was released and there was a dedication to me. "Because of and in spite of Carole Pope." It was a flop.

Dusty had a huge impact on my life. She was intrinsically a good person, and I never stopped caring about her. She finally bottomed out after going through hell, and became sober in 1985. She wanted to move back to England, but her cats would have had to be in quarantine for six months and Dusty couldn't bear the thought of that. She moved to Holland instead, with her cats. Eventually she girded her loins and moved back to London. I heard "Nothing Has Been Proved" and "What Have I Done to Deserve This," two of the songs she collaborated on with the Pet Shop Boys, in 1987. The songs were hip and brilliant. Neil Tennant, the Cole Porter of the eighties. Dusty's interpretation of his glib and urbane lyrics were set against Chris Lowe's synthesized dance grooves. Her voice sounded ethereal. She had a career resurgence and was introduced to a whole new audience. The fags loved her. I must have played those songs a hundred times over.

Then I heard, through Vicki, that Dusty had breast cancer. I got hold of one of Dusty's many phone numbers and called her. She was so reclusive by this point that it was difficult to keep tabs on her. We talked about her cancer and what an ordeal it was. She said she was in remission. We lapsed into silliness. It was good to hear her fabulous laugh. Dusty made amends for her behaviour during our relationship. She said, "I'm sorry for the way I behaved when we were together. You know I loved you." I told her I loved her and that I'd forgiven her long ago.

Several months later, Vicki told me that Dusty had bone cancer. Vicki was exhausted, constantly flying back and forth between London and New York dealing with Dusty's business affairs and her illness.

In March 1999, I'm recording in a studio in Niagara Falls. I am taking a break and decide to check my messages. There is one from Vicki, saying, "Call me whenever you get this." I call her at her office in New York. Vicki says, "I wanted you to hear this from me. I didn't want you to have to read it in the papers. Dusty died in her sleep last night." The next day, I'm on a flight to L.A., thinking about Dusty and whether I should go to the funeral. I think that I absolutely have to go.

It is surreal. It is like watching a film: driving in slow-motion through the wooded hills of the English countryside, sitting in the back of a limo, making polite conversation with Tris, a very sweet man I've just met. I'm dressed up like I'm going to see my ex-lover. I want to look good for her. It's been a long time. Then it hits me. Another wave of the nausea that hasn't left me for the last week. I feel her pain leaving an imprint on my body. There is a tightness in my chest. We turn off the road at Henley-on-Thames. We pull into a parking lot next to the Church of St. Mary the Virgin. The street is cordoned off and thick with mourners. We enter the church and hear her music coming from speakers, the ethereal sensuality of her voice floating through the church. The air is suffused with the scent of flowers. The funeral begins. Priests in purple and gold robes move to the altar, followed by a choir.

Elvis Costello gets up and speaks about his admiration for Dusty. He says she was the greatest white soul singer who had ever lived. Elvis reads a letter from Burt Bacharach, who is devastated by her death. He had wanted to record an album with her but she had been too ill. Lulu speaks about her friendship with Dusty. She claims they have been friends for thirty years. She talks about Dusty's hand gestures when she was performing. Dusty used to write lyrics on her hands and rotate her wrists in a circular motion so she could read them. Neil Tennant speaks about recording with Dusty, how in awe the Pet Shop Boys were of her. How shy and unsure of herself she was. What an incredible perfectionist she was. The choir sings the hymn "Jerusalem," the bittersweet lyrics written by the poet William Blake. *And did these feet in ancient time, walk upon England's mountains green.*

My heart is a dead weight in my chest.

The coffin is unloaded from a horse-drawn carriage, and pallbearers carry it into the church, followed by mourners, including Vicki, Nona Hendryx and Dusty's brother, Tom, her only surviving relative. I lose it then, and Tris grabs my hand and holds it tightly. I always thought I would see her again, that we would reminisce about our insane time together, but Dusty had shut herself off to die.

Her next door neighbour speaks about the day Dusty came over and announced that a series of tests she had just undergone had revealed there was no hope. The cancer had won. He says she had accepted the inevitable. I hate to think of her suffering. I can't wrap my mind around that one. She was so resilient and strong. I thought she would outlive me. The horror of all this is how young she was when she died.

Dusty was a treasure. Too late, she had received an O.B.E., and two days after she died she was to be inducted into the Rock and Roll Hall of Fame. After the funeral, Tris and I walk up to the altar and look at the floral tributes. We start to read cards from Paul McCartney and the kids, the Rolling Stones. It's all too much to process. We walk out of the church. Tris tells me that some Catholic friends of Dusty's said that she'd be sitting up in heaven drinking ambrosia.

There is a reception after the funeral. In some beautiful hotel, with beautiful polite waiters passing around glasses of champagne. The room is full of old queens with bad comb-overs. We all wander around shell-shocked. Vicki and I hold each other. Her eyes are hidden behind magenta-framed sunglasses, and she looks drained and exhausted.

Tris and I attempt to drink ourselves into a stupor. It doesn't work. It turns out that Tris runs a record company and desperately wanted to work with Dusty and Burt Bacharach, but she was too ill. I talk to Nona Hendryx, reminiscing about falling up the stairs with Dusty at a hotel in Paris. I meet the Pet Shop Boys, Chris Lowe and Neil Tennant. They know all about Dusty and me. They are incredibly sweet. *If only she knew how much she was loved.* The phrase reverberates around that room like a mantra.

I had let her voice caress me for years before I met her. I had fallen under its silken spell. The most erotic thing we would do in bed was this—I would beg Dusty to sing to me. She would put her mouth up to my ear. The sound of her voice, so intimate and close, washed over me like waves of pure pleasure.

I like driving in a van with the boys after I've played a gig. It's pitch black outside and your eyes follow the hypnotic white line of the highway. The conversation covers the spectrum from childlike monosyllabic grunts to esoteric revelations. Then there are the garish orange walls of a Ho Jo's. The mattress that sinks in the middle. The one channel on the TV, and somebody hot-wiring it so you can watch free porn. Or the good hotels with the king-size beds that make you feel empty. The flat endless prairies. You wonder how anyone can live out there, so isolated and alone. An airport at six a.m. when you've been up all night partying and your eyeballs feel like they're bleeding. The sound checks at the venue, the sound-man who always says it will sound better when the club is full of people. Having a total fit onstage because you can never fucking hear yourself above the band. You're not singing, you're screaming. The stench of the dressing room. The floor of the stage, which you really don't want to look at too closely.

There's something addictive about performing in a dank beer-soaked bar where you're afraid to touch any surface for fear of contracting a new strain of legionnaires' disease that mutates in Naugahyde. We worked in so many of those places. Some nights, the audience would stare at us like slack-jawed idiots, their eyes glazed over in a state of incomprehension, but most of the time we became ecstatically one with the crowd.

People were aching for something new, shocking, sexual, intelligent—something that touched a chord. And we delivered.

The dark side of this was the stalker fan. Jittery, sweaty people with no lives who became obsessed with you. God forbid they would find out where you lived. The microphone was my prop, my lover. I caressed it. I slid my cunt up and down the mike stand in a not-so-subtle form of masturbation. Kevan was always covered in a layer of sweat, switching from guitar to keyboards and back. We worked with a virtual smorgasbord of musicians. Each one came with his or her idiosyncrasies. If they had wives or possessive girlfriends, there was angst to be had, played out in a series of ball-breaking confrontations. When we toured, our road crew picked up girls by asking them if they wanted to meet me.

One of my favourite kinds of fans are the disgruntled straight girls. The best pickup line I ever heard was "I'm here with my boyfriend, but I don't really like him." Another line that annoyed the band was "I really like your organ player," to which we'd all reply in unison, "We don't have one." Once we played at the Sea Way Motel, and Clive Smith brought his friend Eric Idle to the show. They were working on a project together. Between sets, they came to our cruddy dressing room, and Eric decided to make an understated punk statement. He lit the paper ice bucket on fire. We all stood there and watched it burn and then went out to play our next set.

We did a gig at Kingston Prison for Women. The audience was composed of inmates swathed in prison couture, some branded with self-inflicted primitive tattoos. They were herded into the room by bleary-eyed jaded chick prison guards and one hunky man. We wondered what kind of a role he played in disciplining the prisoners. Some women had their arms around their special ladies. We launched into our show, and most of the audience stared at us stone-faced. They didn't get it. Afterwards Jo-Ann and I walked around and asked everybody what they were in for. Usually it was for murdering their old man cause he'd been cheatin' on them. Many of the inmates were Natives. Every country has some group they like to oppress and in Canada the native peoples fill that niche.

Our most infamous gig was at a place called the Chimney, in 1976: six nights a week, three shows a night, for nine weeks. Wherever I go in this world people come up to me and claim they were at one of those shows. Kevan figures hundreds and thousands of people showed up at this bar, which seated maybe two hundred. What was amazing about that gig was that it introduced Rough Trade to the most diversified audience we ever had. The stage was located in the middle of the room against a wall. Acoustically it was a nightmare. (Hey, club owners, build the stage at the *end* of the room. It sounds better and the entire audience can see the performers.)

Our long-suffering soundman was nicknamed Mr. Juicy. He was assisted at that gig by the fifteen-year-old Steve Webster, who would later play bass in my solo band.

Kevan and I commandeered the stage, all sexy and sulky, tricked out in our little outfits. Kevan would dress like a sailor or a pimp. I went for saucy bondage attire. I wore a skin-tight, black, pseudo-leather rig with a harness and fetish heels that I could barely hobble across the stage in, or I opted for tight silver Fiorucci leather pants and a punk T-shirt with a lurid boy-on-boy S&M scene depicted on the front. Our bass player at the time, Happy, couldn't play unless he was wearing clogs, which Kevan and I detested. We were such style queens. We had a tag team of drummers during those nine weeks. As the gig progressed, we started to notice clones of me showing up in the audience, which I found a little scary.

We had one fan, called Andy, who came to all our shows and danced like a wild whirling dervish. Noah James, a journalist friend of ours, started calling him Fred Hysterical. We had this song "True Confessions," the lyrics a parody of fifties pulp novels. Of course there was a whip reference and Andy would always volunteer to be whipped by me. I was never without my riding crop. I'd light into Andy real hard, and he loved it. He'd proudly display the red welts I had placed on his body. One night, a drunken Elizabeth Ashley, in town with some stage show, tried to upstage us by projecting her husky vodka-fueled voice over the band. That bitch was loud. Brenda Vacarro showed up one night and stared at my cunt through an entire show.

Toronto's finest started to appear at our shows, itching to bust us for obscenity. But as long as I didn't actually touch any part of my body that they considered dirty and immoral, they restrained themselves.

By then Toronto punk bands like the Vile Tones, inspired by the Sex Pistols, were slashing their bodies with razor blades. But actual bloodletting, I guess, was inoffensive and didn't warrant police intervention.

People would throw drugs and notes with their phone numbers on stage. Sometimes I'd pick up girls I didn't know. That was very wrong—and yet I was compelled like some panther-like she-bitch in heat. I know you want dirt, so picture this. I take someone, whose name has escaped me, up to my room on Earl Street. We enter the house. It's dark and June has gone to bed. Calvin, June's intense Jamaican boyfriend, who is several years younger than her, is skulking in the hallway. He likes to listen to the zany lesbian hijinks that go on in several of the girls' rooms. Sometimes he walks around naked at night.

Whoever I've picked up is expecting me to be a bad-ass dominatrix. She wants rough sex, and I give her what she wants, while a voice in my head is repeating, *Get her out of here.* Then, mercifully, it's over, and one of us opens the door to go to the bathroom and almost takes Calvin's head off— he's kneeling next to the door.

On the other hand, everyone who lives in the house likes to congregate in the bathroom and listen through a heating vent when Calvin and June get it on.

Though I eventually started having an open relationship with a girl nicknamed Jada, I had a revolving door policy going on. I became the female equivalent of a swinging bachelor in a penthouse pad. My love life was like a bad sitcom. I was sneaking one woman out of my room before the next one showed up.

We actually started to get TV gigs. From 1975 to 1977, there was a late-night show on CBC called *Canada After Dark*, hosted by the mild-mannered Peter Gzowski. It was a Canadian version of *The Tonight Show*, but with a budget of, oh, I don't know, maybe twelve dollars a night. Elaine was the assistant producer. She had her finger on an incredibly hip pulse. The eclectic line-up of guests included a very young Robin Williams, the Runaways with Joan Jett, Devo, Lina Wertmuller, Buckminster Fuller, Fran Leibowitz and us. We were not censored in any way. Nobody batted an eye when we performed a song called "Dyke by Default," which was basically a litany of names of actresses and literary figures I outed. It was all about getting the best camera angles. You've got to love the CBC for that.

One night before a show, I was sitting in the green room in my bondage rig chatting to Buckminster Fuller, telling him how much I loved his geodesic dome. The tiny mayor of

Toronto, David Crombie, who was also a guest that night, was sweating as I towered over him. I had the distinct impression that he wanted to be punished for being a bad boy.

Any touring company off Broadway or on their way to Broadway would inevitably find us. We were turning into a kinky tourist attraction. Several male chorus boys invited me to see Raquel Welch at the Imperial Room, which was like a Vegas showroom without the decadence. It was located in the fabulous Royal York Hotel. The promoter who booked the room, Gino Empry, was famous for his bad hairpiece. I didn't understand how a non-singer non-dancer like Raquel got to do a big Vegas spectacular. But when I saw her, I realized that with strategically placed male dancers who had a basic knowledge of quantum physics hauling her into position and with the creative use of mirrors and strobe lights, you got the illusion that Raquel had a modicum of talent. (I did, however, worship Raquel in the film *Myra Breckenridge*, by Gore Vidal. Raquel, as Myra, and her alter ego, Rex Reed, get to terrorize plenty of man hunks. My favourite moment in the film is when Raquel straps on a dildo and fucks some poor man up the ass.)

Jack Richardson, the legendary Canadian producer, the man responsible for classic albums by beefy boys like the Guess Who and BTO, checked us out at the Chimney. He decided he wanted to record our music or, rather, wanted to try an experiment with us. His idea was to record us live off the floor. We'd play one whole side of the record without stopping, and then the other, while the album was mastered simultaneously in another building. This process was called direct-to-disc recording. The sound it produced was very live because the integrity of the music was not compromised and no sound quality was lost. It was the way albums had been recorded in the fifties before the use of tape machines, hence the term "cutting a record." After seeing us, Jack thought we could pull it off. The band members made a group decision to record the album and split the profits, which the distributor still owes us. (You bastard.)

We rehearsed in the basement of a church to get into the groove of playing both sides of the album perfectly without stopping. Then, in the summer of 1976, we went into Nimbus Nine, Jack's studio on Hazelton Avenue in Toronto. Jack had a greying beard and was chubby, funny, sensitive and low-key. I'm sure he'd dealt with every drama that a musician's ego could dream up. We set up and recorded a total of fifty-three takes of eight songs, both sides of the record, in two days. Jack sat in with us and played percussion, with a shaker made of two taped-together Styrofoam coffee cups with some beans inside.

It was exhausting. Most of our takes were near-perfect, but there were plenty of technical problems to contend with. There were glitches in the room where the record was being mastered. The most annoying part was that Jo-Ann and I couldn't hear our vocals very well and the head engineer, Brian Christian (he was a real character), couldn't seem to rectify the situation. He was condescending about it because we were women. We were hyperventilating by the end of the recording. George Graves, who actually cut the disc, deserves a lot of credit for the sound. During a break in recording, Michael Fonfara, our keyboard player, got married, dashing down to City Hall to tie the knot with a go-go dancer he'd met at Trude Hellers in New York. (The general consensus was that the union would not last.) *Absolute Sound*, an audiophile publication, still lists *Rough Trade Live* as one of the best pop albums of all times. (Let me add that it's great purely from a sonic point of view.)

One night the Stones were in town, but we were performing so I missed the show. At the end of the night, a certain dealer, let's call him Bill, asked if I wanted to meet up with Mick and the others and then go to an after-hours bar. The drinking laws sucked in Toronto, but if you wanted to party all night there was a plethora of booze cans. We picked up a rather petulant Mick in his suite at the Windsor Arms Hotel. Mick had a compact body and a tight little ass. I tried not to stare at his infamous lips. Bill whipped out some rocks, which he pulverized into thick lines in a very Zen-like ceremony. Hundred dollar bills were produced and rolled up. We hoovered the blow into our bodies. From then on the conversation became scintillating.

We met Ron Wood out on Bloor Street and walked down a dark alley into a very upscale booze can. All the Stones were there except for Keith. They didn't order drinks—they ordered bottles of vodka, which they drank neat. I sat squashed between Mick and Ron like a piece of luncheon meat. Mick was oozing sarcasm about the bar, and behaving like a spoiled brat. Why didn't that surprise me? Ron Wood was sweet, not a great intellect, just one of the lads. Charlie Watts was the most articulate and intelligent. I tried to remain cool and ignore my screaming inner groupie. We put a dent in the gross national product of Bolivia that night.

We opened for the Tubes at Maple Leaf Gardens. Marilyn designed an outfit for me, made out of black patent leather with a clear plastic see-through ass, which got all foggy and steamed up so you couldn't see anything. I had two bleached streaks in my hair that were dyed red. It was a high to play in such a large venue, but there was a surreal quality about the whole experience. I was used to having some kind of eye contact with the audience.

The Tubes are very theatrical and their show is choreographed; in addition to the band members, they had male dancers. There was a hot girl singer in the Tubes, named Re Styles, who all of us were salivating over. The Tubes asked me to sing "White Punks on Dope" with their lead singer, Fee Waybill. I stood on stage between two of the Tubes' dancers. I spread my legs and put each foot on top of one of each dancer's platform shoes and belted out the song's chorus.

Kim Cattrall lived down the street from me. We literally bumped into each other one day and started hanging out. She had just finished working on a film called *Tribute* with Jack Lemmon and Robby Benson. She invited me to the Toronto premiere and party. I brought along Tim Blanks, a friend of mine from New Zealand. The party was full of Toronto's WASP-y higher echelon, the bratty offspring of families like the Eatons, the Walkers and the infamous Wookey brothers, whose father had grabbed up most of Yorkville's prime real estate. (Tim and I are total snobs and love that crap.) We charged the buffet table and started piling succulent mounds of shrimp on our plates. Half-hidden behind the ice sculpture, I watched some rich blue-rinse women jamming food into their purses and prodded Tim. "What's that about?" we wondered, none too discreetly. Kim dragged me away to meet Pierre Trudeau. He was around sixty at the time and a total babe, oozing charisma. Eventually Kim was summoned to Canada's capital by Pierre, where apparently nothing much transpired. Then she married some Swiss prince, and I didn't see her for years.

A beautiful art deco dance hall, the Palais Royale, sat on the polluted edge of Lake Ontario. The fact that the building was still standing was so atypical of Toronto. Michael Budman and his partner Don Green were the co-creators of Roots, the

Canadian clothing empire. Michael was a friend of Gilda's from Detroit. Around 1978, he and Dan Aykroyd started producing shows at the Palais. We'd perform there with guests like Nona Hendryx and the Clichettes. They were always fabulous events. Mary Margaret O'Hara opened for us a couple of times, well on her way to cult status. Her stage presence alone was enough to make you say, "what the—?" She sang passionately and stumbled around in a way that was disturbing yet mesmerizing. Singers like Jane Siberry were very influenced by her style.

John Belushi was lured back to Toronto to do a gig with Danny at the Palais with the Stink Band, which was really a pseudonym for the Blues Brothers. Belushi had a real hate on for Toronto ever since the Stones had been busted for possession, and he flew into Toronto Island on a private Lear jet. During the show, Belushi looked at all the photographs of musicians that covered the walls of the Palais Royale and said, "I can't believe that people like Glenn Miller played here." He was compensated for the show with two glass vials.

In 1979, I got a phone call from composer Jack Nietzsche's office, summoning me to New York for a meeting about a top secret film project. The film was called *Cruising* and was directed by William Friedkin (*The Exorcist*). The gay press was in an uproar over the impending release of this film because it was about a serial killer who preyed on gay men. Serial killers don't confine their killing sprees to the straight world; I wanted to see the film before I made a decision whether or not to get involved. Nietzsche had arranged the rock masterpieces Phil Spector had produced, and had also worked with the Stones. I sat with the film editor while we screened the film on a moviola. Al Pacino played a cop who goes undercover into the gay ghetto to find a serial killer who picks up tricks, fucks them and then kills them. He gets drawn into the gay lifestyle and ultimately becomes aroused by other men. The murder scenes were disturbing for the time. It was intense, but we decided to go for it. The film is now a gay cult classic. We wrote several songs for the score, one of which was "High School Confidential." I thought Mink De Ville, who was also working on the film, could sing it, but Jack passed on it. I decided I would perform the song and sing it just as it was written. The lyrics were about a high-school student (me) lusting after a chick in my school. We recorded two songs, "Shakedown" and "Long Distance Runner," in New York with Jack. He was embroiled in a sex scandal at the time. His live-in lover, Carrie Snodgress, had accused him of rape, claiming he had violated her by inserting a handgun into her vagina. During the time we spent with him, he didn't seem to be able to accomplish anything without the aid of an assistant.

While we were in town, we opened for Mink De Ville at the Irvine Plaza. He was a piece of work. He had a big, slicked-up pompadour and dressed like a sixties greaser. He wore Cuban heels and black stovepipe pants. He was never without his wife. She had a black beehive hairdo with blond streaks in it, and wore thick black eyeliner and white lipstick. Maybe they were big fans of *West Side Story*? Mink wrote great R&B style songs and had a gravelly voice. We toured with him later in Holland, where he was escorted to the stage nightly by a minder.

Back in Toronto we did a sold-out show at the Roxy. Bernie Finkelstein showed up. We knew him from Yorkville days, when he used to manage Kensington Market and the Paupers. He had a label called True North, which was a politically correct, intellectual boys' club with artists like Bruce Cockburn and Murray McLauchlan. Bernie was a character. I liked him the first time I met him. He was such a manager, and I mean that in the most positive way. He really believed in the artists he represented. He was short with a big belly. Bernie was full of stories about the music scene. When he told us he liked the show, I said, "Why don't you sign us, darling?" Bernie said, "Okay, I will." The next day we went for a meeting at True North's offices with our expensive New York attorney and started to hammer out a deal.

The title of our first album, *Avoid Freud*, was my comment about the fucked sexual mores that afflicted most of Western society. The album quickly went platinum. We had a number-one hit in Canada with "High School Confidential." There is a line in the song, "She makes me cream my jeans when she comes my way." Chum-FM, the biggest station in Canada, actually paid for us to go back in the studio to clean up that line. There were two new versions, one where I just say she makes me "mmmm," and the other was suggested by my friend Marge Gross: "She makes me order Chinese food when she comes my way." When I sang the song, I'd run my hands down my body mock-seductively and grab my crotch while singing the line. This was years before Madonna and Prince started playing with their pussies on stage.

In 1981 we were asked to perform on the Juno Awards. We were dressed from head to toe in leather. Kevan, Terry and Buckey wore heavy eyeliner. We did a run-through of the song while the director and crew eyed us warily (the CBC knew us so well). But we were good little deviants until the actual show. Sandy Crawley had graciously consented to dress up in tacky drag and saunter across the stage when I sang, "She's a cool blond scheming bitch." Something came over me during the cream my jeans line. My hands went straight for my crotch. I couldn't help it. People screamed and applauded. The CBC were unfazed. Later Anne Murray said she'd watched the show with her family and they were amused by my zany antics.

Many years later, k.d. lang told me that as she watched the Junos that year, she had been sitting at home in Edmonton plotting her total domination of the world. She saw me and was inspired. She said, "This is amazing, this woman is doing something that no other woman has done before, she's blatantly singing about a chick." "High School Confidential" was mind-blowing because it was so out there. Many straights didn't get the double entendre, and gays embraced it as an anthem. k.d. said it had a big impact on how she presented herself. "Seeing you set a tone for me that I could be out, no question. I was inspired to be as outrageous as I wanted to be."

Soon after the Junos, we appeared on *SCTV* in a skit called "Pre-Teen World," a parody of a kid's show with Andrea, John Candy and Rick Moranis playing the hosts. They grilled us with inane questions about "The Rough Trades," like "What's your favourite colour?" We performed "High School Confidential," while they looked on. I had a great time in the makeup department staring at Polaroids of the incredible makeovers they performed on the actors to make them look like the celebrities they parodied.

One of the highlights of my television career was Rough Trade's performance on *Solid Gold*. I thought it was a tacky stupid show, and yet I was compelled to watch it. To appear on it meant you'd made it in some ways; you were reaching mainstream U.S.A., the lowest common denominator. I could never get enough of the hosts, Rex Smith and Marilyn McCoo. I had the impression that they hated each other's guts. The icing on this cheesecake was the Solid Gold Dancers. When I heard we were doing the show, I was horrified at the thought of those dancers gyrating around me. Don't get me wrong, I love dancers, just not anywhere near me on a TV show. I had two rules concerning TV appearances: no dancers and no dry ice. I pretty much never got my way. But the single from our second album, "All Touch/No Contact," was making its way up the *Billboard* charts, and we had to work it, baby. Michael Ameen was at the show's taping. He was the vice-president of Rogers and Cowan, who were doing our publicity. He was a sweet hyper guy, originally from Boston, and was wildly enthusiastic about the band.

Backstage, we met Rex Smith. I went Hollywood and fawned all over him saying I'd seen him on Broadway in the *Pirates of Penzance* and that he was fabulous. We did a no-frills performance that I was happy with. Even on *Solid Gold*, we still had an edge.

Canada was musically segregated in those days. There was a wide diversified cultural expanse between Toronto and the west coast, Toronto and the east. Musicians had to deal with the indifference (bordering on contempt) that people in each place had for each other. This was in the days before syndicated radio and MuchMusic bridged that gap.

We shot a TV variety show in Montreal; it was big, garish and splashy and I didn't understand a word anyone was saying. Robert Charlebois was on the show; he recorded in English and I was a fan. Quebec has its own subculture within Canada of French-speaking artists. They sell millions of albums in Quebec and France, and the rest of Canada has no idea who they are, except for that Céline chick. Andy Gibb was also on the show. We were all staying at the same hotel. After the taping, we ran into him in the hallway as we were making our way to our rooms. He wanted to score some blow and hang with us. I passed—I wanted to take a sauna with a friend who was staying at the hotel. I was shocked at Andy's appearance. His eyes were glazed over, and his skin was pasty and sweaty. Spending time with someone that strung out made me want to preach, but if I did I would have come off as a hypocrite, especially if I was sitting next to them getting high. The drug culture had spiralled into a no-win situation. I was doing it then and everyone I knew was doing it. Coke is such an insidious drug that you get to the point where you're cheating death every time you use it. Unfortunately, death won with Andy.

In 1983 we were asked to open for David Bowie. He was launching *Serious Moonlight* in Toronto, his most commercial tour ever. He had just recorded "Let's Dance" with producer Nile Rogers. Rogers had an unbeatable track record for turning out hits, and this Bowie album didn't require any serious soul-searching or introspection to appreciate. It was all about tax breaks, numbered Swiss bank accounts and a house in Geneva. There was so much conjecture about Bowie's sexuality. His open marriage to Angie Bowie was complicated and volatile. She resented his obsession with Iggy Pop, with whom he had partied in Berlin, where both shared a brief love affair with the trappings of Naziism.

After what seemed like interminable preamble, we signed some kind of deal with the devil, CPI, the promoters who were putting on the tour. Our first show was at the CNE in Toronto. The audience was about 60,000. We were only allowed to use part of the stage and could not have as many lights as Bowie—not that we needed them, since it would still be daylight when we hit the stage.

Clockwise, Mom, Diane, Elaine and anti-social me in Cape Cod.

Howard and I in the summer of love. ▶

Zack, my sixties inspiration. ▶

The Bullwhip Brothers.

▲
On stage at Grossman's Tavern — Kevan, me,
Peter Hodgson and Marv Kanerick on drums.

Flyer designed by Clive
Smith for the Colonial. ▶

Divine and me promoting
Restless Underwear in 1980.
▼

◀ Singing "Auto Erotic Love"
at the Chimney.

Kevan and me on stage at the Edge.
▼

[JOHN ANDERSON]

◀ Divolution — me, Brenda,
Dianne and Suzette.

Torch Showcase

Song Stylings by Carole Pope, Brenda
Donahue, Dianne Lawrence, Suzette
Couture.

Sunday July 25, 9pm
A Space 85 St. Nicholas Street (Yonge & Charles) Toronto
Admission $3.00 Information 964-3627

High Art.
▼

[ISOBEL HARRY]

Avoid Freud — Rough Trade immortalized by Jorge Zontal.

Weapons — Kevan and
me looking studly.

Rough Trade at home.

[JORGE ZONTAL]

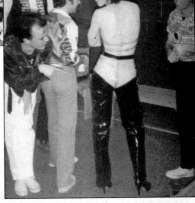

Kevan inspecting my ass backstage at Maple Leaf Gardens,
opening for the Tubes.

[MARILYN KIEWERT]

Backstage with Tim Curry in 1979.

[AISLIN, THE MONTREAL GAZETTE]

Howard, my beautiful brother.

Howard with gal pal
Jennifer Grey. ▶

Clash of the divas — Dusty, me, Nona and Adrienne at the Rough Trade farewell show, RPM, 1986.

Me with my Amazon Bitches on the set of "Territorial."

Bonding with Anne Murray during the recording of "Tears Are Not Enough," 1985.

[DIMO SAFARI]

 Gina.

LaDolceGina

Rehearsing backstage at the Winter Garden Theatre for *Quiet Please, There's a Lady on Stage*. Laurie Hubert, me, Maggie Moore and Shirley Eikhard.

David Ramsden and me backstage at the Winter Garden Theatre.

Backstage, before the show, "We had a vision," to quote Mariah Carey. Bowie was coming down the hallway, the image of an untouchable rock god. He was impeccably dressed in a sea-foam-coloured suit that complemented his eyes, one green, one blue. His hair was quite possibly spun from gold. He was fresh from shooting *The Hunger*, a film that was a total wank-fest for me. Bowie plays a 300-year-old vampire, but who cares about that? Über-babe Catherine Deneuve is also cast as a vampire. She seduces an innocent doctor portrayed by Susan Sarandon and they DO it.

Attached to Bowie like a frightening body appendage was his Yoko, muse and protector, Coco Shwab. She was as tenacious as a pit bull. You couldn't get near David, because she would put the evil eye on you, and her gaze could slice you off at the knees. She glanced at me, and her eyes said, "Don't even think about it." Bowie and his entourage swept by us in maddening slow motion.

Our retinas still burning from the splendour that was Bowie, we checked out our dressing rooms. Then we went to get free food. There were none of the usual cheese trays with food that you could mould into Play-Doh-like shapes, and luncheon meat you could hurl at the wall and it would stick. There were sushi chefs, a fully stocked bar and all manner of perks and obsequiousness. We were loving the alien.

When it was time for us to play, we gazed out on sweating masses melting in the humid Toronto weather. We were decked out in ensembles by Parachute—squares of black linen sown together by disgruntled workers in third-world sweat shops. My ensemble was accessorized by leather gauntlets. Let's get something straight, the eighties were a fashion travesty and I was one of the worst offenders. We took the stage and launched into songs from our new album, *Shaking the Foundations*, which was and still is my favourite. On both sides of us, varilights projected geometric images on our bodies. We'd replaced Terry and Buckey with a more aggressive rhythm section; Jörn Andersen was on drums and Howard Ayee on bass. Our set was comprised of songs about lust, repressed sexuality, the oppression of gays and this crazy fucked-up world. My dark lyrics were the antithesis of Kevan's upbeat grooves and that made our sound work. Thinking and dancing, we had it down by then. Halfway through our set, I noticed Bowie standing at the side of the stage. I could have thrown up from fear, but opted for the much more positive and narcissistic, "Oh, my gawd, David is looking at me. I'm being watched by David Bowie." We piled off the stage after our set. We were so high we actually committed a band hug.

When Bowie hit the stage, I stood riveted in the wings. He is a master of re-inventing himself. I had seen him work before. The performance that stands out for me was the 1977 *Station to Station* tour, in which he was the thin white duke crooning like Sinatra, lit by blinding white spotlights shooting up to the sky in columns, the kind Albert Speer designed for Hitler at the Nuremberg Rally. The incarnation I was watching now was a more accessible Bowie. He had surrounded himself with musicians I would kill to work with. The two front men in the band were Carlos Alomar, who supplied ambiance on guitar, and Carmine Rojas on bass. We knew Carmine because he had worked with Nona Hendryx. Carmine wore a sarong, which was very sexy. Carlos was dressed like an Indian gentleman, Nehru all the way. Backstage before the show, they had bitched to us about how badly they were paid. David had his own private jet, a 707, fitted out with accommodations for the band and a private chef, so spare me.

There were two backup singers, Frank and George Sims. Tony Thompson was on drums, and Earl Slick played lead guitar. David stood on the lip of the stage singing "Modern Love," shaking one leg like Elvis. The show was an amalgamation of music and theatre. While performing "Cracked Actor," Bowie was seated in a director's chair, wearing dark glasses; like a new-wave Hamlet, he sang a soliloquy to a skull. "Hey David, what dyke through yonder window breaks? 'Tis me."

During a break halfway through the show, David came up to me and we started to talk. He was sweet and wanted to dish. He knew I'd been with Dusty Springfield, but he had me confused with one of her other girls. He told me he really liked Rough Trade, which meant we could do more dates with him. He put his arms around me and we hugged. He was so slight, I could have picked him up and carried him. Bowie grossed $2.3 million from that show.

Kevan and I thought we had died and gone to some touring heaven. After the shows, we hung out with Carlos and Carmine, who were sharing a hotel suite. Like spawning salmon, the groupies piled into their rooms. Eventually one bunch would leave and a whole new shift would file in. This went on all night. Bowie would show up at about four in the morning. I was always too bagged to deal with anything by then.

The tour culminated for us in Vancouver. Our photographer friend, Chick Rice, came backstage to visit us and brought along a beautiful, androgynous Chinese boy who was a classical pianist. David kept popping out of his dressing room to check him out. We'd done about six dates and were asked to continue touring with Bowie to California and then to Australia and New Zealand. It was a once-in-a-lifetime opportunity for us to get exposure before thousands of Bowie fans. We called Bernie and he approached CBS about giving us tour support. There was no way we could continue without some financial help. CBS didn't think it was worth the investment. We were crushed by their lack of support. It was a slap in the face to us as artists and the beginning of the end for us. We felt like we were beating our heads against a wall.

The Rough Trade Farewell concerts took place in Toronto and Montreal in 1986. We were doing three shows. The final concert was to be taped in Montreal for a CBC special. We'd asked Dusty and Nona to be our guests since they'd both sung on Rough Trade albums. Those shows were the last times I saw Dusty. Our first show was at a club called RPM in Toronto. There was a little tension among the divas in the dressing room. Dusty was still more of a diva than Nona or me. She was a little put out that most of the attention was on me. The club was hot and smoky and packed with people.

The Clichettes opened for us. The girls came out wearing flesh-coloured costumes of naked male rock stars, with hand stitched penises attached to their bodies with Velcro. Their performance was hysterical. Even though some of the audience threw beer bottles at them, they were pros and dealt with it. One of the highlights of that show was their interpretation of the Paul Anka tune, "You're Having My Baby," which they sang in male drag. After their set, Louise Garfield wandered into Dusty's dressing room still dressed in her naked suit. She started telling Dusty what a big fan she was. Dust just stared at her—she'd missed their set and had no idea what to make of her appearance.

We got up on that stage and played our songs. It was a bittersweet experience. We had a kickass band. Tony Springer was on guitar. His style of playing is very Jimi Hendrix–like. Howard Ayee was on bass and Tony Craig was on drums. Nona and I plowed through songs like "Territorial" and "Shaking the Foundations." The band did a version of "Transformation," which Kevan and I had co-written with Nona. They loved working with her because she's such a pro. Then Dusty sauntered out and sang "Soft Core." The audience loved her.

Our last two shows were at the Spectrum in Montreal. It was sheer joy to work there, though Dusty offended the makeup man when she lugged a giant suitcase into the dressing room, opened it and spilt the contents onto a table. Then she sent him out to buy pink hair dye. The crowd was hip and decadent in a truly French-Canadian way. A CBC crew was filming both concerts. Halfway through our show, a curtain on the stage that was too close to a light caught on fire. We tried to ignore it, hoping it would magically be taken care of; we didn't want to stop in the middle of a song. Cut to our producer, Sandra Faire, and her husband, Ivan Fecan, the head honcho of the CBC, running into Dusty's dressing room, which is thick with smoke. Dusty is sitting there unconcerned, calmly smoking a cigarette. Ivan broke a window and Sandra dragged her out of the room.

Cut to us, I don't know what we were thinking. I scanned the audience for the CBC crew and yelled, "Hey, the curtain's on fire." The crew were all French-speaking. They were busy drinking, smoking and hitting on chicks. No one in the crew acknowledged us or the fire. The smoke was getting intense. We stopped the show and ran off the stage. A fireman appeared and aimed an extinguisher at the flames. We went back out and continued the concert. Dusty floated out, looking blond and fragile. She was much more relaxed for this show. We started joking and it was all sexual innuendo. I said, "Who's gonna be on top?" Dusty said, "I'll be on top, no you be on top." Dusty started to sing. Her soft sensual voice was like liquid.

I'm not sure if we should have disbanded Rough Trade that soon. It was just so difficult for us. The lack of a Canadian star system is not just negative space: the Canadian media tend to denigrate artists after they achieve a certain level of success.

On top of that, I was typecast by the Canadian media as this evil dominatrix/raunch queen. Talk about low self-esteem. Every time we got a distribution deal in the U.S., it was sabotaged by powers beyond our control. Boardwalk declared bankruptcy in 1983; our contract was passed over to a third party who released us a year later. For a band that was just starting to do something Stateside, a year in contract limbo was the kiss of death. Bernie's hands were tied. We wanted CBS Records, who distributed us in Canada, to pick us up in the U.S., but we were completely frustrated by the machinations of the industry, and it never happened.

In the end, Kevan and I both felt like parodies of ourselves and that is not a healthy way to function as an artist. If we had it to do all over again, I think we should have taken time to regroup and reinvent ourselves. We needed a break, not an ending. But from where we were standing, that view wasn't clear.

THE ME DECADE

I'm so over me, I don't want to write about me. That me was
so self-obsessed; her hair kept getting bigger along with her
body and her ego. In the eighties, when it was all about me,
the cult of me loomed large on the horizon and life was one
big, trendy party. One of the perks of my own celebrity was
access to events where I came in contact with sights such as the
grim spectre of Nancy Reagan's oversized head, up close at a
fashion show for the wives of presidents and prime ministers.
At the time the free-world glitterati were gathered in Toronto
for a trade summit. While their husbands wreaked havoc with
the world's economy, the wives had to be trundled off somewhere, so why not sic all the Canadian fashion designers on
them? We were scarcely past the three security checks before
the premier of Ontario sidled up to me and asked if I would
sing "High School Confidential." In some circles, as a musician you're considered just slightly better than the help, and
the rich and powerful expect you to entertain them for free, at
the drop of a hat.

The eighties was a decade of puerile self-indulgence carried
to outrageous levels. It was all about the right wines and
trendy restaurants and yuppie food emporiums like David
Wood and Dean & Deluca. The spectre of AIDS was there in
the eyes of men who covered themselves in makeup to hide
the signs of Kaposi's sarcoma, but we couldn't cope with the

reality of that, and why should we, when we could numb everything with more wine and more lines and more sex?

The eighties was a fourteen-year-old supermodel wrapped in diaphanous layers of black on black fabric, coked out of her head, stumbling down a stairway. It was rolling around naked, tossing your wild mane of hair, like a heroine in a Jackie Collins novel, tangled up in three-hundred thread count Egyptian cotton Pratesi sheets. Yes, the eighties was a time when Moses Znaimer thought he could yell at me from across a crowded room, "Are you still gay?" like it was some lingering disease I had contracted.

The eighties didn't start out well. John Lennon was shot and killed, and Ronald Reagan was shot and lived. At the time I remember thinking, "Is this an omen of how this decade is going to play itself out?"

The eighties was nouvelle cuisine and waiters religiously reciting descriptions of dishes as if they were offerings to the gods. It was presentation over substance, layers of blood-red carpaccio with confit of squash, pomegranate and kiwi, orzo with pine nuts, finished with spirals of coriander. Whatever delicacy you chose was egregiously expensive and always left you hungry for more. The eighties in Toronto was the Parrot, where chef Greg Coulliard held court, and the Clichettes, dressed in shimmering white chiffon dresses and teased bouffants like a sixties girl group, sashaying through the restaurant on its opening night lip-synching "Thank You and Good Night." Following his unfathomable gypsy-like sense of whimsy, Coulliard gathered up his tent and moved from restaurant to restaurant, and we followed him like the food junkies we were. He had us wired to his addictive cuisine, which never varied; only the names changed.

The eighties was all about labels and brand names: Bottega Veneta Frusen Glädj´e Lancôme Armani Clarins John Paul

Gaultier Matsuda Issey Miyake Manolo Blahnik Paloma Picasso Thierry Mugler Chanel Claude Montana. It was restaurants: Café Luxembourg Three Small Rooms Un Deux Trois The Four Seasons Le Cirque Café des Artistes The Courtyard. It was hotels: Morgans The Windsor Arms The Plaza The Carlyle The Pierre The George Cinq Browns. And the best of all scenarios, Leona Helmsley getting dragged off to jail for tax evasion. It was Barney's Holt Renfrew Bergdorf Goodman Creeds Bendels Saks Fifth Avenue Harvey Nichols and Harrods.

Still, in my case, the eighties was about winning three Junos in a row and beating out Anne Murray as best female vocalist. The first time I won, in my acceptance speech I thanked "my wife, Kevan Staples." I sat at a table with the beaming Bernie Finkelstein, Kevan and some record company executives who were into me solely because I was the prize-winning piece of meat that night.

Après Dusty, I hightailed it out of Cabbagetown and moved into an art deco apartment on St. Joseph Street, which Tim Blanks immediately renamed Fagu-Strasse because it was full of boy bars and was ear-shatteringly noisy on the weekends. Sometimes I could hear people rutting like dogs right outside my back window. I'd hang back in the darkness of my bedroom and watch like the voyeur I am. I liked the idea of living in a sex ghetto and witnessing the sense of urgency and desperation in the faces of people who were intent on getting off as fast as possible.

I started seeing a therapist, but dumped her when she confided in me that she used to swallow ground glass. I found someone else, and we'd talk about how torn I was about my notoriety. I couldn't walk down the street without being recognized. Sometimes I loved the perks of fame, but mostly

I felt like it was an invasion of my privacy. I couldn't even go to a grocery store without someone hitting on me. This shrink wanted me to take some heavy-duty mind-fucking meds. I tried them for a minute, but they made me feel like I was losing what was left of my mind. I hated therapy because it seemed to me like an exercise in self-indulgence. I was so sick of talking about me. As soon as I got over myself, I snapped out of my funk.

I was really disillusioned with women and projected my disastrous relationship with Dusty on everyone I met. I remained painfully celibate for a year. Finally, I picked up a girl with blond slicked-back hair who drove a Harley, and we went to my place and broke my sex fast.

I began working with Kevan, writing songs for our third album. The themes were dark and sensual. "Shaking the Foundations" had a gospel chorus of three women wailing in the background. Even though we'd achieved some success, we hadn't become complacent. We were still political animals voicing our disillusionment with the lack of consciousness around us. I was outraged by the avarice and greed that surrounded me, even though I bought into it, shopping for useless crap I didn't need, filling some kind of emotional void. I let myself go there and tap into that anger by letting the words take me over in a stream of consciousness until it resulted in something solid that I could articulate.

I wrote lyrics for a song entitled "Endless Night." I raged on about what it's like to be gay, to be treated as a second-class citizen and exist in a climate of thinly disguised tolerance, which is an insidious part of the fabric of straight society. I've played both sides and I know what I'm talking about. Anthropologist Margaret Mead stated that every mammal is instinctively bi-sexual. Why do straights get to dictate the way we behave in bed? I was upset by the indifference of gays who didn't use their political power to instigate change. That indifference eroded any power we had as voters. We were still the niggers in this scenario. I was sick of the stigma and self-loathing attached to our sexuality, as if sexuality defines what kind of person you are. That thought process is so dangerous and wrong.

Kevan and I asked Nona to sing on several tracks. There was a song called "Territorial," about lust and jealousy, that she wails on. I was never happy with my vocals because I can't ever seem to open up enough. For me, singing is all about unleashing your emotions without any interference from pesky grey matter. A song called "America: Bad and Beautiful" dealt with what was then my love-hate relationship with America. There was also a song inspired by my affair with Dusty, called "Beg for It"—Brechtian and bitter.

While Nona was in Toronto, the Talking Heads came to town, so we decided to go to their concert. Backstage before the show started, Nona, who had worked on the Heads' most recent album, *Remain in Light*, introduced me to the band. Tina Weymouth, the bass player, was pregnant. She said she loved to rest her bass on her stomach—her unborn child loved the vibrations it felt went she played. David Byrne was a little nerdish and slightly uncoordinated, but when he stepped on the stage he was transformed. He was dressed in an outrageously baggy suit. Nona and I stood at the back of the stage, while the Heads performed. The experience was euphoric, and I was one happy chick.

In 1983, Kevan and Marilyn finally decided to make it legal. The wedding was at the Millcroft Inn in the rolling Caledon Hills. Kevan asked me to be his best man. I shared a limo out into the country with Nona and Vicki, who'd flown in from New York. The ceremony was in a tent outside the inn on a perfect summer day, one of those days when the air shimmers with heat and you hear the buzzing of insects. As the bride walked down the aisle, Nona sang the scary eighties hit, "Evergreen," followed by "Amazing Grace." I stood next to Marilyn and Kevan as they exchanged their vows, and handed Kevan the ring. As soon as the ceremony was over, the reverend high-tailed it over to the bar and got totally drunk. The non-traditional nature of the event was too much for him to deal with. The reception was rampant with musicians, including Terry, Buckey, Dave and players from local bands. There were hairdressers and fashion designers and guests with regular jobs who weren't quite as full of themselves as we were. In the middle of the tables were centrepieces that were sculptures of men's tensed arms gripping flowers in their fists. Kevan's grandmother, who had been married for sixty-seven years, gave a speech about giving your partner space.

Bernie asked me if I wanted to go on a promo trip to Australia and New Zealand. We had a distribution deal down under with Big Time Records, the same label Dame Edna was on, and "All Touch/No Contact" was burning its way up the charts. I really liked the insane, hard-drinkin' Aussie guys who ran the label, so I said yes. I travelled by way of Los Angeles, and the flight was a hell ride. We stopped in Honolulu, Fiji, and Auckland because of some engine trouble. I arrived in Sydney eighteen hours later. I was so jet-lagged the ground kept coming towards me. An A&R woman from the label took me to my hotel. There were only two channels on the television: a movie channel that repeated *Mad Max* every two hours, and a channel that played one video, "Come On Eileen," over and over again. I opened my suitcase and a big black dead bug fell out. I flashed back to the part of the journey where I had been awakened from my stupor by a crew of men who sprayed the inside of the plane while we sat on the ground in Auckland.

I had to do interviews every day. The A&R woman gave me some strange white powder to snort, because otherwise I'd pass out. I had a feeling it was ground aspirin cut with Drano. I sat in hotel rooms and made nice with the press; at one point we flew to Melbourne and back, though I saw nothing of the city. I sang live-to-tape on *The Molly Meldrum Show*, hosted by Molly, a very campy, effeminate man. We dished with each other about other celebs. I noticed that the weather was beautiful and warm, that Sydney reminded me of Toronto ten years earlier, and that there was a hit song on the radio called "A Dingo Ate My Baby." (The Aussies were obsessed with a trial involving a housewife accused of killing her baby. Her defence was that a dingo did it, which they discovered was true only after finding her guilty and locking her up.)

I sort of knew three people in wallaby land: one was a male hustler; the others were Eddie Rayner, from the band Split Enz, and his girlfriend, Raewyn. When I finally had some time off, I went out with the rent boy to sample Sydney's night life. We hit the street and got yelled at and propositioned by whores standing on balconies, displaying their fleshy merchandise. We strolled down to Bondi Beach, which was very white, blue and sexy. We got some dinner, and then he took me to a string of gay bars where middle-aged drag queens, Dame Edna clones, put on their nightly entertainments. I had never seen so many homos—the city was teeming with them. I grew very confused. Aussie men were butch and chauvinistic and yet they existed side by side in a city of queens.

I finally got taken to the zoo by the nice A&R lady. I loved the wallabies, like little deer who can hop. I realized I was in a vegetative state. I hadn't really slept the whole time I'd been in the land of toilets that flush backwards.

When Big Time was through with me, they put me on a plane to New Zealand, where I was supposed to drop by Warner Bros. Records, the label that Rough Trade was signed to there. Descending over Auckland, from the moment I saw the sheep look up, I was hooked on volcanoes, glaciers, mountains, those sheep and a familiar but strange English vibe. After the plane landed, I went for dinner with more A&R people. The air smelled sweet; I wanted more; I wished I could stay longer. I spent one night there. In the morning they poured my limp dishrag of a body onto the plane to Canada.

For some ungodly reason, around this time Rough Trade was offered a Pepsi commercial. Did we spend sleepless nights and go through any serious soul-searching about selling out? Not really—we were both realistic about the fact that there is only a small window of opportunity to make cash when you're in a band, and you're a fool if you don't seize the day. We said we'd do it. I confess, it was for the money. Jeremiah Chechick directed the commercial. (Afterwards, he relocated to Hollywood to direct real films, like *Christmas Vacation*, starring Chevy Chase.) We wrote a snappy Pepsi-swilling jingle and shot the thing. We had to drink Pepsi while the cameras rolled, but they watered it down so it would photograph better, reflect the light and all of that. They provided us with pails so we could spit it out between takes. There were male dancers with their heads wrapped in bandages like the invisible man, jerking around in that frightening robotic new-wave way, while we performed the song. The bandages were trouble. Nash the Slash, a local Toronto musician who always performed with his head concealed by bandages, claimed he owned that look. We had a meeting with the ad agency. I said, "Doesn't the bandage thing belong to the studio that produced the original *Invisible Man*?" A tall charming Pepsi exec said he thought it didn't, but Pepsi's attorneys thought otherwise. Pepsi pulled the commercial after minimal airplay. We were not amused, and even less amused when half of what we made went to the Canadian government.

I am out on the frozen tundra of Toronto's Bloor Street. The city planners have created a wind tunnel so intense that when you're hit with a blast of winter wind it feels like tiny knives with serrated edges slicing off pieces of your flesh. Your eyes water as you blindly try to navigate your way down the street. In the winter you can ride the subway and, if you're lucky, live the winter months underground like a member of a tribe of mole people, and surface only to run screaming into your house.

I am shopping for overpriced yuppie food at Holts, and I meet a girl named Adrienne, working in the food department. She's a princess who has embraced all that that implies, and is sexy and funny, her body lush and ripe. She has the whole booty thang going on. She tells me she has a friend she wants me to meet. I ask for a detailed description of this woman, and then I say, "Sure, what the hell, I'll meet her." Adrienne arranges a dinner at her house. I show up and this scary, voracious-looking woman is sitting there. I dislike her on sight. I say hello to her, and she practically has her tongue down my throat, which is a big turn-off. Never touch a Leo until they touch you. I mumble some excuse and take off.

Still, I started to see Adrienne as a friend. She began to grow on me. She was an expert in pop psychology and was working it. I was still damaged goods from Dusty. Adrienne was such a hustler; she was moving in for the kill and I didn't even see it. One night we were together in my apartment and an unspoken sexual tension took over. We worked our way into the bedroom and, about eight hours later, we got up and went to a party across the street at Robert Gage's hair salon. We staggered into the party, stunned and dishevelled, like coal miners blinking in the daylight. We headed straight for the food, loaded up on carbs, and crawled back to my place. We stayed in bed for three days.

Tim Blanks came over, and we shot videos on the roof of my building. He was dressed in the rag look we were favouring that month. I was in a contest that Sony was sponsoring, the object of which was to shoot some avant-garde performance-art type thing. Well, that was *my* object. I taped all my friends, including Jorge, and shot them from flattering angles so they looked fabulous. I swung the camera around the roof and zoomed in on buildings and the street below, and Tim launched into a facetious commentary about Toronto. Little did we know he would end up with a successful television career. I loved being with Tim because he was witty and catty, and I liked the way he turned a phrase. At that time, Tim lived with Lukas Kleanthous, a fashion designer from Cyprus who was once in the army and had quite probably blown people away. He was a big blond bear and designed fabulous leather clothing.

Rough Trade was planning a video for a single called "Crimes of Passion." I'd just seen *Blade Runner*, and I decided I had to have a band of black makeup over my eyes like the android Daryl Hannah played. The single was about two gay boys fucking and a woman playing with herself, but still the song was a hit.

I sat in a room with a casting director named Karen Hazzard, and we auditioned cute boys who had to pretend to seduce one another. I got a vicarious thrill out of watching some of them blush. We picked two pretty young boys who were students at Ryerson Polytechnical Institute.

On the day of the shoot, the band walked onto the set, which was minimal and ready for business. There was a bed and some windows suspended by fishing wire. We had two costume changes, one designed by Kansai Yamamoto, the other by Kevan's wife, Marilyn, a ripped-up rag thing—white material tied in knots and wound around the body in some semblance of clothing. I got to have the eye makeup thing (as soon as I saw the video, I was sorry).

We shot scenes with the band; Kevan and I were voyeurs who walked through the scenes. A sexy girl played with herself, then enticed a boy into her bed and blew him away. Then two boys, named Johnny and Eddie, made out in bed, where a spurned lover, Vinnie, discovered them and stabbed Johnny. The video got minimal air play—I wonder why?

After the fact, Kevan said we should have shot the video using stop-action animation with Barbie dolls, which I thought was a brilliant idea but a little late. The video made its way to various gay bars and took on a life of its own in the netherworld of Benelux countries. The single zoomed up the charts.

Kevan, Marilyn and I are on board the Trans Europe Express from Holland, where Rough Trade just finished touring with Mink De Ville. Mink was paranoid the whole time, and I can't remember if we even spoke to each other. He was joined at the hip to his minder and looked spaced out. On stage, he was transformed into a sexual punk with an R&B aesthetic.

We're on our way to Paris, and I feel like I've died and gone to Euro heaven. The whole credo of the eighties was built on an insatiable lust for items that became obsolete almost the minute you acquired them, hence the term conspicuous consumption. The next day, we're on our knees in a warehouse rummaging through cardboard boxes of Claude Montana's soft butter-like leather jackets and pants while Claude flicks his eyes over us, a tad disdainfully, and chats with his assistant. We try to hide our barely controlled hysteria. The jackets are being given away for a hundred and fifty dollars a pop!

We stay in a hotel on the left bank. I just want to leap about the streets of Paris like a maniac. I wish I could speak French; people look right through me when I say, "Je suis désolé parlez pas français," although they do understand English when you ask, "How much is this?" I'm fatigued by the amount of shopping that's going on. It's too much. I'm no longer a willing participant. The designer boutiques are overwhelming.

Every night we try a different restaurant, though we always order the same thing: steak frites with chocolate mousse for dessert and lots of red wine. One evening we meet up with Michael Budman and Diane Bald, who have an apartment in Paris near the Tuileries. We go out for dinner and Michael is smarmed over by the maître d', like the millionaire Roots god he is. The next morning I tear into the Louvre, wanting to get a quick gander at the enigmatic smile of Mona. I fight my way through throngs of people. The painting is small and enclosed in glass because it's so priceless, and you can't get anywhere near it because it's blocked by a thick wall of tourists. It's so claustrophobic in there, I give up trying and jog out of the museum past the statue *Winged Victory* into the sunlight.

We head out of Paris on a tour bus to explore the palace of Versailles. Our tour guide is a beautiful French woman, who seems to have some Louis XIV and XV issues; she takes us through rooms I have seen only in Deborah Turbeville photographs. I'm fascinated by the hall of mirrors and the bedroom of Marie Antoinette. I really want to see the bathrooms, but maybe they didn't have any. I feel an affinity to decadent French royalty, perhaps because they were so foppish, like me. Our guide shows us orange trees and implies that the courtiers of the sun king, Louis XIV, defecated in the soil. We explore the grounds of the palace. There are fountains with statues corroded with the patina of age, grottoes and wooded copses. Every time we stop at a particularly beautiful and secluded spot, our guide, in her heavily accented English, exclaims, "And zees is where ze king would meet his favourites." After the third time, Marilyn and I are trying not to laugh in her face.

We visit the Arc de Triomphe, Napoleon's wet dream homage to himself. The red granite walls of this monument are covered with scenes of NB performing heroic, albeit dictator-like, acts. The tourists seem intent on discussing NB's dick size, and an inch and a quarter seems to be the general consensus. I'm mad for Bonaparte because he was a Leo and a control freak. I think of him as a style queen because of the Empire look that he and his wife, Josephine, inspired. For the men, tight pants, polished black boots, ornate high-collared jackets and swinging shag hair cuts. For the women, diaphanous gowns with pushed-up breasts like an offering. I believe the fashion statement they were making was "Do me." I love Empire furniture. It's all about divans, where a girl can recline while she's serviced by her courtiers. I'm held in the thrall of Paris; the French, however, are another matter. They are slim, stylish and disdainful of us all.

We fly back to Toronto, wearing layers of new clothes, and try to persuade Canada customs that we barely did any shopping. I want to break out an Oscar for the performance Kevan puts on for the bemused customs officials.

I sort of shack up with Adrienne. She spends nights with me but keeps her apartment. We have tempestuous breakups every few months. I run wild, and then I start to miss her sense of humour and her intellect. All through our relationship, I'm jonesing for another woman who is completely unattainable.

It's so much work being a lesbian. Multiply that by a thousand when you move in with one. You have to operate at a totally unrealistic level of sensitivity. One wrong look or word can spell disaster. You have to develop the hands and seductive skills of a trained courtesan, and you must be attuned to every nuance, every shift in the wind of emotion. Sometimes it's worth it; sometimes it's hell on earth.

Adrienne and I cannot really commit to one another. I'm not sure either of us wants to. It seems to be a marriage of convenience. I feel like I'm in a holding pattern and I've just settled for this. I want passion. It's the drug I crave more than anything. I'm a fool for love, and all the baggage that goes with it.

We are somehow introduced to producer Barry Pearson and director Les Rose, who want to shoot a video with us. Barry has some investors, doctors and dentists who need a tax break; they are willing to invest in a video and a documentary about the making of the video (that's the tax loophole). We decide to shoot a video of "Territorial." Les comes up with the concept of a post-apocalypse city, very Duran Duran, *Road Warrior*-ish. Steven Shach designs a cartoonish, Mussolini-military look for me, with big shells sticking out of my shoulder epaulettes. There are two warring factions. I command an army of Amazon warrior bitches, and Kevan is a warrior who leaps around and executes a series of cool ninja moves. He begins to study the arts of a Ninja with a boy named Nip Kichs. We shoot in an abandoned factory space that used to be a Massey-Ferguson assembly line. There are plenty of extras, semi-clad boys wrapped in Saran Wrap and strategically placed rags.

They are playing android-like creatures who are hanging from hooks. I have no idea why—it's a video and logic doesn't figure in the picture.

I'm surrounded by beautiful, buffed, toned women with crossbows, dressed in a grey version of the rag look that just won't go away. I'm supposed to walk by boys suspended on hooks, leading my posse. During the first few takes, there is trouble because the lights are too hot, and the Saran Wrap is curling and disintegrating on the boys' flesh—ouch. Then there is some business with a geisha in a Japanese tea room. Kevan and I appear to be sharing her favours, indicated by a series of quick cuts that imply nothing and everything. There are shots of Kevan and the Ninja having their choreographed fight. To push this thing over the top, there's a real live horse, which Nip rides down a ramp and along the length of the space. The film crew frames a beautiful shot of the horse and rider reflected against the factory windows. Les, the director, has a thing for horses. The burning flesh problem is fixed, and the director has me strut by the rows of Saran-Wrapped boys, and tells me to caress the flanks of the Amazon women, as if they were my property. That part is cut because we have trouble getting it shown on television.

I fly to New York on a whim and spend a week seeing and meeting divas. The first stop is a trip to Long Island with Vicki and Nona to see Tina Turner. She's on the cusp of her comeback. It's the same act she's been doing for years, but any minute now her career will take off, under the guidance of Roger Davies, the Yohji Yamamoto–wearing Australian who manages Olivia Newton-John. After the show we make our way to Tina's dressing room. She looks amazing. Her legs are polished ebony columns of muscle. She starts talking about jazz guitarist

George Benson's new nose job. She says, "Why do black people get white people's plastic surgery? What's up with George getting a white nose?" Doing that to yourself, she says, is a betrayal of your race. This is right before witnessing the horror that Michael Jackson will become. He looks fine in the "Thriller" video, but he has to push it. Imagine the self-loathing.

A couple of nights later, Nona and I stand on the stage at the Winter Garden on Broadway watching Patti LaBelle work. During her show, she accidentally kicks off one of her Maud Frizon shoes into the audience, and her drummer faints in the middle of a song and has to be dragged offstage and replaced, all without stopping the show. Patti introduces Nona and me to the predominantly black audience, which is very gracious of her. She sings more notes than my brain can handle, twists every sound that comes out of her mouth into a dizzying arpeggio. After the show, she's all about food and cooking for everybody in sight. She says she loves my hairstyle, and the next time I see her she has it.

The topper to the diva week is Aretha Franklin. I've wanted to see her forever, but she cancels her concerts all the time. She has no stage presence to speak of until she sits down at a white grand piano and sings "Spirit in the Dark." Suddenly she's alive and in the moment—it's so obvious her roots and her soul belong to gospel. Unlike Patti, she doesn't give it all away. When the high priestess of soul works a song, it has meaning. In the basest terms, there's some foreplay, instead of a constant wanking stream of ejaculation.

We start work on another album called *Weapons*. It's all about sex and love (surprise). We write an ode to the sixties called "Paisley Generation." It's the first funny song we've written in years. In the studio, before the session, the band performs a ritual; we each do a bump, we want to be a bit fucked-up, which seems appropriate for the subject matter.

We record the song in one take, trying not to laugh out loud or we'll ruin it. We deliberately play the song badly. We go insane working on overdubs, trying to cop the sound of the Beatles and Jimi Hendrix. Kevan and Gary Gray spend hours spinning a plate and letting it fall, endlessly recording takes of the sound to match the outro of the Beatles song, "A Day in the Life." (Sound sampling hasn't been invented yet!)

When we shoot the cover with General Idea, Kevan and I run around half-naked, looking pretty buff and bronzed thanks to our makeup man. Jorge photographs our bodies and parts of dancers' bodies, which he then integrates into a grid pattern design. The album cover is an erotic wall of flesh.

I go to Europe again, with Adrienne. The trip starts out well in London and Holland, but somewhere in Italy, things start to get ugly between us. There is a slow subtle poison seeping into our narcotic-like love. Italy is an earthly paradise, although it still seems to be governed by a zany bunch of fascists. Florence, the shoe capital of the world, is Adrienne's idea of heaven. It is the city where the Médicis, my favourite dysfunctional family, lived their kinky incestuous lives. We stay in a picturesque *pensione* and start fighting. We go to see Michelangelo's *David*. A group of American gay boys scream, "Isn't he beautiful!" as they stand at his marble feet and run their eyes slowly up his body, lingering on his sex, then coming to rest on his sensuous marble face.

On the train to Rome, we drink red wine and look out onto the rolling hills of Tuscany. We pass through small towns and pull into the infamous Stazione Termini. The city is like a whore, sensuous and overripe. Countless boys on Vespas zoom by like extras in some bad sixties movie. We get our asses pinched, and men follow us down the street, salivating over

Adrienne's rolling hips. The Spanish Steps are crowded with people who are in our way as we try to shop. Adrienne falls on her knees in front of the Fendi boutique like it's a shrine she's reached after an arduous religious pilgrimage.

The Coliseum is full of stray cats; I imagine the Christians being thrown to the lions. We are startled by the beauty of blond Italians with blue eyes, like statues. We walk the streets for hours, stopping only for a glass of wine or the sugar rush of a gelato. At the Vatican I'm recognized by several tourists, some of the thousands of Italians who live in Toronto. I happily sign autographs for people who ask how my dad the pope is doing.

At night there are more fights. I hate fighting, I'm no good at it. I get violently angry, then I shut down and no longer feel anything.

We make our way to Venice. It's a spectral city—it looks like the end of the earth; it looks like my dreams. I imagine living there in a doge's palace surrounded by water. At night it's frustrating trying to find your way through the labyrinth of dark claustrophobic streets. I love floating on the septic canals and passing under the Bridge of Sighs. We are exhausted from fighting. There are surreal blond children on the beach at the Lido. (The lesson I learned from this journey is that a trip with your lover can exacerbate the nicks in your relationship until they become open wounds.)

When I think of the eighties, I feel sick about the money I spent. All I did when I wasn't working was travel and shop. In Tokyo, it's all about the style and presentation of clothes; minimalism rules. You walk into a boutique and are faced with a simple cement slab. A piece of clothing by Yohji Yamamoto is laid out like a fashion corpse. Tokyo's streets are laid out in a numerical system that is beyond my comprehension. Some stores have western names. The Japanese are trying to use hip American expressions, but they get it all wrong. Everywhere I go in the world there is this kitschy idolatry of Americana, which has nothing to do with reality. I think it's sad and funny.

I'm travelling with Nona and Vicki, who called me out of the blue and said, "Hey we're going to Japan, wanna come?" Nona is doing a show at the Parco department store, three bunker-like buildings in the middle of Tokyo's Shibuya-ku district. We're there on the anniversary of the bombing of Hiroshima— you know, the bombs they didn't need to drop but decided to anyway, just to see what it would look like. Everywhere I walk, there are chalk outlines of bodies drawn on the streets. It makes me feel ill. Caucasian men look like Neanderthals next to the Japanese. The only white women I see are supermodels, which makes the city more surreal than it already is. Nona and her band are performing in a club on the top floor of the stores. Ryuichi Sakamoto, one of the great contemporary Japanese composers, shows up to catch her set. While hanging out backstage, I teach a Japanese girl some jive American obscenities just to hear her repeat them to Nona's band.

I jog around the moat that surrounds the Japanese Imperial Palace; the circumference of the palace is seven kilometres. There are cranes standing in the water. Every time I cross a street, ten thousand people seem to be waiting on the other side. I explore the Buddhist temples in the middle of the city, and I feel like I'm stepping into another world. Some have wooded gardens with lush trees and lily ponds. I visit a cemetery. The headstones are natural slabs of rock in zen-like settings. The graves are tended by the families of the dead every Sunday. I sit there in silence and reflect on life. Nona, Vicki, a couple of A&R men and I go to the kabuki theatre. Men play all the roles; nothing has changed since feudal times. The play is about a blind girl, and the actor who portrays her is a study in feline grace. I sit there with my breath caught in my throat.

In 1985 the Ethiopian people are being ravaged by famine. Every American mega-star is somehow affected by this. Following the lead of England's Bob Geldof, and the Live Aid simulcast he organized (which raised millions for the cause), the Americans get together to record "We Are the World" to aid the famine victims. I prefer the Spitting Image parody of the song.

Not to be outdone in this outpouring of humanitarianism, the Canadian music business gets in on the action and records "Tears Are Not Enough" (or as Adrienne so succinctly put it, "Ten Beers Are Not Enough"). Megalomaniac producer David Foster is running the show; Bryan Adams and Jim Valance, the songwriting team from hell, whip up a power ballad. Two gods, Neil Young and Joni Mitchell, descend from Mount Olympus for the cause. The lineup also includes Geddy Lee, Burton Cummings, Anne Murray, Corey Hart (the sweatiest guy I've ever met), John Candy, Catherine O'Hara, Gordon Lightfoot, the fat guy from Loverboy, and the rest of us. Every Canadian artist you've never heard of is at the session. Foster is out of control; he makes Paul Hyde of the Payolas and me do fifty takes of a part that was right the first time we sang it. Years later, we are both still pissed at him. In the video they shoot while we're recording, Paul and I look like we're gonna implode. I guess we didn't leave our egos at the door. During breaks in the recording, every chick singer in the place hovers around Joni Mitchell, just happy to be breathing the same air as her, except for Jane Siberry, who starts talking about cows. I see Joni's eyes glaze over in incomprehension. I smoke a stogie with Anne Murray, and we try to guess the names of some of the singers we're working with. I think that about sums up the Canadian star system. Her dry observations about the day amuse me, and I love her for it. The event turns into a love fest, despite itself.

Adrienne stands in the bedroom yelling at me loudly, but it's nothing to do with us this time. She's worked out the fact that she wants to get married and have babies, and the last time I looked I didn't have the proper equipment to be a husband and father. The split is mutual and overdue.

For our first album, Bernie cut a deal with Manta, and we're locked into recording there. I started bitching about it back then—because I wanted a different sound on every album— but my diva tantrum fell on deaf ears. Now Kevan and I both want to work with another producer in another space. We have a meeting with Terry Brown, a Brit who produced the Rush albums. He is very low-key and cool. He wants to experiment with us and record our album on a big empty sound stage. He tells us he'll set up his board in one corner of the room, the band will work in the middle of the space, and we'll get a very live sound. We like his approach; we go into a Phil Spector mode, constructing songs that will be a thick, multi-layered wall of sound. The name of the album is O *Tempora* O *Mores*. At the outset of the recording, we have problems with our drummer Jörn; he is being terrorized by his wife, who has a psychological choke-hold on him. He's a mess and can't play the material, and we have to replace him with a drummer named Tony Craig. Our band is now comprised of three black players, and it's apocalyptic.

———————

I've been having a flirtation with Lisa Dal Bello. She has a singing voice that some goddess has given her to use during her time on this planet. I could sit and look at her for hours. She is very beautiful but doesn't have any conception of how beautiful, so she wears too much makeup and tries to distort her appearance. She has a recording deal with EMI, and the world could be her oyster if she'd let it. We like the same books, the same music and each other. She is straight but curious, and our relationship starts to change—slowly there is more body contact between us, it starts to get intimate, and there's an insinuation of things that might happen. In the middle of this tease, she goes on tour in Europe and falls in love with her new guitar player, and it's over before it begins.

On the subject of girls, the first time I met Sandra Bernhard, she was in Toronto shooting a film called *Beer* and didn't know anyone. Elaine called me and said I should call her and show her the town. We went out to a movie starring Sally Field; the plot was something about a farm, an idiot savant and some yelling. We were sitting in the audience making cracks and being as obnoxious as possible when Sandra's arm snaked around me. I froze—I wasn't attracted to her body; I was attracted to her unfaltering ego. I wished I had the innate sense of self she has. Her philosophy is "Fuck all of you, I'm beautiful dammit," and it has taken her a long way.

O Tempora O Mores is the first album of ours that is only moderately successful. Only one song endures, "On the Line," which I still perform now. In a moment of frustration and weakness, Kevan and I have had it; Rough Trade officially decides to call it quits. To get out of our deal with True North, we have to record a best-of album with two new songs.

So many people I knew in the eighties had the same mindset, smug self-confidence bolstered by a false sense of security, like an ego out of control. In 1986, thanks to June Callwood, a social activist who's been kicking butt since the sixties, we snapped out of our self-obsession. With the death of Rock Hudson, AIDS became a *cause célèbre*, as the arts community came together and, adhering to the old slogan, "We look after our own," did a benefit to raise money to build Casey House, the first AIDS hospice in North America.

In New York, Howard had become involved with ACTUP, the AIDS Coalition to Unleash Power. Their motto was Silence = Death. Through demonstrations and civil disobedience, they made the public aware of the U.S. government's mismanagement of the AIDS crisis. They wanted pharmaceutical companies to abolish double-blind drug studies and release new medication immediately. There was no time. Howard also started working for an organization that helped children with AIDS. He met a man named Michael, who would be the death of him.

After Kevan and I break up, I'm frightened and exhilarated all at once. I expect things to happen for me right away. I want to move to England, New York or L.A. I get a new band together. Steve Webster, the bass player, acts as the music director. He plays his bass so loudly that every woman singer he's worked with says that when she stands in front of his amp, her labia vibrate, and hey, we're not complaining. He used to play with Billy Idol and has endless stories about him. He also used to work for Rough Trade when he was fifteen, and he claims I ignored him. I did.

We try various guitar players, and they're all uniquely psychotic. We settle on one, Tim Welch, who carries a small piece of steak wrapped in tinfoil around with him. Every once in a while he takes it out of his pocket, opens the packet and talks to the atrophied piece of meat like it's his pet. I fall in love with him right then.

We hire a drummer who has serious drug problems but plays brilliantly. We can always tell if he's using because his face turns blood-red like the top of a thermometer. Tim, Steve and I look at each other on stage, half-expecting to witness a big brain aneurysm and be sprayed with blood. We go out on the road to Halifax with two roadies named Sid and Elvis. Steve gets a thrill from asking Sid to bring him useless hard-to-find things, like a map of Albania. We get up on stage to do the show and, sure enough, Sid has photocopied a map for Steve, and it's lying at his feet. Steve and I scope out the women in the audience and lust after the same ones. We check out the dykes in the audience, who stand at the side of the stage and study me with their heads slightly tilted. I call them "knowing lesbians," and he says, "No, they're knawing lesbians." We do gigs whenever possible, the worst one in a bar where we share the bill with strippers. The boys call them peelers.

The gig that still makes me laugh was at Club Soda in Montreal. The audience was predominantly gay. A girl came up to me after the show and said she wanted to come out to her mother, so I signed an autograph to her mother with the inscription "Your daughter eats pussy."

Steve lived with a phenomenal woman named Fuge, and their stunning, gifted daughter, Tokyo. I'd known Fuge since the late seventies, when she and her best friend and soulmate, Torch, had a band called the Time Twins. Fuge was one of the most unique women I've ever known, wise beyond her years. I loved being around her. She was bright, articulate and not as superficial as the rest of us. (She died of breast cancer in 1992.)

For two years in a row, Paul Shaffer and I co-hosted the Casby Awards, which translated as Canadian Artists Selected By You. The Casbys used to be called the Uknows, but the much more prestigious Juno people got real cranky about that. David Marsden, who used to work as a deejay for a station called CKEY under the pseudonym of Dave Mickey, was the mastermind behind the Casbys, a televised vehicle for Canadian and international alternative music and musicians to be heard. (David was the first overtly gay man I'd ever seen in Yorkville back in the sixties, browsing through forty-fives in a record store; he had a shimmering blond pompadour and was wearing a metallic blue mohair suit. He looked so out of place next to the rest of us in our bell bottoms and beads. David always liked to push the envelope.)

Marsden was instrumental in launching CFNY, the most cutting-edge rebellious radio station in Canada in the eighties. Its play list was diverse, modelled after pirate radio, stations that broadcast without a licence and played what they felt like: unsigned artists, people too avant-garde to get air play anywhere else, world music, dance, imports, whatever. If they liked what you were doing, you could always count on them for support. There was a big audience out there who was bored with the same generic stuff you could hear on every other station. CFNY was one of the forerunners of college radio today.

Marsden was the one who approached Shaffer and me about hosting the first televised version of the Casbys, and we both thought it would be a blast. (Paul is an expert on music trivia and kept teasing Marsden about a single he'd released in the sixties as Dave Mickey called "Granny Kitsch.") Paul couldn't leave New York because of his gig on *Late Night with David Letterman*. He'd been the music director of that puppy for what seemed like three hundred years. So I had to fly down to write the Casby scripts, working with Paul in sexy expensive hotel suites, which the CBC paid for (love you). My favourite hotel was the incredibly trendy Morgans, which was the first project Steve Rubell and Ian Strager embarked on after Rubell got out of jail for tax evasion over the creative bookkeeping methods he used at Studio 54. Paul and I got stoned and wrote introductions that we knew the CBC would censor. We didn't really care; we made each other laugh. It was one toke over the line, sweet Jesus.

The first taping takes place at the Harbourfront Convention Centre. Paul and I swan out onto the stage, we're very glitzy in colourful silk suits, and my hair is a monolith. All of our introductions and stage banter border on insulting. My whole shtick is about wanting to fuck everybody cute in the bands we're introducing. We are fans of all the bands who are on the show, especially their hairstyles and eyeliner; however, we're a little puzzled by Luba and Gowan, because of their choice of names. Also, Gowan has some weird moves going on that are, to say the least, unsettling. I suggest to Marsden that he give a lifetime achievement award to Kensington Market, and he does. The band shows up and is just as charming and spaced out as if I were having a sixties flashback. Bobby Curtola, our version of Frankie Avalon, also gets an award. The first Casby show is a hit. Yes, perhaps there was a clash of egos, a frisson of friction between some of the musicians and the hosts and the producer, Sandra Faire. But it can be tense, taping live television.

In 1986 we taped the Casby show at a theme park called Canada's Wonderland. I checked out the program so I could relive it in my mind. The cool eighties thing was to pose at a forty-five degree angle in promo shots, like you were about to fall over. Why? The stage was an outdoor amphitheatre, so of course it rained during the show. I went to a notorious Toronto fashion designer named Winston Kong, who whipped up frothy creations for socialites, and borrowed a gown, a long black sheath with evening gloves. I wanted to work my inner drag queen. The opening of the show was a meaningless production number with dancers leaping about in clouds of dry ice. I had to walk down a stairway in heels, which required all my motor skills. Dry ice makes the floor slick and wet and gets into your lungs and chokes you to death if you're trying to sing live, but who am I to get in the way of art?

After the intro, things kept getting stranger. A band called General Public were missing a member, so they propped up a cardboard cut-out of him and did their number. Another solo artist, from the band Boys Don't Cry, had been stood up by MuchMusic veejay Erica Ehm, who was supposed to sing backup with him. I found myself on stage cursing her name as I mouthed lyrics for a song I didn't know along with this cute Brit boy wrapped in a poncho. *I want to be a Cowboy, I want to be a star.* I kept telling myself, "Nobody's watching." I remembered something my mother used to say: "We're just a tiny speck of dust in the middle of the universe."

Helen Shaver came backstage in the middle of the taping. She'd just finished filming *Desert Hearts*, a film in which she plays an uptight straight girl who is seduced by a cowgirl on a ranch in Reno where she is waiting for her divorce to come through. She told me she wanted to do something to shock the audience. Well, all right. Paul and I go out and do our closing monologue. I suggest we go off and have sex together. I pick him up in my arms and start to carry him offstage. Helen appears clutching a bouquet of flowers. I drop Paul unceremoniously. Helen and I fake a passionate kiss, and we walk off arm in arm. People go nuts. Women ask me if Helen and I are an item. I say, "I don't know. Ask her husband."

After the show, Shaffer and I fall into a limo. We're heading back to the hotel after the show at Canada's Wonderland and, for some strange reason, two of Prime Minister Brian Mulroney's assistants are riding with us. Mulroney bears a striking resemblance to the cartoon character, Dudley Do-Right, and, like most Canadian prime ministers, is the butt of many jokes. The assistants start bragging to us about what a great job perk diplomatic immunity is, meaning they just breeze through borders and have access to some fine dope. Throughout their conversation Paul and I look at each other while he eggs them on; they continue to incriminate themselves.

At the Harbourfront hotel I go to Paul's room, where he, Dave Thomas and Eugene Levy have been hanging out. Marty Short had just put them through a mind fuck by knocking on the door of their room, disguising his voice and pretending to be an officer from the RCMP, looking to bust them. This was the city where Keith Richards had been busted. Paul slowly opened the door and there was Marty grinning maniacally at him. Paul flipped out.

The Canadian Opera Company calls me to ask if I want to be in an opera. Strangely enough I happen to love opera, especially anything sung by Maria Callas, who is the diva incarnate. This opera, *Patria*, is an avant-garde work by R. Murray Schafer, a composer who has a firm grip on the Canadian grant tit. Whatever operatic extravaganzas he comes up with, and we're talking about one production that took place on a real lake, seem to be funded by the Canadian government, no questions asked. My people talk to their people. I show up for the first rehearsal and sit at a table with the main cast, R. Murray Schafer and Christopher Newton, who will be directing the actors. There is an undercurrent of hostility in the room. R and Chris apparently hate each other's guts, but we're pros, so we soldier on. I'm playing the part of Primavera Nicholson (the name makes me crave pasta). I get to write my own lyrics to R's music, a rocker chick aria in 23/17, a time signature that requires math skills I don't possess. There is a real diva in the production, Jo-Anne Kirwan Clark, who I love at first sight. She is very undiva-like, with a sweet disposition and long, cascading Rapunzel-y hair that falls down her back almost to her feet. There were supposed to be two opera divas in the production, but whoever the other one was, she had some issues with someone involved in the project. She blew into our first rehearsal for a minute, spat some French-Canadian venom in our general direction and took off.

I do not pretend to know the inner machinations and work-ings of the *theatre*, but after that day, I know the opera world is a seething hotbed of intrigue. We start to rehearse this epic: the cast consists of about 125 people, including actors from the Shaw Festival and Ryerson and a twenty-eight-member choir who will sing their parts in Morse code. The whole ménage is completed by an orchestra.

I immediately bond with the actors from the Shaw, who are going into this thing with a sense of humour. The names of the characters in the opera—D.P. the Characteristics Man, Sappho Silikens, a hermaphrodite policeman, and Amadeus

Nagy-Toth-Toth, for example—add to the confusion. The rehearsal turns into one big party for the cast, but not so for Chris and R, who sit on different sides of the Joey and Toby Tanenbaum Opera Centre, commandeering their own divisions, as it were. The opera is about alienation and non-communication in the video age.

We try out some scenes, reading lines in between the Morse code notes of the choir and the atonal shrieks of the orchestra. It's a giant musical jigsaw puzzle. When the real diva sings, I just want to listen to her. Why can't this whole thing be about her and her voice? During my aria or whatever you want to call it, I spaz out in front of the orchestra and sing my punkish rant. After three weeks of rehearsal, somehow this thing comes together and starts to make sense to us. On the opening night, we're all running around backstage and I suddenly know why my mother loved the theatre. It's the biggest high in the world to bond with a herd of crazy thespians; it's mad, darling. And, unlike rock 'n' roll, there are no cheese trays or tubs of iced Labatt Blue—we all get flowers.

We perform the opera, and the audience is understandably more than a little confused. I know I would be if I was sitting out there watching this go down. My big complaint is that nobody gets stabbed or poisoned, or jumps off a bridge, which is very unopera-like. *Patria* gets glowing reviews; music critics wax poetic about the multi-faceted context, innuendoes and sub-plots of the production. Were we all in the same room? At the opening night party, we can't get drunk enough.

I take off to Los Angeles to meet with Michael Ameen, who is kind of managing me. At least, we've committed to a six-month trial period, because I go through managers like toilet paper. He is just as wired as ever, but is knowledgeable about music and the way the industry operates. He is well-connected and all about networking. He takes me out to a party at the Hollywood Race Track, some fundraiser; Bette Midler's a co-chair, but she's in the hospital giving birth to her daughter, Sophie. I get a taste of Old Hollywood. The guests include Merv Griffin and Dick Clark, who are so tanned they resemble the undead cleverly disguised in layers of pancake makeup. I meet Barry Manilow and his partner, Gary, and also the songwriter Carol Bayer Sager, who is with Burt Bacharach. I say hi to Joyce Bogart and Bruce Bird, who once ran Boardwalk Records. Under the fluorescent lighting, everyone seems slightly sinister and unnatural looking. Throughout the evening Michael is hyperkinetic, like Speedy the Alka-Seltzer Boy.

The next night we go to a party at the house of Allee Willis, a songwriter who wrote "Boogie Wonderland" and who, in the nineties, will write the theme for *Friends* (which pushes her publishing royalties into the stratosphere). She looks like a cartoon character with her zigzag red hair and glasses. Her house is from the thirties, originally built as a party house for MGM. There are ten-pin bowling balls embedded in the yard. The theme of the party is "Russia." Outside the house, we meet Pee Wee Herman, dressed as a Cossack, wearing a big fur hat and a caftan. He looks so cute. He and Michael share a joint.

Allee has rewritten the lyrics for a bunch of sixties pop songs to fit into the Russian communist party theme, songs like "Red Rubber Ball" by the Cycle. Later she hands out sheet music and there is a singalong. The guests include boys from Devo, Pee Wee, Tony Basil (the choreographer responsible for introducing breakdancing into mainstream consciousness) and Sandra Bernhard. Allee has just written a song for Debbie Harry called "French Kissing in the USA," and the video is playing on a TV in one of the cartoon-style rooms.

I've been toying with the idea of moving to L.A. for years. I can see that it's stupid and vacuous, but people are so open to writing and performing with each other—on the chance that one of you might make it, and then they'll be an integral part of the mix. I start thinking seriously.

Back in Toronto I'm sitting in my pathetic excuse for a studio trying to figure out how to program my Yamaha drum machine. It's my way of procrastinating. I need some motivation to write. Bob Ezrin calls me about a recording project he's working on with David Gilmour and Pink Floyd since Roger Waters has left the band over "creative differences." I think it's a dick thing.

Gilmour is looking for a lyricist to collaborate on a new Pink Floyd album. I was never a big fan of Pink Floyd, but Bob brings over some albums and I listen to them intently. It's obvious to me that Waters was the engine that drove the band; trying to fill his shoes would be a mammoth undertaking. I start playing with concepts and working on some lyrics and then fly to London to meet Ezrin and Gilmour. I stay with Bob in Holland Park, a very upscale part of London. Elton John lives down the street. Bob tells me the house we're staying in is where Jimi Hendrix OD'd.

We drive out of London to Gilmour's studio, which is in a houseboat anchored on the Thames. The interior of the boat is art nouveau. Gilmour is all charm and intellect. He has as many guitars as Nigel Tufnel in the film *Spinal Tap*, only this is serious. I listen to him record a rough track and I'm blown away by what an incredible player he is—who knew? The most fun I have with Bob and Dave is when we go round to the pub and throw back a few pints of Guinness. I like Gilmour. He lives in a house that was once a place for romantic assignations between Edward VIII and Wallis Simpson. He tells me he gave Kate Bush one of her first breaks.

I spend a few days writing lyrics and dealing with the album concept. I feel under intense pressure to come up with the goods. I'm also aware that this is a boys' club and I only have a visitor's pass. Gilmour does demos of a couple of songs with some of my lyrical contributions, but that doesn't mean anything.

While I'm in London, I have a meeting with Barry Reynolds, who played guitar and co-wrote all the songs on Marianne Faithfull's brilliant *Broken English* album. I'd sent him some of my stuff to see if he had any interest in working with me. It's February and very budding blooms and spring-like outside. I meet him in a restaurant for breakfast, and he already stinks of Grand Marnier. I can't help but notice that Van Morrison is at the next table. Things get weird right away. Reynolds keeps telling me he wants to *be* with me, and I say, "You mean *work* with me," and he says, "I want to *be* with you" and this goes on for some time. It's obvious to me and, pretty soon, everyone in the restaurant, that Reynolds is a sex fiend who likes to drink at ten in the morning. I keep trying to blow him off, yet somehow he follows me home, and Bob kicks him out.

That was the topper to an intense and frustrating two weeks. Gilmour ends up collaborating with a guy, and everyone makes millions of £s except me. In an article in *Penthouse* magazine, Roger Waters vents about his departure from Pink Floyd, then goes on to list the lyricists Gilmour had attempted to work with. He pays me a backhanded compliment, calling me "one of the finest Canadian contemporary songwriters."

I'm forced back to my bachelorette lifestyle, and once I wrap my head around it, the idea is daunting. I go to a really disgusting dyke bar and pick up a nineteen-year-old and bring her home. Her alabaster swimmer's body is beautiful. She is very sweet and naïve, but our liaison is short-lived, as we don't connect on an intellectual level. I'm being facetious as usual.

I get a grant from FACTOR, an organization that helps fund musician's recording projects. I go into the studio with Steve Webster and company and record a couple of songs, one of which is a ballad I've written with help from Kevan, called "I'm Not Blind." Musically, it's tame for me, but the lyrics are as intense and bitter as ever. I get a distribution deal with some dishonest coked-up guys; Murray Ball releases it on the RPM label and we work it on radio. A producer friend applies for and gets a VideoFACT grant, which is a fund that enables artists to make videos, and Deborah Samuels directs my first solo video effort. She makes me look like a pretty hot unit. The song is not a big hit but continues to generate income after it gets placed in some film and television projects. A friend of mine named Mark Nathan, who works at Atlantic Records, takes on the always thankless and intimidating job of managing me.

My last conscious memory of the eighties is of a beautiful, soignée woman named Gina. Steve Webster and John Whynot, who is now also in my band, do a little matchmaking. They think we would like each other. I call her up and we go out on a date. Gina looks sweet and sensual in a clingy dress by the Toronto design team of Zapata. She teaches art to children and sings backup with Jane Siberry. Siberry is a complex piece of work, both brilliant and annoying, like a series of neuroses strung together in one dysfunctional package, but achingly beautiful music comes out of her. There is a line in one of Siberry's songs, "Gina says I remind her of the dog, the way I just did that." She is Jane's muse of the moment. She tells me road stories about her adventures with Jane, and all the stories involve Jane, Gina and Rebecca Jenkins eating too much garlic, sitting on the tour bus, and how the sheer stench oozing out of their pores annihilates everyone in their path. Gina is sweet, womanly, a child and a philosopher all rolled into one, and we fall in love. I get lost in her. She is spiritual, which is a refreshing change for me, and she makes me remember what that felt like. When she cooks for me, it feels like it comes from a place of love.

Gina says, "Being in Toronto in the winter is like being trapped inside a dirty baby food jar." We become intrigued by the thought of going to L.A.; we're tempted by the promise of success vacillating before us in a maddeningly seductive way. Gina wants to try acting, and auditions for a school called the American Academy of Dramatic Arts, which is canvassing for students in Toronto. She reads a scene from *Dangerous Liaisons* and gets accepted into the school. Gina packs up her belongings and heads for the campus in Pasadena, California. Two months later, I follow her.

L.A. Is My Lady

I find an apartment for Gina and me on Larrabee Street in the middle of West Hollywood, an upscale boys' town down the road from Tower Records and a stone's throw from the Chateau Marmont. I fantasize that I'll be lounging there poolside with various celebrities. The apartment is a one-bedroom condo, and my new landlord is an articulate, deceptively uptight-looking man who wears Clark Kent glasses. It turns out he runs a company called Doc Johnson, which manufactures sex aids. He hands me a catalogue, and I open it and scan the contents. He's got the usual dildos and things; I spot a plastic acu-jack, a pair of man's lips with a mustache that you can shoot your load into. Even though man-on-man love turns me on and every lesbian I know gets off on gay porn, I find the idea of ejaculating into a disembodied hunk of plastic with a mustache the act of a very desperate person. Therein lies the difference between the sexes.

Gina and I dump our suitcases in our pad and go out to thrift stores to find some furniture. Our stuff is still in storage in Toronto; we're testing the waters before making a real commitment. We embark on what becomes a never-ending adventure—discovering Los Angeles could take years. Even something as mundane as going to a grocery store is overwhelming. We both feel like refugees from a Third World country where you can't buy thirty varieties of ketchup.

Canada and the U.S. have just signed a free trade deal but, to paraphrase Marilyn Monroe, Canada got the fuzzy end of the lollypop. We find massive stores with inane names like Pic and Save, and Smart and Final filled with acres of junk that we simply must have.

I look at things in a whole new way with Gina; there was none of the tension between us that I felt when I was in L.A. with Dusty. Gina is open to her surroundings, and we find beauty lurking everywhere. We drive through the deserted tree-lined streets of Beverly Hills. They are flooded with purple paper wisteria; there is the scent of magnolia blossoms; night-blooming jasmine hangs in the air. The ultimate high is driving up to Mulholland, pulling over on an embankment and staring down at the view you've seen in a million movies: the otherworldly glittering lights of L.A.

Like two little kids, we stare awestruck at the La Brea tar pits as they bubble and regurgitate next to the L.A. County Museum. There is a full-scale model of a woolly mammoth standing on the banks of the black primordial ooze, so we're reminded of where we come from. As you make your way east, the stores become more exotic; there are Botanicas selling spells, potions and loteria candles. Downtown, the streets are populated with real live human beings, walking around. We drive by abandoned art deco theatres and lethal sky scrapers. Main streets like La Cienega, Pico and Sepulveda are named after families of the Spanish land barons who first settled here, lording it over everyone in their sprawling ranches, oblivious to the body count of the Indians who lost their lives building their churches and missions. Think of those days as a Latin version of *Bonanza*. Those men were fooled by the deceptive greenness of the land; they had no idea that they had settled on an arid desert.

———————————

Howard calls from New York to tell me he's tested positive for AIDS. For the past few years he's been in hell, watching all his friends drop like dominoes around him. He was riddled with guilt because he wasn't sick, and part of him wanted to be. That is an incomprehensible idea to me. I want to fly to New York to be with him, but he's very stubborn and doesn't want me to. I file all this information away someplace deep inside, and part of me starts waiting for the inevitable to happen. I talk to Elaine; we feel angry and powerless. As yet, there are no drugs available to stop the downward spiral.

In November the Berlin wall comes crashing down, and then Gina and I have our first sad little Christmas in L.A. We barely know anyone, and nobody in their right mind spends Christmas here. We find a Santa in a fake snowy grotto in Larchmount Village, the main street in Hancock Park, which looks like Small Town, Anywhere, U.S.A.

I start to write music and record demos. An old friend of mine, John Capek, who used to live in the same house with Kevan and me, is writing a solo album that he is going to record in South Africa. I write the lyrics for three songs, enjoying the unique challenge of writing world music for other artists to perform. Networking is essential if I want to meet musicians in this 'burg. And you have to play live if you want to try to get a record deal. It's blatantly obvious. People here are obsessed with their careers, and although they might collaborate with you, it's depressingly difficult to maintain friendships.

———————

Every weekend Gina and I go on excursions into nature. We pack picnic lunches and trek up into the mountains or to beaches. State parks in California are an oases from the feeling of inertia you sometimes get from the day-to-day monotony of life here. These escapes alleviate some of our malaise.

When you're walking along the spine of a mountain top, stopping to let geckos dart across the trail in front of you, you forget everything. Watching Gina stopping to pick aromatic sage from blue-green bushes. Hearing the warning sound of rattles from the snakes lurking in the tall yellow grass in Topanga Canyon. Trekking through muddy paths in forests in the spring. Climbing down to the bottom of a canyon to find a waterfall. You lose yourself looking out at the ocean, where you'll probably see dolphins or seals, and you get hypnotized by the waves pounding the rocks at a deserted beach. It's then that you realize you've been sucked in. California has a way of insinuating itself under your skin, and in spite of yourself, you end up feeling a very strong attachment to the place.

Our social life picks up when Andrew Alexander starts up a branch of Second City in an old theatre in Santa Monica. Robin Duke and Andrea Martin are cast regulars and Catherine O'Hara does guest spots. (The male members of that cast are now starring on hit sitcoms.) It's a kick to watch this West Coast incarnation of Second City perform, but the audiences are small. Santa Monica turns into a beachfront ghost town at night and hardly anyone drives out to see the show. In L.A., it's all about location, location, location. You get the impression that most people go to bed after dinner in this part of town; all signs of social life come to a grinding halt when you see the sun dip into the ocean as you swill martinis at your table at the Ivy on the Shore.

I'm driving along Santa Monica Boulevard in West Hollywood, on my way to the gym that we've joined. It's infamous, because they shot the eminently forgettable movie, *Perfect*, starring John Travolta and Jamie Lee Curtis, on location there. Everyone calls it the Sports Erection, because it is full of man pussy on the prowl. The men hog all the weight machines. This is a *Stepford Wives* city for gay boys. They drive by me like beautiful zombies, all in the same, black status-symbol cars displaying the same pretentious elitism. Are they programmed by some queen dressed in Gucci, who dictates their every move? Yes, I think they are. When you move to L.A., you get with the program. You're sucked into an idyllic fantasy world of health and fitness. Even I swear off drugs and all manner of hedonistic pleasures. It seems like sacrilege not to.

Gina tells me she's doing a play entitled *No Exit* by Jean-Paul Sartre. "How appropriate for L.A.," I whisper under my breath. I go to the theatre on the corner of Santa Monica and Hudson to see it. Gina is playing the part of Inez, a slightly sinister closeted lesbian dressed in acid-green pajamas who is stuck in a hotel room in purgatory with a man and a woman she secretly desires. After the performance, the director is going to give the actors notes. I tell Gina I'll meet her at home later. She walks me to our car, and I sense rather than see something in the darkness, out of the corner of my eye. I feel something cold on my neck; it's the barrel of a gun, a very big gun. Two black men, one of whom is holding the gun on me, start screaming at us: *"Gimme your money, gimme all your money."* I get very calm, cold even. I pull out my wallet and hand them twenty-five dollars. "That's all I have," I say. The other man runs his hands over Gina's body. I hate him. "What about you," they say to her, "you got any money?" She tells them her wallet is in the theatre. They tell her to go get it. I do not want to be left out here with the two men. I say, "There's a bunch of people in there." Gina walks toward the theatre. They make me sit in the car with the gun pressed to the back of my head. I'm still calm, but I begin to wonder what it feels like to have your head blown off. My life is waiting in the wings ready to flash before my eyes. I sit there in limbo for I don't know how long, and then I feel the pressure ease off my neck. I slowly turn around, and the two men have taken off. Just then Gina runs out of the theatre followed by the actors. Gina and I begin to fight.

"How could you leave me out here with those two guys?" I ask her.

"What was I supposed to do?"

We go back into the theatre and drink lots of beer with the guys. We don't even bother to call the cops, since everyone says it's a waste of time. From then on every time we see a black man in a lonely spot we flinch in fear. I don't want to live like this. Eventually the terror subsides.

I visit my friends Alain and Natasha, who live in a cramped apartment in Hollywood with a ménage of green finches, cats and recording equipment. They are driven musicians who have been struggling forever to get a break. They keep getting signed to labels and then dropped. Natasha is Russian, with a sexy Slavic face. Her speaking voice is low and tinged with an accent. She has a very healthy ego, which I am completely in awe of. I have a firm unshakable belief in my talent, but I'm fucked-up about the rest of me. She has no doubts. I vow to be just like her, which is an ongoing project of mine.

Natasha was a child prodigy; she began playing piano at age three and toured Holy Mother Russia. Alain is Swiss-Argentinian and a guitar virtuoso. The music they write is a combination of influences—the Beatles meet Les Voix Bulgares with Motown grooves. I relate to them because they are a couple bound together by their art, and they live and breathe it every waking minute of their lives. Their tenacious single-mindedness will eventually pay off. Bands like Soundgarden and Pearl Jam ask them to open for them. What's really funny is that they are so opinionated—about comedy, of all things. Just recently Natasha and I were having a conversation about comics and Natasha stopped me dead with "Carole, No. Jackie Mason is the greatest living comedian." What can you say to that?

I start to record demos wherever I can. There are so many Canadian engineers working in the studios here, it's a slam dunk to hook up with somebody I know and grab some free studio time. I actually eke out a living by getting some songs placed in low-budget television and movie projects.

Gina gets a part-time gig as a hostess at Café Largo, managed by a man named Jean Pierre, who is French but still seems like a nice guy. There are some mondo bizarro shows going on in this club. There is a bad poetry night, where young actors like Justine Bateman, from *Family Ties*, get up and read angst-ridden crap about issues like changing agents and losing credit cards. I can't sit through more than a couple of these poems; it's so painful even the thrill of celebrity can't hold me.

I much prefer John Fleck, an outrageous performance artist who crawls around on the stage wearing diapers and screaming. He supplements his income by playing child molesters on cop shows. On Halloween, Alexis Arquette appears as a phantasmagorical figure in the guise of a faun or Jessica Rabbit.

Henry Rollins, who seems unnecessarily angry, emanates so much testosterone off the stage you get knocked up by sheer osmosis. My personal favourites are a trio of motley drag queens called Guys or Dolls; the best of the three—a queen named Giselle. She does not make a particularly attractive vision as she makes her entrance wearing a plastic fruit–laden Carmen Miranda headdress and armed with a basket of tortillas. She walks through the audience, lip-synching to the Sinatra version of "South of the Border." In the middle of the song she starts tossing tortillas into the audience. They slap against the sides of people's heads. She has a strong right arm. The audience counterattacks, and soon food is flying everywhere. We're holding our sides, doubled over in pain from laughing. This is the real lunatic fringe of L.A. All of this inspires Gina to start singing. She has a sexy Marilyn Monroe kind of voice. She puts together a jazz trio, which I christen La Dolce Gina, and she starts doing gigs.

I fly to Vancouver to sing at the opening ceremonies for the Gay Games. There are thousands of athletes from around the world competing. I'm emotionally torn by the event, first because it's the biggest display of solidarity I've ever seen between the international gay, lesbian and transgendered community and, second, because it segregates us from the straight world.

We've been in L.A. for a year, and we have to find a new apartment. I come across a funky place right on Fairfax. Our neighbours are all good-looking air-headed boys and psychotic girls, except in the apartment directly across from us, where there is a nuclear family. Matt McDuffie, his wife, Cassie, and their four-year-old son, Ian, seem so out of place. They are so real and down to earth, and we fall in love with them immediately. They're struggling just to make the rent. Matt is a talented screenwriter trying to catch a break; Cassie is southern, womanly and cooks Cajun gourmet meals. Ian is a child prodigy: every word out of his mouth is a gem of wisdom; he is wise beyond the scant four years of his existence. Gina and I can't get enough of him. We take him out on dates to the farmer's market, to see the animals in the petting zoo, and thrill to everything that comes out of his mouth.

I start gigging at Largo. I've played everywhere that matters in L.A. by now. I have a band comprised of drums, bass, guitar and keyboards. I've already gone through what seems like three hundred musicians. They're disposable, like chick singers. We're sharing the bill with Lypsinka. I'm so over drag queens, but John Epperson is unique. His persona is that of the tough bitch in fifties musicals. His act is an exercise in dementia. He edits various campy pieces together in a sound montage that he lip-synchs to, and for some reason it's riveting. I go to the washroom and run into the supermodel Iman, who has bleached her hair blond. I hear her say to someone, "David is mine now." Meaning her husband, Bowie. The boys, whoever they are, and I, get up to play. I've compiled some new material that I'm somewhat satisfied with. Thierry Mugler and Iman are sitting at a table up front. I yell out to Thierry that I wore one of his suits on my first album cover. I add that he had a way with shoulder pads. It's great to play in L.A. and not have the rep of Rough Trade to deal with; nobody's expecting anything and people dig the show. I've long since given up the hope of being discovered or signed; I'm singing because it makes me feel alive. After our set, I'm invited to join the trendy ones. Iman sits there and looks beautiful and doesn't say much. Thierry is very sweet, and we talk about photography. He may even be straight. I'm almost tempted to set aside my distrust of the French.

When we first moved here, everyone was into this guru chick named Marianne Williamson; now it's Marianne who? Gina is studying Kundalini yoga; she wants to wrap a towel around her head and be one with the Sikhs. They are a bunch of rich white people, which should set off a warning signal somewhere in her consciousness, but it doesn't. I tell her I don't think the quest for enlightenment involves riding around in a BMW and overcharging for chiropractic treatments.

Gina takes us to a dinner party at Bob Blumer's, up in the Hollywood Hills. She and Bob are old friends. He manages Jane Siberry and is the imperial wizard of networking. Jane Child and her boy-toy are at the party. She is a Canadian singer who lives in L.A. and had a big hit single called "Don't Want to Fall in Love." She has long blond hair extensions that fall down her back, and her lower lip is pierced with a silver ring. We start to talk, and have an instant diva-to-diva connection.

We begin to feed on a strange fascination we have for each other. Jane owns a house in an area of Hollywood called Whitley Heights, where Satanists used to live in the twenties. While exchanging recipes and roasting sacrificial lambs over barbecue pits, they changed all their addresses into numerical combinations of sixes and nines so they could be closer to the anti-Christ. Jane's house is a Goth mansion with Victorian furniture and a grand piano. One room is constantly being uploaded with recording equipment, including a Fairlight, a high-maintenance hybrid of a synthesizer/music work station. You have to phone Australia to speak to a technician when it breaks down. Jane is an expert at using this demonic piece of equipment.

Jane's closets are overflowing with vintage dresses, and she drives a Citroën, which is a hydraulic lemon. Her brother Ricky is staying with her. I really like him. He's a talented musician and songwriter but confused about what the hell he's doing. Jane's boyfriend, James, also lives with her. Jane is a rock 'n' roll Norma Desmond wandering around her mansion, and I feel like an ineffectual William Holden. I grow slightly afraid that I might be discovered lying face down in her swimming pool.

We're both intrigued with Old Hollywood. We drive to the Hollywood Cemetery, and I photograph Jane from the back, standing facing the reflecting pool outside Marian Davis's mausoleum. Her hair extensions almost reach her ankles. I want to say to her, "Why are you wearing these things in your hair? They smell like dead Barbie dolls." But I hold back, realizing that I'll have to be subtle about it. She has two women who come in and change her extensions; sometimes when I go to her house I see her old hair lying in the garbage. Jane is recording a new album at home, and she's looking for an engineer. I introduce her to my friend Mike, who she loves; he becomes ensnared in the Jane web, and he's in and James is out. Jane is truly the epitome of everything diva-like. Looking back, I think I developed a crush on her that petered out into indifference because she was just too much work.

I write a couple of musical cues for the *Coneheads* movie Dan Aykroyd is starring in. I hire Lisa Dal Bello, who moved to L.A. around the same time as we did, and Natasha, Gina and Jane to sing on these two pieces that are supposed to be over-dubbed by the Conehead women. Jane puts on a performance, staggering into the session, pretending she has a hangover and is really out of it, when in truth she isn't. She is intimidated by all the diva power in the room and has no reason to be, because she has an incredible voice and all the chops any singer could want. We all watch her little show, but when we get down to recording the cues, she is a pro. I do not pretend to know the inner workings of any woman's mind, even though I am one.

I fly to Toronto to work with David Ramsden, who is a singer-songwriter. He's doing a series of shows called *Quiet Please, There's a Lady on Stage*. This one is taking place at the Winter Garden, an old circa 1920s theatre that was hidden on the top floor of another theatre called the Elgin, and had been abandoned for years. It is quite spectacular; the ceiling is full of tree branches and lights, like a camp fairyland. I share the stage with David, Shirley Eikhard, Jane Siberry, Rebecca Jenkins, Maggie Moore and Laurie Hubert. Siberry, in her ongoing role as the ultimate diva, tries to upstage everyone by changing into a series of outfits that only she finds whimsical and humorous. As an ensemble, we sing backup on one of her songs called "The Valley," which just reinforces for me how brilliant she can be. The night is uplifting, sad and sensuous.

Kevan, Marilyn and their daughter Sacha are in the audience. Sacha's take on blond sex-bomb Maggie Moore is that she looks like a living Barbie doll. When Rebecca Jenkins sings, Kevan is moved to tears; she has that effect on people. We party at Ramsden's place after the show. He's mischievous, decadent and never seen without a cigarette or beer in his hand. His whole schtick is a faux bitterness; his speech is peppered with insane expressions like "Cock of Christ." Every girl singer he comes in contact with loves him because he is so generous and easy to work with.

Maggie Moore and I tour Casey House, the AIDS hospice. We meet the people who work there, who, of course, are completely dedicated and wonderful. We go from bed to bed talking to the patients, some of whom are suffering from dementia and can barely form a sentence; others, who are lucid, seem blindly optimistic that they will get to go home soon. There is still nothing, no drug, to prolong their lives. When we leave there, we are drained and speechless.

Back in L.A., Gina is on my back about everything because she can't figure out what she wants to do with her life. Her curse is that she is multi-talented; she finds it hard to settle on one thing because she is skilled in so many. I've started going through all kinds of hell, re-evaluating my life and my commitment to her. We both wonder what we're doing in Los Angeles.

I'm flying back and forth between Toronto and L.A., doing gigs and trying to put together an album. The horrible sentence "I need space" comes out of my mouth. This does not mean I don't love her; I do. We decide to live apart, and Gina finds an apartment down the street from me. Sometimes I'm so overwhelmed by living here, I lie on my bed, all zombie-like and immobile, like a dormant sausage, my limbs too heavy to move. This place is so insular that you are forced to become introspective. Lacking enough social stimuli you really have to deal with yourself, which can be frightening. That's probably why the city is full of self-help groups and twelve-step programs. Humans are fragile, and in this unforgiving cut-throat industry, baby, it can all come tumbling down.

It's dusk in L.A., and the sky is magenta. The evening started innocently enough. I'm on my way to the opening of a new Roots store in Beverly Hills. Michael Budman and Don Green are throwing a reception on Beverly Drive in the heart of the shopping area. I'm with Gina, and we move around the room looking like experts in the art of networking. Dan Aykroyd enters, followed by his wife, Donna, and their nanny, who is holding their daughter. I'm having a conversation with Lynette Walden, an actress who is starring in a sexploitation film I'm co-scoring called *The Silencer*. I'm trying not to stare at her breasts, which were not there in *Mobsters*, the only other movie I've seen her in. In the campy *Silencer*, Lynette, a hitwoman, runs around in skintight black outfits, clutching a big phallic gun, blowing people away, right after set-ups illustrating what creepy little maggots they are and why they deserve to die. She delivers lines like a bad-ass Mae West. It's so wrong for the film, which will mercifully go straight to video. Gina and I both went to the set to watch the action and got hours of entertainment out of it.

There are other Canadians at the party. I usually steer clear of them. They tend to hang out in cliques in L.A.: perhaps they're intimidated by Americans. We quickly become bored and head home. I walk into my apartment and turn on the TV, and the news is frightening.

I run outside and look down the street at the skyline of L.A., and the city's on fire. The acquittal of the four LAPD officers charged with beating motorist Rodney King has brought things to a head; the city is erupting like a Vesuvius, volcanic ashes of hate spilling down over all of us. The sky is filled with smoke. As far as the eye can see, new fires are springing up in the darkness. Helicopters strafe the deserted streets with searchlights, and the wail of sirens fills the air. The Crips and the Bloods, two L.A. street gangs, are blowing each other away and setting buildings on fire. Gangs of people are smashing store windows and looting them. Some store owners open their doors to the looters, then torch their own places, so they can collect the insurance. On television newscasts, we see people carting off truckloads of stereo equipment and TV sets. Blacks descend on Korea Town because they hate the Koreans for coming to L.A. and setting up successful businesses. The store owners are armed and ready. Some twenty-five hundred businesses in that neighbourhood are looted or destroyed. Governor Pete Wilson calls in the National Guard and declares a curfew. We have to be indoors by nine p.m. or have a good reason why we're not.

It takes three days to restore a semblance of order in the stunned and abused city. We're numb with shock, along with everyone else in this city of angels. We can't stand the feeling of being caged in, so we get in the car and drive up to the mountains, only to find that all the state parks are closed. Gina and I walk in anyway, and other people have the same idea. We hike through the silent mountains, united in our quest for a few hours of sanity. In the aftermath of the carnage, more than a thousand buildings are damaged or destroyed. White people start a migration out of the city. We feel like witnesses to the beginning of the apocalypse.

I visit Howard in New York; he looks pale and drained. I take him out to lunch and love him unbearably. I feel more intensely now than ever that we are part of each other's flesh. He says he's had enough of New York and has decided to move to San Francisco. He is in so much mental anguish. He tells me which of his friends have died lately, and I'm overwhelmed with sorrow because I knew all of them. He takes me to the Guggenheim Soho Gallery to look at the work of Andres Serrano, whose *Piss Christ*, a shot of a crucifix submerged in urine, has shaken up the art world. The whole show is about the expulsion of bodily fluids; there are shots of male ejaculation. The artist is making a statement about AIDS. This exhibit has pushed Senator Jesse Helms over the edge; he is outraged that the NEA funded this project. I'm overcome by the power of Serrano's art, especially his photographs of the dead taken in a morgue. One photo is of a child wrapped in a shroud. All you can really see is part of the baby's face and its long eyelashes, which look so alive.

Howard packs up his collection of tapes, records and CDs and heads to San Francisco. Gina and I go up to spend Christmas with him. He seems fairly healthy and is taking large doses of medication and vitamins—he is optimistic about things. He has participated in various drug trials and is a walking encyclopedia when it comes to the latest medical breakthroughs. He can't take AZT because it's carcinogenic and his system can't tolerate it. Howard adores Gina, but who in their right mind wouldn't? We cook a big turkey dinner and nurture him. He shows us around the city and takes us to the Castro to see an art film. Gina and I both pass out from boredom because the film is so long.

The House of Blues opens in L.A. It's located up on Sunset and has a corrugated tin roof like some shack in the Mississippi Delta. Dan Aykroyd is one of the partners in this venture. The interior is filled with priceless art and religious statues representing every kind of deity known to man. To celebrate the opening, there are parties for a week. I'm somehow at one of these things, hanging with the A-list of showbiz royalty. The place is packed with the beautiful ones. Jack Nicholson with Rebecca Broussard, the mother of his babies (a relationship that lasted, what, a nanosecond?), Warren and Annette, Bobby De Niro, Bette, Whoopi, Jeffrey Katzenburg, Steven Spielberg, the Boss is jamming onstage . . . I'm unfazed by it all, because I've seen them around the 'hood. I only care about kitschy celebs like Joan Collins, who I once tried unsuccessfully to inspect minutely at the Beverly Center. I run into Valri Bromfield, and together we find Bill Murray, who is stoned and effusive, with a bottle of red wine jammed into the front pocket of his jean jacket. He's handing out big fat cigars to us girls. The Ellen DeGeneres of old walks by with a boy date pretending to be straight (we all laugh at that, and wonder where Jodie is).

At five the next morning, I'm rudely slammed into consciousness. I feel like I'm being tossed around in a clothes dryer. I realize it's an earthquake, and I drag myself out of bed to stand in a door frame until it subsides. I crawl back into bed and slip back into a stupor. I'm slammed into consciousness again. This is a really bad aftershock. Stuff starts falling out of my kitchen cupboards. I assess the damage. Only the things I care about are broken.

The phone rings. It's a radio station in Toronto, and they ask me if I'm going to stay in L.A. after this quake. I'm all stupid and somewhat indignant at having my privacy violated. I say, "It's just a quake, they happen all the time, and how did you get my number?"

I hear my neighbours congregating outside. I step out in my green plaid pajamas, which they make fun of, the bunch of style queens. Nobody has any idea how big the quake was. A group of boys says they're going down the street to the French Market to get breakfast. The rest of us discuss the size of the quake, reeling off numbers like 5.2 and 6.3. This is something you get quite adept at after you've been in L.A. awhile. The breakfast club soon returns and reports that everything's closed and the power is out all over. We are surrounded on all sides by a black void.

I crawl back into bed for a few hours, and there are about two million more aftershocks. I wake up to the ringing of the phone—Gina's calling to see if I'm all right. I spend a good two hours checking on friends; some of them are trapped in their apartments, which have collapsed on them. Pat Dorn, an A&R person at Warners, who works with Jane Child, calls. He has a cellphone and is working his way out of his place, which is full of amps and speakers that have trapped him. He's coping; he's just traumatized like everyone else I talk to. Jane calls and wants me to come and crash at her place, but she's in the hills and I feel safer down here, which is really quite ludicrous because all of Los Angeles is riddled with fault lines. Another friend, Amy, who lives in Santa Monica, woke up to see the sky above her filled with stars. She thought she was dreaming until she realized that one side of her apartment had caved in. She's shaken up but all right.

I walk across the street to the supermarket, where people are standing in line to buy water and candles. We are always being lectured on quake preparedness, and now here people are, stocking up on supplies after the fact.

The epicentre of this 6.9 quake was in a town called Northridge. The city of Santa Monica is right on the biggest fault line. Gina and I drive out to the beach to survey the damage, which is extensive. For the next three days we have no power, and everyone who lives in my building spends a lot of time sitting outside talking and drinking heavily. The building, a series of row houses, was constructed in the twenties and has withstood several quakes. I'm reminded of an old Cass Elliot song called "California Earthquake," and the chorus: "I've heard that the fault line runs right through here." I sing it for everyone I know, but no one thinks it's funny except Howard.

More people move out. God knows the thought of moving looms large in my mind. Los Angeles is touted as a desert paradise, but it's an ecological nightmare. Residents must endure torrential rains, mudslides and flooding in the winter, and raging wildfires in the summer. Real Angelenos are like lemmings forced to do battle with nature in order to hold onto whatever piece of paradise they've found. The only real concern on the part of politicians is to rebuild the Santa Monica Freeway as soon as possible, because people gotta drive. Little mention is made of the thousands who have been made homeless because of this disaster. On television newscasts, I watch the seemingly brainless, bouffant-haired newscasters and spin doctors drone on about the freeway, which looks like it was blown up in the middle of a demolition derby. California is a paradox to me, part paradise, part police state. I begin to wonder about this thing called democracy. It seems to be a word Americans like to throw around when they're not getting their way.

I fly to Toronto to take part in a tribute honouring Gilda Radner, with the original cast members of *Godspell* and Second City. A surprise guest, Marvin Hamlisch, who worked on Gilda's live show, is going to play her character Emily Litella's favourite song, "Memories" at the end of the show, which will prove to be a tearjerker. Kevan and I perform "Birds of a Feather" with Paul Shaffer and his band. Backstage we both support an overweight John Candy, who is not looking well. He's hanging onto us and is sweating and nervous about the prospect of going out in front of a live audience with the Second City kids, who are planning to do some scenes. Success has not changed John at all. If anything, he's become more vulnerable. He loves smoking cigars, and his favourite drink is still a triple rum-and-coke. Art imitates life: his appearance is now painfully reminiscent of Johnny LaRue, the hard-living sleazeball he played on *SCTV*. His life is encumbered by a massive and draining entourage, and he makes his home in a compound in the Pacific Palisades. We try to calm him down by telling him how much everyone loves him, and that all he has to do is show his face to the audience and they'll go wild.

Later that spring, at a lawn party honouring nominees at the annual Oscar party at the Canadian Embassy, Robin Duke is in the middle of reading a tribute to John when the ground rolls beneath us in an aftershock. Visitors to L.A. jump up from their tables and scream, while the rest of us sit there oblivious to the undulating green lawn.

I find a new apartment on Laurel Avenue, a beautiful street. Apparently, F. Scott Fitzgerald and Dorothy Parker once lived here. My new pad is in a fifties building, a spacious one-bedroom with a large tiled bathroom. I settle in and concentrate on getting work scoring films, and continue my never-ending search for a manager.

Just when we think the tense racial climate is cooling down, the whole O.J. circus starts up. The day that Nicole Simpson and Ron Goldman are murdered, I'm working on a film. A woman who dated Ron Goldman says he told her all about O.J.'s fits of rage, and she just knows O.J.'s guilty. The line is drawn in the sand. All the white people I know know somebody who has first-hand evidence that O.J. did it. All the black people think it's a frame. Five days after the murders, O.J. and his friend Al Cowlings take off in his white Bronco in what turns into a slow-motion freeway chase. People stand on the side of the road and cheer him on. O.J. is captured and thrown into jail, and he claims he's "one hundred percent not guilty." Our lives are inundated with the soap opera of the murder trial. In this drama, Simpson is Othello; Marcia Clark,

Judge Ito, Johnny Cochran and Chris Darden are just some of the members of the ever-expanding cast. Even with the introduction of the infamous "bloody glove," I find it no surprise when he is acquitted by a predominantly black jury. If this had happened in Canada or anywhere else, the man would be toast, but the American justice system seems like a joke to the rest of the world.

I'm intent on putting an album together. I do a remix of two songs I've recorded at A&M, a studio that is the love child of Herb Alpert, the A in A&M. I only know him as the horn player from Tijuana Brass. There's a gigantic multifaceted boulder of a hundred thousand dollars worth of crystal in all the studios in the place. The rocks emit cosmic vibes and look like hunks of furniture you'd find in Superman's Fortress of Solitude. This is one of the things you've got to love about this town. When I finally have five cuts together, I grow intent on pulling together a video.

I get in touch with a filmmaker named Ellen Seidler, whose very erotic film, *Et l'amour*, I'd seen at Outfest at the Director's Guild. We decide to attempt to do a film of a song I've recorded, called "Love Strikes Hard," which I can then use as a video and Ellen can enter into gay and lesbian film festivals. We want to make it sensuous, cutting to two women kissing and making love, while I walk the streets of San Francisco, singing and looking angst-ridden. I foolishly think the climate towards lesbian sexuality has changed, and as long as the video is not too graphic it should get some air time on MuchMusic. I fly to San Francisco to shoot the thing. Ellen is still missing an actress to play one of the lovers. I zoom over to meet her, straight from the airport, and we rifle through 8 x 10 headshots of women. A girl shows up who is supposed

to work as a production assistant. It's a Hollywood moment—
we both look at her and ask her if she wants to be in the film,
and she does. An actress named Fontana drops by, who Ellen
has already cast. She is feisty and ready to bare all for art; I
like her attitude.

The next day we're shooting at the Presidio, which is
almost deserted since Clinton cut defence-budget spending
and closed several army bases in California. The girls kiss each
other, pulling each other into the darkness of abandoned
bunkers. We go to the next location, which is a bed in the
basement of the video editor's house. The girls make fake love,
and Ellen shoots it. She is wearing a harness and operating a
Steadicam, which is very heavy and physically demanding;
she's doing double duty as a director and camerawoman. I do
several takes of the song, slamming through an empty hallway. The next day we're shooting me singing outside against
graffiti-covered walls. I'm with Elizabeth, the makeup artist,
and we're going to a loft that a friend of hers owns, to re-do
my makeup. The Folsom Street S&M Fair is raging around us
in all its kinky glory. The street is jam-packed with people
dressed in leather and vinyl, wall-to-wall flesh, bodies of every
description celebrating the joys of bondage and multiple piercings. Some are almost naked, some are on leashes being
dragged along by their dominatrix masters and mistresses.
There is every kind of S&M scenario imaginable. It's flagrantly
beautiful and horrifically ugly at the same time. We make our
way to the loft and stand on the balcony, looking down at the
undulating bodies. I wish I had a camera.

Someone puts me on to a manager in Canada. His name is
Nigel Best, and he represents a band called the Barenaked
Ladies. I send him my music, and he thinks there's potential

and that he can relaunch my career. We meet in Toronto. Nigel's a Brit who's full of energy and understands how to market talent, and he *really* wants to work with me. I decide he's one of those managers who think it's all about them—he treats himself as if he were an artist—but I don't care because his track record is so great and people seem to love him. He flies me to New York, where the Ladies are playing at Irvine Plaza. We stay at one of my favourite hotels, the Parker Meridien. We go to the show; the Ladies are an amazing live act, and, strangely enough, I meet record execs I actually like. We carouse all night and I have flashbacks of the eighties. Nigel introduces me to Seymour Stein, the man responsible for signing Patti Smith, the Talking Heads and k.d. lang. He's all over the map, obsessing about some art he's bought and ten thousand other things. Warners and Atlantic are going through some internal upheaval. Stein is a music legend and I wish I'd met him years earlier.

We plan a Rough Trade reunion with Kevin O'Leary, Holly Cole's willing love slave, who works at CBC Radio. He wants to broadcast the show live in Toronto. We pull together a dream band with two of my favourite guitar players, Tim Welch and Ken Myhr, which makes me ecstatically happy, since I always wanted Rough Trade to be a guitar-heavy band. Kevan is beside himself with joy because he misses playing live so much. We rehearse for a week at the Corp, and the songs sound hot.

We ask Scott Thompson from Kids in the Hall to introduce the band in his character of Buddy Cole. We coerce Mary Margaret O'Hara and Moe Berg, from Pursuit of Happiness, to do their interpretation of our songs in the show. The concert takes place at the Phoenix. My past crawls out of the woodwork to attend the festivities. Howard flies in from San Francisco, saying he would not miss this for anything. I don't realize how gaunt he is until I look at photos of him taken that evening. My sister Diane shows up; she hasn't seen Howard in a long time and she's obviously shocked by his appearance.

We take the stage and plow through all the old songs. The band is a solid mass of sound behind me. The audience loves it, and they scream out requests, most of which we play. We are about to launch into "Shaking the Foundations," and I ask if anyone who sang backup on the song is in the crowd. Sharon Lee Williams yells out, "I'm here." She comes up on stage and we dive into the song like no time has passed at all.

A few months later, Nigel organizes a Rough Trade gig in Vancouver at a yearly seminar for the Canadian music industry called Music West. After the show, the band converges on Nigel, who is luxuriating in a decadent white-on-white hotel suite, and we stay there till dawn, doing the things that rock bands do.

I'm in an introspective mood driving along Hollywood Boulevard. I feel sorry for the tourists who flock here from all over the world, taking photographs of the cement imprints of movie stars' hands and feet in front of Mann's Chinese Theater. More and more of the buildings are being bought up by Scientologists. Many of my friends feel that joining this church is like making a deal with the devil. You renounce your sexuality, give them a large chunk of your income—and become famous. Scientology. It's more than a religion. It's a lifestyle.

Nigel wants me to come back to Canada for six months to try to relaunch my career. At first I'm torn, because it seems like defeat to go back to Canada, but I'm so sick of this city I could scream. I take a quick flight back east, to play Gay Pride in Toronto with Steve Webster and Tim Welch. Somewhere around three hundred thousand people attend. There is a group of women who are on before us called the Drag Kings, dressed as the Village People. There's a woman, named Erin, in a cowboy outfit who swaggers around like a boy. I had actually met her the night before but wasn't impressed; today is different. She has the blue eyes of a martyr. Without really knowing her that well, I can see that she's a misguided Joan of Arc who is willing to burn alive at the stake for passion. I figure I'm going to let her destroy me, and write about it later. A whole crowd of unruly women, including me, maraud our way along Church Street. I haven't felt this free in years.

We're getting progressively drunk and disorderly, and we end up at Buddies in Bad Times, a gay theatre on Alexander Street that was once the Toronto Workshop Theatre. Buddies is packed with people celebrating their sexuality. It looks like a scene from Fellini's *Satyricon*; in the darkness, some boys are blatantly fucking each other in a daisy chain. Erin and I press against a wall and kiss passionately. At this moment I feel I could die right here. I let myself become a whore for beauty; I succumb to it without hesitation. Perhaps it's from living in Los Angeles, being surrounded by all the vacuous perfection, but this beauty has intelligence and substance, which makes it all the more seductive. We go down to the washrooms. It's unusual to see Torontonians this abandoned—there's a different girl drama going on in each stall. Around four in the morning, we climb drunkenly into a cab and go to Forest Hill, where Erin still lives with her parents, who are away for the weekend. Yes, warning signals are sounding in my subconscious.

Back in L.A., I start packing. My future is uncertain, but I think it will be that way till the day I die. Gina has found love with a man named Zig who is quirky but real and honest, which is virtually unheard of in these parts. I need a change, and I need to quit beating my head against the wall.

I fly to San Francisco to see Howard, whose health fluctuates up and down. Right now, he has a nurse visiting him daily to give him meds. Howard's roommate is a creep and wants him out of there. He's going to move in with a friend of his named Michael, who he says is loving and completely trustworthy.

He's very thin and weak. I make dinner for him and we talk. He tells me he's frightened of dying and that he's haunted by the thought night and day. He will not go down without fighting, and he is still experimenting with drugs. He gets whatever new medication is available from the HIV trials he's involved in, but so far, his body cannot tolerate any of the medications he's tried. Some of the drug cocktails AIDS patients take have a toxic effect on them. Howard's just started taking antidepressants, which I hope will take the edge off his terror.

On Sunday some friends come and take him to the beach, which he loves. Like me, he is a sun worshipper. I walk around the streets trying to deal with all of this. I meet B.J., one of Howard's best friends, for lunch. His own lover is sick, but he isn't yet. We talk about his fear of death and the fact that he started taking antidepressants as soon as he found out he was positive. He is very funny and pragmatic about things, and says, "If you laid all the men I slept with end to end in a daisy chain they would circumnavigate the earth."

I go with Howard to San Francisco General, which is one of the best facilities in the country for AIDS patients. While Howard gets a check-up in his weakened state, he cruises a cute boy in the waiting room. He tells me it helps keep him alive, but I already know that. Howard introduces me to some of the staff and doctors. I'm moved by how caring they all are. I tell Howard that I'm going back to Canada for six months, but stress that if he needs me, I'll be there in a heartbeat. We make plans to spend Christmas together in Toronto so he can see all his old friends. When Howard is feeling up to it, Elaine is planning to take him on a vacation to Laguna Beach.

I'm about to be released from my endless summer of discontent. I put my stuff in storage and get on a plane to Toronto, not knowing, or even caring, if I'll be back.

I guess I should tell you a little of the vast panoramic drama that unfolded when I touched down in Toronto. First, Erin picked me up at the airport and started vacillating back and forth about seeing me. For you astrology buffs, she is a Libra and apparently they can't seem to make up their minds about anything without weighing the pros and cons on their scales, left brain, right brain, and putting everyone around them through hell.

Then there was Nigel, my new manager, and it was mad, darling. Nigel was a charismatic boy wonder whose major coup was getting Sire Records to sign the Barenaked Ladies. He charmed everybody he came in contact with. We were livin' high; we went to the finest restaurants and showed up at industry parties. I played gigs in and around Ontario. Tyler Stewart, the drummer from the Ladies, sat in with me a couple of times, and I loved him, his contagious energy and the groove he laid down.

Then the cold light of reality hit me in the face. Nigel was into some serious substance abuse. He was married and had three small children; then his wife dumped him and the kids for another man. I knew he was using, but I had no idea how much.

The Ladies slapped him with a lawsuit, claiming he had been skimming money off them. So that was the end of Nigel's ride.

Careerwise, it just rolled off my back. I went on with my life. I was so used to my karma with managers, it didn't faze me. I felt bad for Nigel because he was not intentionally a bad person, but a victim of circumstance. He'd been totally upfront in his dealings with me. I got a distribution deal and released my CD.

I became good friends with Sarah Stanley, the artistic director of Buddies in Bad Times. I told her I had an idea for a show, a homage to the *diva* and her imaginary world, in which a group of women performers would get to act out their sublime and perverse fantasies. I must stress that this was 1995, before the rest of the world hopped on the diva bandwagon. We conceived of a show that would have three singers and one actress and a comedian; as an afterthought, Sarah had the brilliant idea of adding a dead diva who would make a ghostly appearance during the show and blow everyone away. After consuming gallons of coffee and red wine, smoking cigarettes while plotting diagrams and flowcharts, we came up with the loose outline for the show, with a producer and four women we both wanted to work with. We cast Sook-Yin Lee, a veejay on MuchMusic, who is a gifted performance artist, singer and composer. We followed with Mary Margaret O'Hara, legend and cult goddess. Diane Flacks, an actress, writer and icon of the theatre world. Elvira Kurt, a driven comic, the future bane of my existence. And Erin McMurtry, as the dead diva Edith Piaf, and a still painful reminder of the smouldering embers of my dead romance.

Sarah came up with a set that utilized Buddies' industrial space. It was a three-tiered platform with an orchestra pit centre stage for a three-piece band consisting of Steve Pictcan on drums, the lovely Ken Myhr on guitar and Richard Armand on electric cello. They were the musical epicentre of the thing. There would be five divans for the divas to recline on and two male attendants to cater to all our diva whims while we were on stage. There was trouble right away with Mary Margaret. Her father was very ill, and it didn't look like he'd be around much longer. She bowed out of the show. We replaced her with Tamara Williamson, an Irish lass with a great voice and some smouldering political angst. We began rehearsals, and everyone came up with her own interpretation of a diva and got to act out that fantasy on stage. Sook-Yin was a princess with a tinfoil crown, who sang Elvis's "Burnin' Love." Diane was a thespian who explored her inner diva, her face and body transformed during her monologue. Elvira was a bratty schoolgirl, dressed in a school uniform with a very short skirt, who talked about kids and cats as divas. Tamara sang about love and pain with plenty of attitude. I wore a riding habit and just acted like myself. I did a song by Depeche Mode and Morrissey and some of my new material.

The Boy Choir of Lesbos opened the show. Ten women dressed as little innocent boys with flushed cheeks, slicked-back hair and unruly cowlicks, holding candles in front of them, came out of the darkness to the front of the stage, singing "O Come All Ye Faithful" (it was December). Halfway through the boys' song, a blast of music signalled the opening of the show. Colourful banners dropped from the stage, heralding the arrival of the divas. I stood centre stage, surrounded by the others, as we sang the theme from *Bedazzled*, a movie in which Peter Cook plays Satan as a jaded pop star filled with inertia. Only three of us could sing. Elvira and Diane were another story, but they were obviously getting off, which was infectious, and the show *was* about getting to act out your fantasies. Everyone took turns doing their diva shtick. In the middle of the show, way back in the antechamber, the ghostly presence of Erin as Piaf appeared on a platform singing "No Regrets/Non, Je Ne Regrette Rien." Erin's French was impeccable, her voice sounded uncannily like Piaf's.

The second night of the show I realized two things. One, that Elvira was kinda sexy and two, that she wasn't wearing any underwear. This fact was not lost on the band, who had figured it out before they got up on the stage. Boys have a sixth sense about these things.

We slept together on Christmas Eve. I was supposed to see Howard, who was in Toronto spending Christmas with me and his friends, but he was too tired to get together, and so I saw Elvira. Things spiralled out of control at an alarming rate, like they always seem to do with chick love.

Moynan King, Sarah's girlfriend at the time, was the assistant artistic director of Buddies. She was writing and directing a play about a sixteenth-century kook named Elizabeth Bathory, who liked to bathe in the blood of virgins. (She had this zany notion it would keep her young. No honey, sleep with virgins, that'll keep you young.) Anyway, King asked me to contribute to the sound design of this thing, and I was very excited to explore the world of Sufi/Hungarian/ethno music and then write and record vocal cues, singing all the parts and utilizing Erin's out-of-this-world speaking voice to illustrate the sick fantasies I imagined were spinning around in that iron-maiden-wielding chick's head. The play was (I'm being restrained) trouble. The staging made no sense; the actresses spent a good part of the time running along corridors off stage, screaming for Elizabeth's maidservant Dorka. But Elvira and I came up with a killer sock puppet version for our own amusement. The experience made me hungry for more theatre.

Sarah gave me a chance to write and perform a song as the real pope, in *Metropolis*, a play without dialogue based on the Fritz Lang film. As a director, Sarah had a Cecil B. DeMille approach, having mounted productions under a bridge, among other things. The show's staging was unique: there was a large cast of proletariat on the ground level, while officials of the police state raged above them. Subtitles were projected on a transparent scrim that covered the front of the stage.

I did another show at Buddies called "Carole Pope and a Bunch of People She's Slept With," with Ashley MacIsaac, a fiddle-playing boy from Nova Scotia who had a big Celtic dance hit in Canada. There was a small problem. Ashley was returning from a cruise and he was stuck on the *Queen Mary*, which had engine trouble in the middle of the Atlantic; we had to start the show not knowing whether he'd make it in time. He literally appeared in the middle of our set, looking suave and urbane, dressed in a tux. He'd been entertaining the passengers in first class while they were towed into New York harbour, and then he hopped on a plane to make it to the theatre. I was getting blitzed out by this performing business.

In the spring of 1996, the unthinkable happened. Elaine called me and said I should get on a plane to San Francisco. I caught the next flight, but I arrived an hour too late. I called from the plane to find that Howard had died in the arms of his three best friends. Elvira met me at the airport. She'd been working in Los Angeles and drove up to meet me and whisk me to Howard's side. I'd been talking to him every day. One of his lungs had collapsed and he was in the hospital, and all he wanted to do was get out and see a Patti Smith concert.

I was lost. I'd been camping out at people's apartments for months in Toronto, and when I got back I decided to rent something on a month-to-month basis in Toronto's Little Italy. I knew I didn't want to stay in Canada, and I was seriously considering moving to New York. Vicki Wickham had been urging me to give it a try for years. But there was the Elvira factor. She was in and out of Los Angeles, and she really needed to be there for her career, and out of fear? out of love? begged me to move back there with her. So I did.

In the summer of 1998, I performed at the Michigan Womyn's Festival. I never thought I'd end up in Michigan, because it excludes men; using male musicians is not allowed. For years, my boy band from Toronto had been begging me to get a gig at Michigan so they could dress up in drag and infiltrate the place. Picturing what they would look like frightens me.

There are no men allowed on the Land. Sometimes *the Land* is pronounced in tones of awe and wonderment, as if it was a Shangri-La. The Land is located two hours outside Grand Rapids and is 650 acres of trees. Lisa Vogel runs this babe utopia; she is sweet, deceptively shy and in total control of her city of womyn. She could be the lesbian Hugh Hefner if she wanted. She started the festival in 1979 with a tent, a piano and some womyn. As the festival progressed, it added a food tent, a health-care tent and child-care facilities. Lisa was nineteen at the event's inception, and she's dedicated her life to it—it's a full-time job.

Lisa and her co-founders, Mary Kindig and Kristie Vogel, went to other festivals in the seventies, like the Midwest Women's Festival, where women camped out during the week-long event, and the Boston Women's Music Festival, a show-case for women's music. Both these festivals were bare-bones, with no amenities for the women who trekked out to hear the music. Lisa told me it was a drag coming out of these events with a vanload of women, having to search for a bar or restaurant in the nearest town where they could socialize. With dyke naïveté, they hit upon the idea of combining the best of both these festivals so that everything was self-contained on one site, giving womyn the option to stay on the land and providing all services they needed. So the seed for the Michigan Womyn's Music Festival was sown. Two thousand womyn attended that first event, which lasted three days and took place on a tract of land outside Mount Pleasant, Michigan. Now its home is in Oceana County. None of the womyn involved had produced anything before they created their festival, and the festival has evolved into a politically correct event that glorifies everything female. The sound of male voices is absent, and festival-goers don't listen to male music. Even male children are segregated, in their own special daycare centre. The only men who set foot on the land are the shit men, as I like to call them. They show up around two in the morning to hoover out the Porta-Janes.

Through years of trial and error and refining what worked, the whole enterprise is now a well-oiled machine. You get three veggie meals a day. There are two stores, doctors, chiropractors and masseuses—everything a girl could want. This year at least 6,500 womyn attended the event. The festival is multi-generational; many womyn who attended the first festival return year after year bringing their children. No one's special needs are overlooked. MWF's all-encompassing concern for womyn with disabilities prompted them to lay a carpeted trail for wheelchair access that covers the entire site. There are support groups for womyn of colour, Jewish womyn and the deaf. The event welcomes womyn of all sexual preferences, but does have a dominant lesbian culture.

So to do this gig, I had to put together a group of women musicians. I was already working with a woman bass player and drummer in L.A. My all-girl band included Lynn Keller on bass, a Michigan veteran who is an incredibly funky player, having worked with superdiva Diana Ross forever. She has a funny habit of shooting one leg out when she plays bass, like she's kicking a soccer ball. Denise, the drummer, was usually hyped to play. Not this time, though: she had just quit working with Sandra Bernhard after ten years. Sandra was on her way to Broadway to do a one-woman show entitled *I'm Still Here Dammit*. It was bad timing and a bad career move. Denise was having serious regrets about her decision, and somehow I was gonna pay for the shitload of angst, baggage and what-have-you she was lugging around. We were to meet up with Kris Abbott, who was flying in from Toronto. She's a Canadian guitar player I'd always wanted to work with, and she was strictly low-maintenance, thank goddess.

We arrived from Los Angeles at the airport in Hart, Michigan, and were greeted by a surly lesbian who was to take us to the Land. Pretty much all the womyn who carted us poor entertainment types around had attitude problems and, hey, that's *my* job. We shared the van with Ferron, a Canadian lesbian icon, whose music I'd never heard; she hails from one of the Gulf Islands that seems to be populated entirely by lesbians. A percussionist named Maria, who was playing with Toshi Reagon and was a cast member of the show *Stomp*, completed our group. She was as irreverent as I was and referred to women as babes, so I related to her right away.

After what seemed like hours, we arrived on the Land and were greeted by womyn in various stages of undress. The womyn at the gate sported accessories comprised of walkie-talkies, toolbelts and construction boots. I commented, "Oh, this is like the sixties without the guys." We drove along dirt roads through acres of forests past womyn living in tents and RVs. Denise was sweating, disoriented, her eyes darting around in her head—she had the look of a frightened caged animal. The mini nervous breakdown that had started on the flight from L.A. had escalated into something serious. Lynn and I were eyeing each other in apprehension. We thought maybe she'd calm down once we got settled.

We pulled up to the main stage, and I badly needed some air—I couldn't face dealing with anything right then. I charged out of the van in order to catch the last part of Kinnie Starr's performance. I'd just gotten a copy of her CD and was in the process of getting addicted to her music. I sat with a bunch of very sweet laid-back womyn, Canadians, my people. Everybody had wickedly serene smiles on their faces. We sprawled on a blanket in front of the stage and cracked open some beers. Kinnie was a musical revelation; she's part Native American, just plain stunning to look at, and her performance was unabashedly sexual. She liked to confront her audience verbally and physically by stepping out into the crowd and getting in their faces. The Gen-X girls in the audience where salivating over her, and so was I.

After Kinnie's performance, I went backstage and found that Denise had been spirited away by some of the womyn to the "Womb," which serves as a medical tent and a kind of holding pen for psychos. Apparently she hadn't really slept for six days, so she was suffering from severe sleep deprivation, which would account for some of her weirdness. Her care-givers informed me they were not sure if she would be able to perform. What fresh hell is this? We began the daunting job of looking for a replacement drummer. This was an important gig for me, and we had never worked with Kris the guitar player. Fortunately, I was on medication—Zoloft—which had the effect of numbing most of my emotions and giving me a laissez-faire attitude about almost everything except sex, so I didn't fly into a panic. I remained in a state of artificially induced calm. After all my years in this business, I was not amused by unprofessional behaviour.

Denise was not the only fly in the granola at Michigan. Elvira, now my ex-girlfriend, was there with her new flame. I actually thought I would get through the weekend without seeing them together—wrong. Elvira had dumped me for a social worker who worked with disturbed kids—*hmmm, I sense irony*—that she'd met the previous year at Michigan. We had been perfectly happy until Elvira, following her inner-child script, tossed me aside. That coincided nicely with my going through a mid-life crisis. After we broke up, I started seeing a therapist, because I'd plunged into a downward spiral from trying to cope with the enormity of the loss of Howard to AIDS, and on top of that, the loss of Elvira. The two events seemed to melt into one black hole that I was struggling to crawl out of.

I'd also started going through what is the biggest nightmare a woman has to deal with—*menopause*. Say it with me, people, it's a word that strikes terror into every woman's heart. She's lying if she says it doesn't. Irregular bleeding means you're riding the red saddle, as John Belushi so succinctly put it, for three weeks at a time. You're so weak you're crawling around drained of blood, but wait, there's more—you have psychotic mood swings; your skin breaks out. Did you think you'd be using Clearasil in your forties? The topper is, it lasts for ten years!! What's up with that? I don't care how much soy, calcium supplements, tofu, South American yam, Pro-gest, hormone replacement therapy (if you want to flirt with breast cancer), black cohash, ginseng and evening primrose oil you cram down your throat, or what

Germaine Greer crone-tome mother earth–empowering chick mag you read, waking up and looking in the mirror and seeing the lines in your face deepen and the spectre of your own mortality staring back at you is hell on earth—especially if you're an egotistical, Leo rock diva suffering from the chick version of the Peter Pan syndrome.

The one positive thing that happened was that going through menopause made me fearless. Talk about connecting with your inner eighteen-year-old—I did, and she wants to hurl herself into Xtreme sports, flirt with death on mountaintops and start a second career as an assassin. She wants young beautiful women to whom she can impart her wisdom, and with whom she can share her pretty good sexual technique, and she's getting it all. I suddenly realized why everyone, male and female, wanted to bone Catherine Deneuve, who must be pushing sixty. Yes, she's still earth-shatteringly beautiful, but you just know she knows things, secret womyn things. She's worldly, and that is a big fucking aphrodisiac, oh my brothers and sisters.

Back to slagging the ex. Elvira is a talented, driven comedian and exceedingly bright. As always, a lethal combination for me. I was swept away by the way her face transformed when she looked at me. Holding her in my arms was my panacea. Getting dumped stinks. In the aftermath of a relationship all you do is obsess about your ex. Stuck in the quicksand of despair, you torture yourself with the expertise of a dominatrix. What is she thinking? What is she doing? Why doesn't she miss you? You were so there for her etc., etc.

You go through all the stages of grieving; denial, anger, longing, revenge fantasies, depression and, finally, acceptance. One thing is painfully true. The last person she's thinking of is you.

When I first met Elvira, I thought she was quirky, talented and driven, emotionally on a par with an eight-year-old child, precocious and full of herself. I called her Baby-head. She reminded me of an infant whose fontanel has not yet grown over.

The big lesson I learned from our relationship was not to trust anyone who relates to pets more than to other humans. That is a strong indication that trouble lurks down the road.

She often joked that she should come with a manual. I can totally relate to a fear of commitment—I'd been plagued by that fear most of my adult life. I guess I conquered it when I committed myself to Elvira, in some kind of karmic (I hate to go all sixties on you) payback for all the women I couldn't commit to.

I've always been attracted to other performers, which I know is insane. But I can't be with an accountant—they just don't get it. Nobody knows better how you feel than another artist who is also trying to express herself, who understands the art and idiosyncrasies of being completely self-indulgent. Unfortunately, if you're both in the same head space at the same time, neither of you has the inclination to reach out to the other. But I still cling to the belief that it can work if both partners are evolved. Somebody should slap some sense into me.

That first night on the Land, I hung out with Kris and Lynn. Kris is deceptively cute and low-key, has pale Toronto-only-gets-daylight-for-two-weeks-a-year skin, and, most important, plays guitar like a maniac. We stayed on the Land until one in the morning, exploring the woods and various tents with flashlights. We felt absolutely fearless and liberated, like little kids running wild. We had a blast networking with other musicians. I bonded with Maria and with Kinnie who, even though she'd played at Michigan before, was a little overwhelmed by the festival and the desire aimed at her like a heat-seeking missile. We met this amazing black drummer named Boom Boom, who worked with Toshi; she was a real trip, unafraid to say whatever the fuck she felt. We were hoping she could sub in for Denise, if all else failed. At some point Denise staggered out of the Womb, supported by two sweet, nurturing womyn. She had a drug-induced benign expression on her face; they'd given her something to calm her down and help her sleep. She would remain on the Land that night.

We finally took the shuttle to our motel, the fabulous Comfort Inn in Hart, Michigan. We'd opted not to camp out on the Land. That was a mistake; it was exhausting being shuttled back and forth by the surly ones. The next morning Lisa Vogel called my room with news about Denise. It was still touch-and-go, and we needed to cover our asses. I called Boom Boom at her hotel to see if she could fill in.

Back on the Land, the sun was hot and the womyn walked around in total freedom. The band and I went up to the main stage and joked around with the production crew while they set us up. They were fast, efficient and extremely professional. What is it about women techies that turns me on so much? There's something about an empowered self-sustaining woman who has tools and knows how to use them. Sometimes, my ex, Gina, would walk around wearing nothing but a tool belt and work socks, holding a Mikita power drill, and it was such a great image, it drove me wild.

We did a sound check with Boom Boom. She was confident and strong, hit the drums hard and sat back on the beat. We went to the rehearsal tent, which was located across from the communal showers. It was your basic showerheads-and-naked-women-in-the-woods scene. We all agreed it was very distracting to rehearse under those conditions. We started playing the songs in the set, oblivious to everything but the music and the sound of water running down womyn's bodies. But the band was sounding solid. Halfway through the rehearsal, Denise showed up and said she was ready to play. Somewhat reluctantly, we thanked Boom Boom and finished the rehearsal with Denise, who had pulled herself together and sounded good.

Hours later, at dusk, we hit the stage, and the audience was a wall of female flesh. Stage left, Gen-X babes wrapped in sarongs, their bodies studded with multiple piercings, undulated to the beat. The more restrained womyn sat down front. They came in every shape and size and spanned all generations. There were children, excited little girls cavorting through the audience like wood nymphs. It was amazing to perform in that atmosphere, and I would do it again in a heartbeat. A long runway in front of the stage went out into the crowd. At one point I jumped off the stage and crawled onto a womyn and kissed her passionately. When we finished our set, we went back out and did an encore.

I'm now a Michigan convert.

I found out from Christie Degado, the production manager, that some womyn feel so connected to the Land that they scatter the ashes of their dead lovers in the woods. Some womyn have conceived children there, with the aid of a cooler of frosty brews and a turkey baster chock full of frozen sperm. Still others have confided to Lisa Vogel and Christie that they've buried their uteruses and other parts of their anatomy in the soil after having hysterectomies.

Christie told me some funny war stories about the other entertainers working the festival. Karen Finley, who had been there earlier in the week, was a real trip. She arrived on the

Land in a slinky dress and heels. Christie and the others were amused by Finley's wardrobe choice—those spike heels can get caught in the dirt. During her performance, she got naked except for a g-string and covered her body with chocolate. She'd demanded that a shower be available for her backstage so she could wash the goo off her body right after the show. The crew provided a portable shower, but it wasn't good enough for her. The next day during her performance, the candy-coated Finley taunted the audience, offering them a lick to help get the chocolate off her body. She was expecting that maybe one womyn would timidly take her up on the offer. She didn't know who she was dealing with. About twenty womyn charged the stage and proceeded to lick her breasts and crotch, which was not really what she had in mind. Eventually she ended up backstage with a crew of womyn hosing her down like she was an expensive Mercedes in a car wash.

On day two in this rustic paradise, I got to relax and check out the entertainment. Later on, Elvira and I were going to meet up for a talk. There were three different stages on the Land, to support the diversified entertainment. Not only did the festival feature music, there were also plays with elaborate sets, and a crew of onsite scenic artists. I cruised over to the day stage to sit with Maria and watch her ex perform. Maria was coolly and methodically dissing her, which was very funny. We both noticed this womyn sitting across from us. She had dark hair pushed back off her forehead, the most amazing aquamarine eyes and two piercings on either side of her brow. She was wearing a long dress that did nothing to conceal the voluptuous body beneath it. I'd seen her before in the performers' tent, but she'd always disappeared before I could say anything.

I got up to leave for my talk. On the path I met up with the mystery womyn. She complimented me on my performance and said she thought I was sexy. I told her I thought she was hot and said, "Do you want to hook up later? I have to go and talk with my ex." Her name was Jenna, and yes, she'd meet me later.

So I had a talk with Elvira. Now I ask myself why. For some reason, lesbians always want to become friends with each other after fucking up each other's lives. This was the first time I'd questioned the wisdom of that philosophy. Talk about the walking wounded. We just weren't ready. At Elvira's insistence, I hung out with Sara. We sat in the woods and watched a one-womyn show called "The Menopausal Gentleman." I didn't pay much attention to the entertainment. I was scanning the audience. Womyn were lying in groups on a grassy slope in front of the stage and it was very pastoral. Sara and I toured the site to check out the huge trench-like barbecue pits that had to be constantly tended so they would keep burning throughout the festival. It was a heavy undertaking, feeding thousands of womyn three meals a day. Everyone who visits the festival is expected to pitch in and help with the food preparation—everyone, that is, except the entertainers. On the surface, Sara seemed sweet but boring. She'd been thoroughly indoctrinated in the cult of E, and I found that sad. I knew there was a whole other side of her that she wasn't showing me. I told Sara I had wanted to kill her, but now maiming would suffice.

Finally it was time to meet up with Jenna. We strode into the woods and sat outside a tent and drank some beer. She was so easy to be with. I kept stealing glances at her while we talked. She was beautiful and completely wired on music. I murmured a silent prayer to all the goddesses I could think of; just talking to her made me feel inspired. She was twenty-six and the world was this open, ripe magic place to her, and that is infectious—she was like a really hot wood muse. We stood up, taking each other's hand, and walked out of the woods to watch the womyn perform on the night stage. We sat huddled together with other womyn on benches in the damp Michigan night. There was a gospel group called Sweet Honey in the Rock, six womyn wrapped in colourful African robes, who sat in chairs on the stage and unleashed their soulful voices. Following them was an eccentric sister act from New Zealand called the Topp Twins. They were both dressed in tight pants and had big butch pompadours; they played guitars and sang insane songs. Then they changed into dresses and wigs, which on them seemed like very bad drag, and did comedy sketches. I thought they were more like brothers than sisters.

It rained like it always does that time of year in Michigan. Jenna and I ran for cover, and as we huddled together in the shelter of the performers' tent, I realized that this experience and these womyn had restored some of the sense of connection and community that I'd been craving in my everyday life in the outside world. I felt linked to some of the womyn I'd met here like we were members of a secret and evolved society. The next day I was reluctant to leave, and I know that everyone in the band felt the same. It was hard for me to drag myself away from the Land and the girl and the onslaught of feelings. The one thought that stayed with me was that I'd actually experienced a world of Amazons.

It's a convoluted heartbeat away from the New Millennium, which anyone with half a brain knows begins in 2001, and I'm back living in Los Angeles. You've read my cathartic tale about misdirected love, abandonment and a U-Haul. All I know is life is fragile and impermanent, and I want to live in the moment. So bring it on.

I've spent years watching my lovers, friends and this funky ship of fools we're sailing on, seen too much death and not enough beauty, drinking it all in and filing the information away, so I can vent about it in the form of music. That's what I do, that's my purpose. So this chapter is part of my creative process. Could I be more self-indulgent? I don't think so. I want to go off on a tangent about the things that drive me. Imagine you, the reader, are listening to a really long guitar solo that you can tune in and out of, only picking up on the notes and sounds you like. If you want to get to know what makes Carole run, this is it. What follows are the things that inspire me and torment me, as I follow the anti-diva way of life, stopping occasionally to shop.

With the success of mainstream artists like Cher, Shania Twain, Lauryn Hill and Alanis Morissette, an artist who reflects young women's anger and adolescent idealism, the diva is now an entity recognized by society. Unfortunately, artists like the Spice Girls and Britney Spears, and other blond chicks whose names won't matter by the time this book is published, are doing nothing but pandering to the lowest common denominator. Girl power was just another not-so-thinly-veiled exploitation of women's sexuality. I have no doubt that a man came up with that phrase. I was always getting the names of the Spice Girls and the Teletubbies confused, since they both smack of mass-market strategies. Real girl power does not come in such an unrealistic package.

But I'm inspired about women and music, and the women's movement in general. As we plunge into the twenty-first century, how much has really changed? How evolved are we? When I started out in the industry, it was just Anne Murray and me standing on the frozen Canadian tundra. After working at Michigan, I decided I had to explore the phenomenon that is Lilith, and the chain reaction that the Fair set off in the media and the industry and, most importantly, in women themselves. What has manifested out of this adoration and acceptance of women?

My first problem with Lilith was that due to some glaring oversight by all concerned, I wasn't in it—but I'm over it, I don't care. If it wasn't for me there wouldn't be any blatantly sexual chick singers in Canada, but fine, I can live with that. No, my ego isn't that big; it's just that I think I made a somewhat warped contribution to music in Canada by throwing the love that dare not speak its name in people's uncomprehending faces. Yes, I'm slightly put out about the big oversight that Miss Sarah made by not dragging my jaded diva ass up there for one song, but apparently now she's busy making babies in a West Vancouver suburb. Perhaps when there's a Lilith reunion?

Oh, here's Joni Mitchell, let's talk to her. She's the *real* goddess of chick music. "Did they ask you to be a participant in

Lilith?" I ask innocently, unaware that I'm broaching a very volatile subject with her. Joni pulls out a pack of Marlboro Lights, fires one up and kicks back. She pushes away her double espresso and flicks an ash into the overloaded ashtray. "Well, Carole," she says pensively, blowing smoke. "Yes, they did ask me to perform at Lilith, but it went horribly wrong and I did a complete three-sixty, in as much as I changed my opinion as to the validity of what they were trying to do." (This is a re-enactment of a conversation I imagine us having. I couldn't get past Joni's people. I'm still working on it!)

I went to the last date on the Lilith tour in 1998. From my vantage point backstage, I looked out into a sea of young women. There were countless Sarah clones, with their silver barrettes reflecting in the Vancouver sunlight. Henna tattoos adorned patches of bare flesh. This thing is a very positive affirmation of women—or is it? There are no real women rock 'n' roll rebels; no one here is about to follow in Patti Smith's footsteps, standing on a cliff over a chasm of insanity, willing to bare her naked burning soul. The women who are part of this tour are all of a certain genre. Nobody's pushing the envelope; it's safe, sister. No one who is doing this gig would make me fall to the ground and kiss the hem of her garment.

There's no Hole, no L7; there's no Björk, which as far as I'm concerned is the most glaring oversight. I think that little Icelandic cherub is the most idiosyncratic, fearless woman out there. The hardest this thing gets is Sheryl Crow and the Pretenders. Performers like Tori Amos and Shirley Manson, the lead singer of Garbage, are vocal about their dislike of Lilith because of what they perceive as its elitism and its exclusion of certain artists. There are no heavy women rappers, no performance-art pioneers like Laurie Anderson, and obviously there's no Joni Mitchell, the mother and influence of all things Sarah. I'm curious as to why. Lilith does not celebrate the rebel in women—it's all peace, love and don't make waves.

I'm backstage with my friend Yvette, who has just performed on the smaller stage. It's dusk and we're checking out the action, waiting for Sarah to go on. The show runs like clockwork. As soon as Lisa Loeb finishes on the main stage, the lesser-known Wild Strawberries crank up on the second stage. Some of the women standing there watching Paula Cole are appalled when she breaks into her hippie-wannabe dance—it's embarrassing to watch. We all grudgingly admit that she can sing, just *please* lose the Haight-Ashbury shit.

To me, the most exciting part of the show is when people sit in with each other. Me'Shell NdegeOcello, a kickass bass player and brilliant solo artist, is the hands-down favourite with the group of musicians I'm standing with. The players backing the women up are exemplary, especially Cole's drummer and bass player, who are a tight cohesive unit after slogging it out on the road together for years.

I walk out into the audience and around the site, through thousands of people milling about while they wait for the next set-up, past the backstage tents where they feed the bands and crew members. I stop to talk to people, and the vibe is very laid-back. Members of the road crew keep coming up to tell me they worked on the *Serious Moonlight* tour and that Rough Trade blew Bowie off the stage. I'm flattered that they would even remember. Sarah finally hits the stage, and she really *has* an earth-mother womanly vibe. She has metamorphosed into a force to be reckoned with. It's all warm and nice, more like a love-in than a rock concert.

After the show, at the wrap party, I'm roaming around the Subeez Café in downtown Vancouver with Linda Chinfen, who manages Kinnie Starr. I'm suddenly face to face with Sarah, who I met three years earlier at a festival we were doing when she was still walking around shellshocked by her success. Now it has settled on her, and she is open, gracious and seemingly unchanged by all that has happened to her. She tells me if she'd known I was backstage she would have asked me up to sing with her. My fragile, needy ego gets stroked, and I have a flicker of hope that maybe next year . . .

At the Troubador in Los Angeles, I'm at an audition for Lilith '99, with a group of my neighbours, to support a friend named Cynthia who is very driven but painfully naïve about the music industry. In almost every place it played, Lilith Fair tried to seek out some local talent and give them the chance of exposure before their audience. About twenty nervous artists get up and do one song each, while a panel of industry people scrutinize them in their role as judges. Besides giving away T-shirts while the singers set up, the MC keeps insinuating that the mystical Sarah is somewhere in the club watching the proceedings. Most of the women turn out to be pale watered-down Sarah clones. Perhaps four of them are unique, but they get passed over. The artist who is chosen to work the Los Angeles show is a ballsy, Irish Melissa Etheridge soundalike, whose adjective of choice is fucking, and who we will never hear from again. It's a chick singer jungle out there.

I'm visiting k.d. lang in her studio overlooking a busy Hollywood street. Right away we get into a discussion about how Canadian women are kicking butt in the U.S. and rule the world of female pop, and that their incredible success is really part of *our* master plan to infiltrate the American government and take over the country. We laugh about what a betrayal Canadians thought it was if you were a successful artist in Canada and then moved to the States.

We eventually segue into the aftermath of Lilith 1999, and k.d. says she was a little jealous that she wasn't asked to do it. We wonder what the criteria was for picking talent, considering such a large segment of women artists seems to have been ignored. In spite of that, and all my fanatical raving, Lilith has consistently outsold other tours and blown Lollapalooza out of the water. Sarah is officially a goddess. She's been elevated to a position as the Princess Diana of non-threatening babe music, and this event is a celebration of her femaleness with other women, who are clamouring for a role model, someone taking the high ground, who they can relate to. The Lilith audience gets empowerment from hearing artists sing lyrics that speak to them about their femininity and the power it manifests. Women are finally being validated a thousand times over on a large scale.

On reflection, k.d. thinks that with an event like Lilith, "You can't get too diverse—it's too much information for the audience, and the audience is predominantly white." However, the event did prove to a lot of skeptical promoters—who thought you couldn't have two women back-to-back on the same bill—that there is an immense untapped audience out there for women performers.

Kinnie Starr worked on two fairs, and we're having a phone conversation about her experience. "The first year," Kinnie tells me, "there was all this hype around women in music and their new success, negating every other woman artist before Lilith." In 1999, the climate had already changed. McLachlan and artists like Jewel set the precedent for what was acceptable and commercially viable for women artists. I ask Kinnie about her own background. She has only been making music for four years. She got a deal with Mercury in the U.S., but they were devoured in a takeover by Universal and nobody was left at the label who got her, so she got out of the deal. This year in Denver, Kinnie says she was standing backstage looking out onto the Lilith audience while the Dixie Chicks were performing, and she was horrified to see the crowd singing along to what she called "redneck-slit-your-throat kind of music. What is this, Lilith, or *Deliverance*?" We all have our own idea of what we'd like to see out there, and the biggest argument between women artists about the event is who should be out on that stage representing us. In spite of all that Lilith has accomplished, there is still much to be realized by women artists.

There is a noticeable shift going on, specifically with men and music. Our anger is being negated and trivialized. Women are still held and judged under the cold clinical male scrutiny of oppression and control; no matter how you slice it, dice it, dilute it or candy-coat it, we're still found wanting. In 1999, the sales of some of the artists who made it under the Lilith umbrella began plummeting. There had to be a backlash, especially when the mainstream co-opts a movement; ultimately this can be a good thing, because it will weed out the mediocre artists. During the Lilith window of opportunity, any twenty-something girl holding a guitar was grabbed up and signed by record companies. Surviving this cruel but necessary purge will allow developing artists like Fiona Apple, whose second album blows her first one out of the water, to become a creative force to be reckoned with.

Still, anything outside the parameters of the dogma laid down by mainstream radio is now cavalierly dismissed by the male-dominated music media as Clit rock. Women's anger is considered passé, and it's being negated and trivialized. Alanis Morissette and Courtney Love have toned down their music, and some of their fans feel they've copped out. Record companies have stopped adding female acts to their rosters and radio is reverting back to its format of avoiding playing women artists back-to-back.

It's interesting to note that there also seems to be a huge backlash against cute, cuddly, romantic, non-threatening pretty-boy bands like the Backstreet Boys, who carry the banner of crooners for this generation. Do men really consider these boys competition for female attention? I guess nobody's safe from misdirected male rage.

At the 1999 incarnation of Woodstock, women were raped—that is a cold insidious truth that we must deal with. The event was a travesty, touted as a mock love-in put on by uncaring promoters who did nothing while concert-goers camped out in squalor, living in tents surrounded by raw sewage and piles of trash that nobody cleaned up. People paid $150 a head for this. The event deteriorated as anger at being forced to spend three drugged-out days in hundred-degree temperatures breathing in noxious fumes finally exploded. Bands like Limp Bizkit incited people to act out. Whoever started the first fire ignited the angry, volatile crowd into action and caused a riot of destruction. Young men vented their rage by torching anything they could find that would burn.

Teenage boys are into bands like Korn, Limp Bizkit and Kid Rock, who profess to love women, yet spew venom against them with their misogynist lyrics. They're sending out a mixed message, which does nothing but unleash more misdirected male rage. That kind of music is all about receiving rather than giving. How can these musicians claim to love women and yet be stuck in such an unevolved place? The frightening thing is that the women who adulate these bands seem completely unconscious of the real message they're sending, which is that women are sex objects and whores.

Men are threatened and men are freaking out. Young boys go on killing sprees and vent their bloodlust on innocent people. The Columbine high-school killings were not the first whole-sale massacre of students. In 1975 at Centennial High School in Brampton, Ontario, a teenage boy went on a killing spree, wounding fourteen people and killing three. It's no secret that as a society we have become desensitized by the constant barrage of mixed messages, misinformation and images assaulting us. Some of us completely buy into it, into this constant bombardment; still others close off from it—our defence is to shut down when we can't deal with it, and we don't want to know. Life is trivialized, an expendable commodity. Interactive media allows people to deal out death and rack up points for doing so. Mortality is a concept that the young cannot grasp. If we look back, we can all remember experiencing the heady feeling of invincibility in our youth.

A lot of the women I talk to think men can feel the shift towards a matriarchal society and it's making them crazy; it's like a tide pulling at them. This male behaviour affects us on every level. Even science is clued into the fact that a shift is occurring, and scientists are not usually tuned into the cosmos in a spiritual way.

Maybe all this rage and chaos is the impetus for a rebirth. Maybe society is about to hit bottom, like a junkie who has been on a thousand-year bender, and it's manifesting itself in our society and our psyches. There is so much upheaval and unrest in the world, most notably in Africa and Eastern Europe.

But I really can't exclude any country. Oh Jesus, let's face it, we're all fucked in some way. People are struggling to get out from under patriarchal oppression, and omnipotent dictatorship is just not on—no more daddy striding around in his big jackboots, kicking the shit out of any of us. People want change.

The resistance to change is the product of fear of anything new and unfamiliar, and seeps into every facet of our lives. Why are we not united in our discontent? Can we not get beyond sexism? We all feel angry and disillusioned with society. Why does most male anger have to be directed at women? Are we that threatening? We're still perceived by some men as weak, which is so *old*. Those of us who are resistant to change are being dragged kicking and screaming into the future. We are all evolving and our sexuality does not factor into the big picture.

For those who think Jung . . .

If you're still with me, I'd like to deal with the specifics of the role of the artist in all this chaos. What is any entertainer, but an embodiment of their audience's fantasies and desires? The artist uses eroticism and lust, and can take on the role of attacker or victim, or both.

I get to act out while you get to watch or listen to me act out.

The ecstasy of being a rock musician is that you get to release the trickster that exists in our unconscious. (Christian rockers are excluded from this analogy.)

Jung described the trickster, who shows up in various guises in all societies, as the shadow archetype that embodies the dark side of the individual and the collective consciousness, that conceals those wild, untamed impulses that are outrageous, savage and threatening and must be repressed. Society has always found outlets for these dark forces in the form of carnivals, public executions, orgies, even present-day sporting events, political protests and marches. These gatherings are an accepted way of acting out, just as rock concerts are sanctioned excuses for debauchery. We need that, people. An artist's catharsis on stage unleashes a torrent of emotions—pain, passion, lust and unrequited love—and that is what the audience relates to vicariously.

Modern-day tricksters would have to include the likes of Bugs Bunny, Sid Vicious, Lenny Bruce, Trent Reznor, Chris Rock, Marilyn Manson, Courtney Love, Limp Bizkit, and even me. You get my drift. Artists who are androgynous, wanton, twisted and/or satanic appeal to the dark side of our id.

Society, and the male part in particular, needs a creative outlet besides sports—like a rave, only for grown-ups. Events like the Burning Man, an annual five-day bacchanal in the American desert where people get to express themselves in a cathartic ritual with no restrictions, are one way of unleashing the beast and the artist inside. The event culminates in an enormous bonfire, in which a massive fifty-foot stick figure structure of a man constructed from steel, wood and neon is torched, along with most of the art people have created during five indescribable days. The point of this exercise is to construct an intricate, functioning city in the desert and then take it apart, leaving no trace of anything human ever having been there.

Around these parts, it is the closest thing there is to a pagan ceremony. Black Rock City, the temporary home of Burning Man, is located 127 miles north of Reno, in the middle of an empty desert. It's an idealistic society, anti everything in the outside world, that brings people together in the middle of nowhere to form a transient community based on freedom of expression. It's the antithesis of the outside world; no money, no government, no laws and no social inhibitions.

Anarchists, artists, hippies, social discontents and every other outcast who will not get with the program (except for this one) head out to the desert in droves. There is only one rule and that is leave no trace. Anything you bring with you, you take with you—you must clean up your mess so the space remains as pristine as possible. Considering that the majority of people attending this event are blitzed out on drugs and alcohol, it is amazing that somehow, during fleeting moments of sanity, everyone complies with this request.

The days are unbearably hot; temperatures reach about 115 degrees, which limits physical activity. The nights dip down to thirty degrees and the games begin. People make their campsites into art installations. One site looked like a partly submerged submarine sticking out of the desert, another was a sensory environment that you walked through to feel feathers and chains brushing against your body. There were bizarre cars—one looked like a silver fish hurtling through the desert. Another was equipped with a tetra coil that emitted flashes of electricity. One site was a rave with deejays set up in tents, spinning acid house and techno pop while dancers tranced out.

There is no commercialism of any kind, no product place-ment going on the playa, there is nothing for sale on the site. If you want to buy water, juice or pancakes, you have to barter with the currency of art, music or poetry. Whatever form of expression you're into is a medium to gain acceptance in this microcosm of a new society. Here people achieve a kind of bliss and ecstasy which is freeing because there are none of the restraints society places on us. At the end of the five days, when the effigy of a man is set on fire, it symbolizes the shed-ding of all the baggage we have to deal with. The more people get in touch with themselves and find outlets that enable them to express themselves as human beings, and in essence get into the chaos that surrounds us, the more it will ultimately free them. It's all about embracing fear and pain and the unknown.

In my own way I've discovered that fear is a pain in the butt. It's the drunken bore bitching at you in the party of life. Too bad it took me so long to look it in the face. At the moment I feel re-energized and inspired. I'm making music and art for Howard; I tell myself he's up in a Fire Island Heaven looking buff and Dusty drops by and they drink mimosas and gently prod me along.

Anyway, that's how I cope with that tragedy.

The day my brother died I heard his voice in my head, telling me to go to a mountaintop. I thought he was being literal, but now I know that he wanted me to live my life the way he couldn't live his.

With three Juno Awards, a Genie Award, and four Gold and two Platinum records to her credit, Carole Pope is an icon of transgressive music. As the lead singer of the band Rough Trade, Pope, with her songwriting partner Kevan Staples, revolutionized the Canadian music scene from 1975 to 1986. Carole Pope currently lives in West Hollywood, California.